GW01606228

INDIA
by
Al-Biruni

India—The Land and the People

INDIA

by

Al-Biruni

Abridged Edition of
DR. EDWARD C. SACHAU'S
English Translation

Edited
With Introduction and Notes
by
QEYAMUDDIN AHMAD

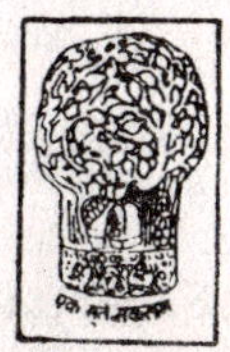

National Book Trust, India

ISBN 81-237-0289-2

First Edition 1983
Second Edition 1988
First Reprint 1992
Second Reprint 1993 (*Saka* 1914)

Rs.42.00

Published by the Director, National Book Trust, India
A-5 Green Park, New Delhi - 110 016

*Contents**

---

* Al-Biruni's own synopsis of the single chapters of the book.

The page numbers of the chapters are of the present abridged edition.

Abbreviations

ACV,	**Al-Biruni Commemoration Volume, 1951.**
IC,	*Islamic Culture.*
II,	*Indo-Iranica* **published by the Iran Society, Calcutta.**
JBORS,	**Journal of Bihar & Orissa Research Society.**
JPHS,	**Journal of Pakistan Historical Society.**

Editor's Introduction

My book is nothing but a simple historic record of facts. *I shall place before the readers the theories of the Hindus exactly as they are, and I shall mention in connection with them similar theories of Greeks in order to show the relationship existing between them. . . .*

Before entering on our exposition, we must form an adequate idea of that which makes it so particularly difficult to penetrate to the essential nature of any Indian subject. The knowledge of these difficulties will either facilitate the progress of our work, or serve as an apology for any shortcoming of ours. . . .

First, they differ from us in everything which other nations have in common. And here we first mention the language. . . . If you want to conquer this difficulty (i.e. to learn Sanskrit), you will not find it easy because the language is of enormous range, both in words and inflections. . . .

Add to this that the Indian scribes are careless, and do not take pains to produce correct and well-collated copies. . . .

Secondly, they totally differ from us in religion. . . . They consider as impure anything which touches the fire and the water of a foreigner. . . .

In the third place, in all manners and usages they differ from us. . . . with our dress, and our ways and customs. . . .

There are other causes. . . . [such as] peculiarities of their national character. . . .

Now such is the state of things in India. I have found it very difficult to work my way into the subject, although I have a great liking for it. . . . and although I do not spare either trouble or money in collecting Sanskrit books. . . .

Ignoring the rather old style of writing, these lines may easily be mistaken as extracts from the introduction of some recent book on India by a foreign social scientist. Actually these have been taken from the opening pages of a book which was written by a man born a little over one thousand years ago. Its author was alien to Indian culture but he made such an extraordinarily conscientious effort to understand it and to present it sympathetically to his own people that he has been rightly hailed as 'the first of the scientific Indologists, and one of the greatest of all times.'[1] The title of the book is *Kitāb fī Tahqiq mā li'l Hind min Maqala Maqbōla fi'l 'Aql ao Mardhūla,* popularly referred to as *Kitābu'l Hind,* and its author was Abu Raihan Muhammad ibn Ahmad, more commonly called Al-Biruni.[2]

Al-Biruni was born in A.D. 973 in the territory of Khwarizm,[3] then under the control of the Samanid ruling dynasty (874-999) of Transoxiana and Persia. He was not born within the city itself but in a suburban area: hence the epithet of Al-Biruni, which has almost substituted his name in popular usage. *Biruni* is a Persian word, meaning 'of or belonging to the outside': in the present context it denotes the outskirts of the town of Khwarizm.[4]

Some early Arabic works, dealing with the life of Al-Biruni, state that Birun was the name of a town in Sindh, and that Al-Biruni was so-called because he was born there. This, however, is a misconception which seems to have arisen because there was a town named Nirun in Sindh, and due to the copyist's error it was misread as Birun and it came to be regarded as Al-Biruni's birth-place.[5] The latter's keen interest in Indian culture was perhaps taken as indicative of his Indian origin.

Al-Biruni was a Muslim of Iranian origin. Not much is known about his early life[6] and upbringing, but he seems to have had very good opportunities of learning during his childhood. He remained an

---

[1] S.K. Chatterji, 'Al-Biruni and Sanskrit', *Al-Biruni Commemoration Volume,* 1951, (hereafter cited as *ACV*), p. 83.

[2] Opinions differ about the correct transliteration of this word. For a discussion see *ACV,* pp. XIV, 195–196, 290. Edward C. Sachau, editor and translator of *Kitabu'l Hind,* has spelled it Al-Beruni, but I have preferred the spelling Al-Biruni, adopted by the Iran Society in *ACV.*

[3] The modern Khiva. A Khanate of Turkistan in Central Asia in the 19th century, it is now part of the Uzbekistan Republic of USSR.

[4] It has also been suggested that although Al-Biruni was born in Khwarizm, his parents were of Persian origin and would have been regarded as strangers to the place; hence the 'Persian nickname of Biruni (outsiders)'. A. Yusuf Ali, 'AlBiruni's India', *Islamic Culture,* Vol. I, 1927, p. 33.

[5] Abdus Salam Nadvi, 'Al-Biruni' (in Urdu), *ACV,* p. 255.

[6] Definite information is not available about Al-Biruni's religious beliefs, and opinions vary on the point.

Hitti, (*History of the Arabs,* 1968 edition, p. 377) calls him a 'Shiite with agnostic leanings' while *ACV* (p. XIV) mentions him as a 'Sunni Muslim by conviction with Ismailian sympathies in religion and universalist tendencies in philosophy.'

avid reader throughout his life. A story is related that even when he was dying and a friend came in to see him, Al-Biruni enquired about the solution of some mathematical problem regarding which that friend had spoken to him earlier. The friend was shocked that he was worrying about such things in that condition. Al-Biruni replied with a great effort, and wanted to know if it was not desirable that he should die with the knowledge of the solution of that problem rather than without it. The friend gave him the desired information, and as he walked out of the room, he heard people crying on the death of Al-Biruni.

Al-Biruni was a great linguist and a prolific writer. Besides his mother tongue, Khwarizmi—'an Iranian dialect of the North with strong Turkish influence'—he knew Hebrew, Syriac and Sanskrit. Of Greek he had no direct knowledge but was well-acquainted with the works of Plato and other Greek masters through Syriac and Arabic translations. Of Arabic and Persian, of course, he had a deep knowledge, and wrote most of his works, including the *Kitābu'l Hind,* in the former language, because it was the international language of the times, the repository of the scientific works of the whole civilised world, and the medium of valuable contributions to different branches of science and literature.

The early years of Al-Biruni's life coincided with a period of rather quick, violent, political changes in Central Asia, and some of these had their impact upon his life and work. He first lived under the patronage of the local ruling dynasty of Khwarizm, the Maimunids, who threw off the yoke of the Samanids around 995. This seems to have adversely affected Al-Biruni's fortunes; he moved out of Khwarizm and lived for sometime in Jurjan (the area to the south-east of the Caspian Sea) in the court of Shamsul Ma'ali Qabus bin Washmgir, to whom he dedicated one of his earliest and most valuable works, *Atharu'l Bāqiya'an al-Qurūn al-Khāliyah.*[1] He seems to have returned to Khwarizm and lived there for some time, when, in 1017, Sultan Mahmud of Ghazni (999-1030) invaded and annexed that kingdom. Among the important personages of the Khwarizm court who were taken to the victor's capital city, Ghazni, was Al-Biruni. Since then he lived and worked there most of the time, until his death at the age of 75 in A.H. 440 (1048-1049).[2]

---

[1] Edited and translated into English by Edward C. Sachau under the title of *The Chronology of Ancient Nations*, London, 1879.

[2] ICI, p. XVI.

Al-Biruni's position in the court of Sultan Mahmud is not quite clear. He was some sort of a hostage, but an honoured one because of his scholarly attainments, particularly his high reputation as an astronomer and astrologer. However, his relations with Sultan Mahmud do not seem to have been very close or cordial. His famous work on India was prepared during the reign of Sultan Mahmud (around 1030) but he refers to the Sultan only on a few occasions and that too very tersely.[1]

It is to this period of his stay in Ghazni that the beginnings of his interest in India and the Indians can be traced. As we know, many important Indian works on astronomy, mathematics and medicine had been translated into Arabic long ago, during the early Abbassid period. Some of these must have been available to Al-Biruni. This is evident from the *Kitābu'l Hind* itself in which Al-Biruni refers to the Sanskrit manuscripts consulted by him, the copyists' errors in some of these, etc. During his stay at Ghazni, Al-Biruni must have had greater opportunities of pursuing his studies on India. The city was the chief political and cultural centre of Islam in the eastern region, and it must have attracted accomplished persons from the neighbouring countries including India. It also contained a number of Indian prisoners of war, skilled artisans and learned men who were brought over in the wake of Sultan Mahmud's invasions on India. Moreover, the Punjab with its large majority of the Hindus had become a part of the Ghaznavid empire. At Ghazni, as also some of the Indian towns visited by him,[2] Al-Biruni must have come into contact with many a learned Indian scholar and *pandit*. S.K. Chatterji suggests[3] that Al-Biruni established some sort of an academic rapport with them through the West Punjabi dialect which he must have picked up, or through Persian which some of the Indians might have learnt.

Al-Biruni refers (p. 194)[4] to a letter which Anandapala of the

[1] In great contrast to this is his attitude towards Mahmud's son, Sultan Mas'ud (1030–1040) to whom he dedicated his greatest work *Al-Qanun Al-Mas'udi fi'l Hai'ah wa'l Nujum*, and paid fulsome tributes. The concluding part of Al-Biruni's life, spent in Mas'ud's court, was one of comparative material prosperity and affluence.

[2] In a rather inadequately noticed passage Al-Biruni mentions some of the towns in India which he actually visited (p. 143).

[3] Article cited above.

[4] This and the subsequent references to page numbers within brackets in the Introduction indicate the pages of the present abridged edition.

Hindu Shahiya dynasty wrote to Sultan Mahmud offering military help to him for suppressing a Turkish rebellion in Khurasan. Anandapala wrote that since he himself had been 'conquered' by Sultan Mahmud he did not want that the Sultan should be 'conquered' by someone else.[1] Such diplomatic exchanges presuppose the presence of persons who knew the official languages used in the courts of Sultan Mahmud and some of the Indian rulers.[2] Connected with this is the question of Al-Biruni's readers not only for the *Kitābu'l Hind* but some of his other books too. That there was a continuing interest in Indian scientific treatises and other works in some Muslim circles is evident from the writing of the *Kitābu'l Hind* itself. Al-Biruni's significant concluding remark that what he had related in that book was 'sufficient for anyone who wants to . . . discuss with them (the Hindus) questions of religion, science or literature on the very basis of their own civilisation' shows that there were such persons. But not so well appreciated is the fact that there were also some Indian Hindu readers Al-Biruni had in his mind. He specifically mentions about his 'being occupied in composing for the Hindus a translation of the books of Euclid and of the Almagest, and dictating to them a treatise on the construction of the astrolabe' (p. 65). At another place he refers to a book, the Arabic *Khandakhadyaka,* which he had composed for a Kashmiri Indian named Sayavabala (p. 268).

It has been suggested that a feeling of shared adversity brought Al-Biruni and the Hindus close to each other.[3] Of this we do not have any direct evidence but; as we know, Al-Biruni was deeply interested in astronomy and mathematics since an earlier period of his life, and he must have taken full advantage of the opportunities of direct contact with Indian scholars during his stay at Ghazni. A considerable body of Indian scientific literature was available in Arabic translations and Al-Biruni would have been familiar with some of it. While living at Ghazni he got additional opportunities of securing first-hand information by personal contact with Indians and by direct study of Sanskrit sources. As we know, he paid visits to and lived in different parts of the Punjab, and the possibility of travels to other parts of India cannot be ruled out. Al-Biruni's serious

---

[1] This is an interesting commentary on contemporary ideas of political behaviour and chivalry.

[2] See Note 46.

[3] Sachau, *Alberuni's India,* Preface, p. XVII.

interest in Indian sciences, religion and philosophy began under these circumstances, and the collection of materials for the *Kitābu'l Hind*, as also perhaps its preliminary draft, was completed during this period.

Various estimates have been made about the number of books written by Al-Biruni. Yaqut (1179-1229) claims to have seen in Merv a list of books written by Al-Biruni which was spread over sixty closely transcribed pages, while another writer mentions that the weight of the books written by Al-Biruni was more than a camel's load! More specific but still astounding is the information given by Al-Biruni himself who mentions the names of 114 of his books in a letter which he wrote to a friend some 13 years before his death.[1] This too is not a complete list. Apart from the likelihood of Al-Biruni having written some more books during the remaining years of his life, there are references to some other titles not mentioned in his list. Regrettably, the bulk of his works has either been lost or is lying unpublished. Only two,[2] the *Athāru'l Bāqiya* and the *Kitābu'l Hind* are available in printed edition, and English translation, due largely to the scholarly devotion of the great German scholar, Edward Carl Sachau (1845–1930).

Sachau was born at Neumunster on 20 July 1845, and served as Professor of Semitic Languages in the University of Vienna (1869) and later as Professor of Oriental Languages in the Royal University of Berlin. He remained engaged with the study of the *Kitābu'l Hind* for long, and some particulars of the editing of its text and translation into English, as also the latter's subsequent editions and translation into languages other than English, may be noted. A copy of the Arabic manuscript was prepared and collated in 1872–73, and Sachau first translated it into German. Later, as the Arabic text[3] was being printed in 1885, Sachau 'translated the whole book a second time into English, finishing the translation of every sheet as the original was carried through in the press.'[4] The English translation

[1] Abdus Salam Nadvi's article cited above.

[2] Muhammad Abdur Rahman Khan's article 'On the Minor Tracts of Abu Raihan Muhammad bin Ahmad Al-Biruni', *ACV*, pp. 171–175, refers to the publication of the text and translation of another work of Al-Biruni, *Kitabu't Tafhim li Awa'il Sana'atu't Tanjim*, by R. Ramsay Wright, London, 1934.

[3] Another edition of the Arabic text based upon a *ms.* copy in the Bibliotheque Nationale, Paris, has been brought out by *Dairatu'l Ma'arif*, Hyderabad, 1958.

[4] Edward C. Sachau, Eng. tr., *Alberuni's India*, New Delhi, 1964, Preface, p. XLVIII.

with exhaustive notes was first published in two volumes in London in 1888.[1] Later, a one-volume edition was published from the same place in 1910. The former was re-printed in Pakistan in 1962, and the latter in India (S. Chand, New Delhi) in 1964.

The book was translated into Hindi by Shantaram and published by the Indian Press Limited, Allahabad, in 1926–28; it was again translated into Hindi by Rajnikanta Sharma and published from the same place in 1967. An Urdu translation in two volumes done by Syed Asghar Ali was brought out by the *Anjuman Taraqqi-i Urdu* in 1941–42. A Russian translation by A.B. Khalidov and Y.N. Zavadovskii was published under the editorship of A.I. Belyaev in Tashkent (U.S.S.R.) in 1963. More recently, the Arabic text has been translated into Bengali by A.B.M. Habibullah and published by the Bangla Academy, Dacca, Bangladesh, in 1974. An abridged edition[2] of Sachau's English translation based on a method different from the one adopted here was prepared by Ainslie T. Embree and published in New York, 1971. In the present abridged edition an attempt has been made to draw the general readers' attention to the approach and methodology of Al-Biruni, the core of his direct observations on the Indian society and sciences, and to some of the significant specific portions which have not received adequate attention.

Al-Biruni's long account is divided into eighty chapters, each with a sub-heading indicating the topic or topics to which it relates. The first chapter is an introductory one in which Al-Biruni discusses the difficulties (difference of language, religious and racial prejudices, etc.) one had to face in preparing a dispassionate account of the Indian society, and explains the methodology adopted by him. This is followed by chapters on Religion and Philosophy (II-VIII), Social Organisation, Civil and Religious Laws, Iconography (IX-XI), Religious and Scientific Literature (XII-XIV, XVI), Metrology, Weights and Measures, Alchemy (XV, XVII), Geography, Cosmo-

[1] The publication of both the text and translation received the patronage of the India Office, London.

[2] This is a photographic reproduction of the 2-volume edition, London, 1888. This process was perhaps responsible for the practical difficulties in deleting unrequired materials from within a chapter, page or paragraph. Several chapters not considered relevant have therefore been deleted, though brief indication of the topics concerned have been given at the end of the preceding ones. The Introduction presents a critical survey of the contents of the work and stresses its significance.

graphy, Astronomy, Chronology and related subjects (XVIII-LXII), Social Life, Manners and Customs, Festivals, etc. (LXIII-LXXIX), and Astrology (LXXX).

There is some degree of overlapping, but these apparent repetitions are not due to any lack of attention, because Al-Biruni himself explains that one could not always adhere to the 'geometrical method', only referring to that which precedes and never to that which follows. One had often to introduce in a chapter an unknown factor, the explanation of which could only be given in a later part of the book (p. 12). Al-Biruni also often repeats certain information because he considered such repetition to be useful. It facilitated the learning of a subject (which in this case was a completely new one), because learning was the 'fruit of repetition'.

The chapters generally begin with a brief, neat,introduction to the topic concerned, then comes the descriptive portion, followed by relevant extracts from the original sources. Care is taken to indicate the differences if any in the original sources, the textual errors due to copyists' mistakes, the correct transliteration and explanation of key-words (p. 12) and the incompleteness of information on any particular subject. On a few occasions Al-Biruni refers to some individual Indians or a group of them from whom he obtained some information. (pp.76, 77 and 222). But he did not accept such testimonies uncritically. He tried to verify such information by asking the same question from different reporters and in different order. He refers to one such case and expresses surprise at the 'different answers' he got from different persons when thus cross-examined. He adds sardonically, 'But lo! what different answers did I get! God is all-wise!' (p. 222).

Al-Biruni honestly notes about the incompleteness of his information on any topic (pp. 60, 70, 74, 117, etc.). However, while he draws attention to insufficient information, he does not regard it as a justification to omit all discussion on that topic; he prefers to record whatever information is available (p. 95). Finally attention is drawn to similar ideas and practices among other nations in earlier periods. All this indicates a surprisingly modern scientific methodology and a comparative approach.

---

[1] Chapter XVI relates to the different languages, scripts and numerical signs current in the different parts of the country, but its concluding portion gives an account of the 'strange manners and customs of the Hindus' which better fits in with chapters LXIII-LXIV.

Particularly significant is Al-Biruni's sociological insight, which is quite evident in the chapters dealing with the caste system, the civil and religious laws, idols and idol-worshipping, etc. For example, in explaining the origin of the caste system he points out that if 'a new order of things in political or social life' is introduced by a strong-minded individual and supported by religious sanction, it gradually turns into the accepted social norm (p. 44). The kings of the ancient period, who were conscious of their duties and obligations, took care to create and maintain the 'division of their subjects into different classes and orders, enjoining upon each a particular kind of work and prohibiting any intermixture between these (pp. 44–45). Any attempt howsoever well-intentioned and by howsoever meritorious a person to transgress these restrictions was punished (p. 228). He also stresses the role of the State in preserving the established social order and adds that harmony between 'these twins, State and religion', has a salutary effect on the society. Again, while discussing the nature of Hindu religious law and the question of its abrogation, he stresses the very important point about changes in law being 'necessitated by the change of the nature of man' and by the fact of the laws becoming too exacting for the people concerned (p. 49).

Al-Biruni also takes note of ancient Indian traditions in which indications of such sociological insight are evident. For example, he approvingly quotes a tradition from Saunaka (pp. 233–234), taken probably from the *Vishnu-Dharma* in which ecological differences and the multiplicity of social organisations have been considered as essential for the development of human civilisation. Mutual assistance which is the basis of civilisation, presupposes mutual differences 'in consequence of which one requires the help of the other.' It is noted further that customs and usages make people live and act in a particular manner, and when to these are added, the weight of religious commands the habits grow more binding, because while the former are open to criticism and modification, the latter are not. To some extent patriotism too is rooted in the attachment of the people to the climatic conditions and socio-religious set-up of the areas in which they have been living.

Attention may also be drawn to Al-Biruni's observations on the causes and utility of wars in connection with his account of the great Mahabharata wars. He expresses certain ideas which seem surprisingly similar to the theory of natural selection and the survival of the fittest, and which indicate some awareness of the need to preserve what is nowadays called the ecological balance. He writes:

The life of the world depends upon sowing and procreating. Both processes increase in course of time, and this increase is unlimited, whilst the world is limited.

When a class of plants or animals does not increase any more in its structure and its peculiar kind is established as a species of its own, when each individual of it does not simply come into existence once and perish, but besides procreates a being like itself or several together. . . . Then this will as a single species of plants or animals occupy the earth and spread itself and its kind over as much territory as it can find. . . .

The forester leaves those branches which he perceives to be excellent whilst he cuts away all others . . . .

Nature proceeds in a similar way; however it does not distinguish, for its action is under all circumstances one and the same. . . . If thus the earth is ruined, or is near to be ruined, by having too many inhabitants, its ruler. . . . sends it a messenger for the purpose of reducing too great the numbers and of cutting away all that is evil. (p. 184).

Turning to the specific topics covered by Al-Biruni, one is amazed by the range of his interest. Though concerned mainly with the religious and intellectual aspects, he writes about many other things too—the social and religious conditions, food and dress, games and pastimes, weights and measures, law-suits and superstitions, etc. At the same time one cannot help noticing the silence on some other important aspects. About the political aspect, it is understandable for they are too obviously outside the scope of his work, and had, moreover, been attended to in other extant works. More difficult to understand is the silence about such other topics as trade, industry, agriculture, arts and architecture,[1] etc.

On social conditions, the chapters on the caste system and the rites and customs which the Brahmans and members of the other castes had to follow (pp. 45–47, 223–229), constitute the most valuable part of the book. No such detailed and perceptive account of the caste system as it prevailed in early medieval India is available in any other non-Indian source. This portion seems to be

[1] There is a brief admiring reference to the construction of ponds with stepped embankments (p. 232). On another occasion when Al-Biruni is mentioning the name of an Indian book on architecture (p. 73) there is a lacuna in the original Arabic text. This is rather unfortunate; the missing portion would have provided us with information on a neglected topic.

based partly on the position stated in the standard religious texts but it throws some new light too. Thus for example, one notices some sort of a pairing of the Brahmans and the Kshatriyas on the one hand and the Vaisyas and the Sudras on the other in regard to some of the things they could or could not do (pp. 47, 229, 240–241).

The reference to members of the different *varnas* living 'together in the same towns and villages, mixed together in the same houses and lodgings' (p. 46) indicates some degree of inter-caste marriages, at least among the Vaisyas and the Sudras. That inter-marriage was common among the *Antyaja,* 'who are not reckoned among any caste, but only as members of a certain craft or profession' is specifically stated by Al-Biruni (*ibid*).

It also appears that the caste gradation, apart from its validity in social and religious matters, had some bearing on other matters too, as for example polygamy[1] and the period of confinement after child-birth. Al-Biruni writes that some Hindus were of the view that the number of wives depends upon the caste; that accordingly, a Brahman could take four wives, a Kshatriya three, a Vaisya two and a Sudra one (p. 240). On the other point, he writes that the period of confinement was 8 days for the Brahman, 12 for the Kshatriya, 15 for Vaisya and 30 for Sudra women (p. 241). It may be remarked here that among the poor people, for whom every working hand was important, the longer period of confinement would have caused some economic difficulty.

On education, regional languages and scripts, too, there are valuable bits of information. We are told about the use of slate (black tablet) and chalk (white material) for writing by the children in the school (p. 86). We also get a description of the manner in which writing materials were prepared from the barks and leaves of different kinds of trees and the methods by which palm-leaf manuscripts were bound and preserved (p. 80). Pieces of silken cloth were also used for writing, though in very special cases (p. 193).

The writing or the alphabet 'of the Hindus' consisted of 50 letters

---

[1] He mentions (p. 86) another very interesting practice prevailing in the eastern parts of the country of loving the younger child more because the eldest one owed his birth to 'predominant lust' while the younger one was due to 'mature reflection and calm proceeding'!

[2] In many a private collection of books and manuscripts the palm-leaf manuscripts are still preserved exactly in the same manner.

which had developed by a gradual process. The large number of letters was due, among other things, to the fact that their language had many sounds which were not to be found in other languages. There follows a very graphic description of the writing of 'the Hindus'— 'The Hindus write from the left to the right like the Greeks. They do not write on the basis of a line, above which the heads of the letters rise whilst their tails go down below, as in Arabic writing. On the contrary, their ground-line is above, a straight line above every single character, and from this line the letter hangs down and is written under it. Any sign above it is nothing but a grammatical mark to denote the pronunciation of the character above which it stands' (pp. 81).

Al-Biruni goes on to enumerate some of the other regional languages and scripts and the areas in which they were used. He mentions one, called 'Bhaikshuki' (p. 81) which was used in Udunpur in Purvadesa,[1] and which was 'the writing of Buddha' [Buddhists?]. It may be noted here that unlike the other languages listed areawise, Bhaikshuki was not the exclusive language of a particular area but that of a religious group living in that area.

The account of the principal festivals (pp. 258–62) provides an interesting reading. Even at this distance of time a present-day reader can identify some of the festivals, such as the *Holi, Durga Puja* and the *Dipavali.* He can also notice the continuity, as well as change, in regard to some rites and ceremonies observed on these occasions. The information available in the ancient and early medieval Indian digests on these points is of course there but Al-Biruni's account constitutes a different, supplementary, category of source-material, and sheds light from a different angle.

Al-Biruni believed that knowledge was truly international, that ideas and major discoveries by whomsoever and wherever made benefited all nations (p. 69). That he believed in the usefulness of spreading knowledge beyond one's own frontiers is evident from what he writes about his being 'occupied in composing for the Hindus a translation of the books of Euclid and of the Almagest, and dictating to them a treatise on the construction of the astrolabe' (p. 65). He also believed that the kings and princes could play an important part in promoting scientific studies because they alone

[1]Sachau rightly suggests that Udunpur might be identified with the famous Buddhist monastery of Udandapuri. It is situated in the present Nalanda district of Bihar. See also note 30A

could free the scholars from material worries and enable them to pursue their studies with contentment and devotion (p. 69). However, 'the present times', Al-Biruni ruefully adds, were not opportune. Neither was royal and princely patronage available, nor the 'public mind' directed towards the sciences. It was, therefore, impossible that 'a new science or a new kind of research' should arise. What existed was nothing but the 'scanty remains of bygone better times.' This remark of Al-Biruni about the arrested growth of Indian scientific studies finds support by the fact that some of the standard works available to, and used by him, were those which had been written centuries ago. Al-Biruni further remarks that not all the rulers and rich men were conscious of 'the nobility of science.' That explained as to why they did not call at the doors of the scholars whereas the scholars always flocked to the doors of the rich (p. 90). At the same time Al-Biruni thought that the kings and princes played an mportant role in promoting arts and sciences for they alone could free the scholars from material worries and enable them to continue their studies (p. 69).

Among the 'Hindu' sciences Al-Biruni devotes special attention to that of astronomy partly because it was 'the most famous among them' and partly because of his own interest in the subject. While admiring their proficiency in this branch of knowledge he stresses the sharp distinction between 'the two theories, the vulgar and the scientific'. The two had got inter-mingled with the passage of time, and that was why in their mathematical and astronomical literature one found 'scientific theorems' mixed up with 'silly notions of the crowd' (p. 11); it was a mixed bag of 'pearl shells and sour dates. . . . of costly crystals and common pebbles' (p. 12). That was because they did not apply 'strictly scientific deduction' (p. 12). At another place, Al-Biruni mentions some of the factors responsible for such an attitude. Among these were a lack of courage to hold firmly to one's convictions, as Socrates had done (pp. 11, 218), pull of social ties and fear of social odium (pp. 217–18).

Al-Biruni also writes about some other 'Hindu' sciences, such as alchemy, metrology and medicine. Under the first-named, he refers to the use of the processes of sublimation, calcination and waxing of talc. He, however, comments sarcastically on the pseudo-science of *rasayana* whose adepts sought to make gold out of baser metals, and condemns 'the greediness of the ignorant Hindu princes for gold-making.' They would resort to even inhuman practices such as killing of children by throwing them into fire if some misguided practitioner of *rasayana* were to tell them about some such wild 'scheme of gold-making.' Finally, Al-Biruni observes that 'the Hindus' cultivated numerous other branches of science and literature, and adds with characteristic modesty of a true scholar that he could not 'comprehend' them all with his limited knowledge.

In religion, too, a distinction had to be made between the beliefs of the educated class of the Hindus and those of the common masses. The former's conception of God was strictly monotheistic—'God. . . . is one, eternal, without beginning and end, acting by freewill, almighty. . . . living, giving life, ruling, preserving'. On the other hand, there was the widely prevalent practice of idol-worshipping among the masses. But Al-Biruni does not just denounce it, but tries to understand it and to explain it to his readers. He points out that the popular mind had an aversion to abstract thought and leaned towards the sensible world. This led to the setting up of monuments and making of idols to preserve the memory of, and show veneration to, prophets and sages. With the passage of time the circumstances of the origin were forgotten but the practice remained, and a feeling of veneration for the idols became ingrained among the people (p. 52). It is evident that Al-Biruni in spite of his personal feeling of abhorrence is trying to give his readers an objective account of the practice of idol-worshipping among the Hindus.

Matters of economic interest are comparatively less attended to but Al-Biruni's insight into such diverse things as the economic reasons for the importance of Somanath (p. 214), the prohibition of cow-slaughter (p. 238), the prevalence of prostitution (p. 242), etc. is remarkable. He explains that Somanath had become so famous because it was a harbour for sea-faring people and a station for the traders operating between the East African coast and China. As for cow-slaughter, it was prohibited because of the manifold utility of the cow for agricultural and domestic purposes. Regarding the prostitutes, he observes that kings used them as 'an attraction for their cities, a bait of pleasure for their subjects, for no other but financial reasons.' The revenue earned from them as fines and taxes was spent on the army.

There is an incidental but important reference which shows that political expediency rather than religious sentiments often guided the actions of some of the early Muslim rulers. Mentioning the conquest of Multan by Muhammad bin Qasim, Al-Biruni writes that the conqueror let the idol remain where it was (though after desecrating it) when he learnt that the temple and the idol were the cause of the accumulation of treasures in the town and of its flourishing condition (p. 53). More telling is the account of the sending of 'golden idols adorned with crowns and diamonds', captured in Sicily during the Caliphate of Mu'awiya (651–680), to Sindh for selling them to the princes of that country. The caliph did not feel any scruple about making money out of the sale of 'objects of abominable idolatry' because he was looking at the matter from 'a political, not from a religious point of view' (p. 56).

The references to principles of taxation and the ideas regarding the division of income (p. 235) also deserve notice. The emphasis on maintaining sizeable reserves for emergencies, 'to guarantee the heart against anxiety', as Al-Biruni puts it, explains the habit of hoarding and non-investment in trade and manufacture. Also to be noted is the reference to religious restrictions on occupational mobility and to the desirability of Brahmans not taking to trade 'except in case of dire necessity' and then also in the trade of clothes and betel-nuts only (p. 225). Trade was undesirable for the Brahmans because it involved 'deceiving and lying'. 'Usury or taking of percentages' was also forbidden, except in the case of the Sudras who could charge interest upto 2 per cent (p. 236). That Al-Biruni had an eye for significant bits of information from amongst legal and other details is evident from his reference to the hermaphrodite being reckoned as a male being for purposes of inheritance.

While giving an account of the physical geography of the country Al-Biruni seems to have an eye for everything, ranging from the shape, size and make of rocks and stones (p. 94) to the anthropological features and costumes of the people (p. 96). In the geographical portion of his account, he depends not so much upon extracts from books, as on scientific observation and calculations. The description of the main routes[1] to the different parts of the country and the calculation of distances between the important towns (p. 95ff) constitute a very important portion of Al-Biruni's account, but its proper utilisation requires the arduous work of identifying all the place-names and working out the exact Indian equivalents of the units of measurements used by Al-Biruni.

---

[1] Al-Biruni mentions sixteen important routes originating from Kanauj, Mathura, Anhilwara and Dhar. He probably obtained this information from the military and civil officers of Sultan Mahmud who were more familiar with that part of the country.

Sometimes, very valuable pieces of information are given by Al-Biruni while discussing a rather unconnected topic. Thus, while describing the 'alphabets of the Hindus' used in the different parts of the country, and referring to the '*Karnata*' used in Karnatadesa, he mentions that the group of soldiers in Sultan Mahmud's army called the *Kannara* were recruited from Karnatadesa (p. 81). Again, while writing about the constellation of the Great Bear he states that 'our time' (*i.e.,* the time of the writing of *Kitābu'l Hind,* or A.H. 421) corresponded to 952nd year of the Sakakala (p. 180). This provides indirect corroborative evidence on the concordance of the Saka era with the Christian era, and supports the view that it commenced in A.D. 78. As we know, A.H. 421 corresponds to A.D. 1030, and 952 added to 78 yields 1030. At another place, while discussing the methods of determining longitudes, he lists some of the towns in India which he had visited and of which he had determined the longitudes himself (p. 143). This information, which has not received adequate attention, has a bearing on the question of Al-Biruni's travels inside India, on which opinions differ. For example, while writing about the divisions of time, he mentions the clepsydrae, a mechanism for determining the passing of a unit of time called *ghati,* which he had seen at Peshawar, and to the endowments made by pious people for administering these clepsydrae (p. 156).[1]

The most remarkable feature of Al-Biruni's account is the conscientious and sympathetic approach to the subject of his study. To realise the significance of this approach one has to bear in mind that the book was written at a time of recurring military clashes and increasing ideological and emotional hostility between the Hindus and the Muslims. At times he uses rather harsh expressions about some of the Indian customs and practices, and he is particularly critical of what he considered as some sort of a superiority-complex, and an attitude of insularity, among the Hindus (pp 10–11, 85) but he takes care to add that such things were not peculiar to the Hindus alone but were common among other peoples too, including the pre-Islamic Arabs. He further explains that they appeared so strange to an outsider like him because there were no such parallels in his own society (pp. 85, 88).

[1] We know of similar arrangements made in the time of Firuz Tughlaq (1351–88), and Babur (1526–30) too makes an admiring reference to a similar arrangement he had seen in India. The testimony to the continuity of the practice shows that it had been working since long.

Also, very significant is Al-Biruni's concluding remark that his book was meant for those who wanted to discuss with the Hindus 'the questions of religion, science or literature *on the very basis of their own civilisation*' (p. 272, emphasis added). Much stress is nowadays being laid by Western scholars to try to understand Oriental cultures on their own terms and on the basis of the indigenous sources. It is a measure of Al-Biruni's greatness that he made such an attempt, fairly successfully, about one thousand years ago. In fact, it is this discerning and basically appreciative approach to the understanding of an alien culture on its own terms which lifts Al-Biruni's account much above anything else written on India in the medieval period.

In this abridged edition of Sachau's English translation all the chapters have been retained in their original order, as also all the direct observations of Al-Biruni's on different topics. A considerable portion of the book relates to astronomy, astrology, chronology and related subjects, and to Al-Biruni himself this perhaps was the more important part of his account. However, much of this is not of any particular interest to the common reader, and has been rendered obsolete by recent scientific progress. On the other hand, greater interest is now attached to the portion relating to social organisation, manners and customs, fairs and festivals, the legal system and topographical details, etc. The editing of the text has been done accordingly. The deleted portions are mainly those which contain technical details of astronomy and astrology, legends and stories, and reproduce long extracts from original sources (except where they relate to some significant subject). Such portions are of interest only to the specialists. The contents of the deleted portions have been briefly indicated within square brackets, and the numbers of the pages (New Delhi 1964 reprint) thus summarised given in square brackets.[1] At a few places there are cross-references, where Al-Biruni refers to some matter on a preceding page. In such cases the corresponding page number given in small brackets is of the present abridged edition. Smaller deletions covering matter within a page or two have been indicated by three dot marks.

Explanatory notes[2] have been added on some of the books and authors cited by Al-Biruni and on technical terms occurring in the

---

[1] With Chapter XLIX, Volume II commences, and the pagination begins with 1.

[2] Footnote numbers are not printed in the body of the text in Sachau's English translation; they are arranged page-wise at the end of the book. I have, however, given the footnote numbers in serial order in the text and arranged the notes at the end of the book.

text. Some of these are based on Sachau's own annotations spread over 150 pages of the book. It was not considered necessary to retain or to summarise these because many of the notes are of a specialised, philological interest. Also, some of these needed updating in the light of recent researches. For the convenience of those interested in following up any particular part of Al-Biruni's observations, a selected list of relevant articles has been given. The index gives special attention to the portions regarding social organisation, religion and sciences, etc. A map showing the extent of the empire of Sultan Mahmud, including the Indian portion of it, has also been added. An attempt has thus been made to present the kernel of Al-Biruni's account in such a manner as to render it meaningful and enjoyable for a common man to read this great work.

Sultan Mahmud and Al-Biruni symbolise two different aspects of the contact between the Indian and the Islamic civilisations. While the former stands for the immediate, external and destructive results, the latter represents the long-term, internal and constructive impact. Unfortunately, the common reader, not excluding those interested in history, know more about the invasions of Sultan Mahmud on India than about the scholarly study of the Indian society by Al-Biruni. If this book could be of some help in correcting the tilt and restoring the balance it would have amply served its purpose. I feel happy and encouraged by the fact that this revised second edition of the book is coming out within only two years of the first one. Some additions have been made in the extracts from the text, and the Editor's Introduction, Select References and Notes have also been revised.

I am indebted to my friend Paul Jackson, S.J., who has transliterated into Roman script the Greek words occurring in the English translation. I am thankful to Professor Yogendra Mishra, former Head, Department of History, Patna University, for some useful information on the Hindu calendar which helped me prepare the Notes on the Festivals (pp. 288–90), I am also thankful to my colleague Dr R.N. Nandi, Reader, Department of History, Patna College, for the help he gave to me in preparing some of the notes, and the time he spared in discussing several other matters requiring elucidation. My son, Imtiaz Ahmad, Lecturer, Department of History, Patna College, helped me by preparing the Index and seeing the book through the press.

Q. AHMAD

LIST OF GREEK WORDS IN THE TEXT

Greek words transliterated in the Roman Script as they occur in the text are given below along with the page numbers of this abridged edition : the words are separated from each other by (–) if more than one occur in a page.

Page	*Greek Words*
16	*to lanthanein – he dunamis – sophia*
17	*philasophos – philosophoi*
17	*mousai*
19	*en praxei – en dunamei – hule – dunamis – praxis*
19	*hule*
21	*hule*
23	*en praxei – en dunamei*
24	*dunamis – praxis*
32	*ta onta*
42	*hule – hule – en dunamei – hule – hule-hule – hule*
76	*charistiones*
80	*i.e. tomaria*
92	*he oikoumene – okeanos*
107	*aither*
109	*klimatia*
134	*oikoumene*
135	*oikoumene – oikoumene – oikoumene*
137	*geographia*
138	*oikoumene*
142	*oikoumene – oikoumene*
144	*hule – hule – hule*
145	*phusike – akroasis*

153	*hule – hule – hule*
270	*tropikon – stereon – disoma*
	kentron – epanaphora – apoklima
272	*ta meteora*

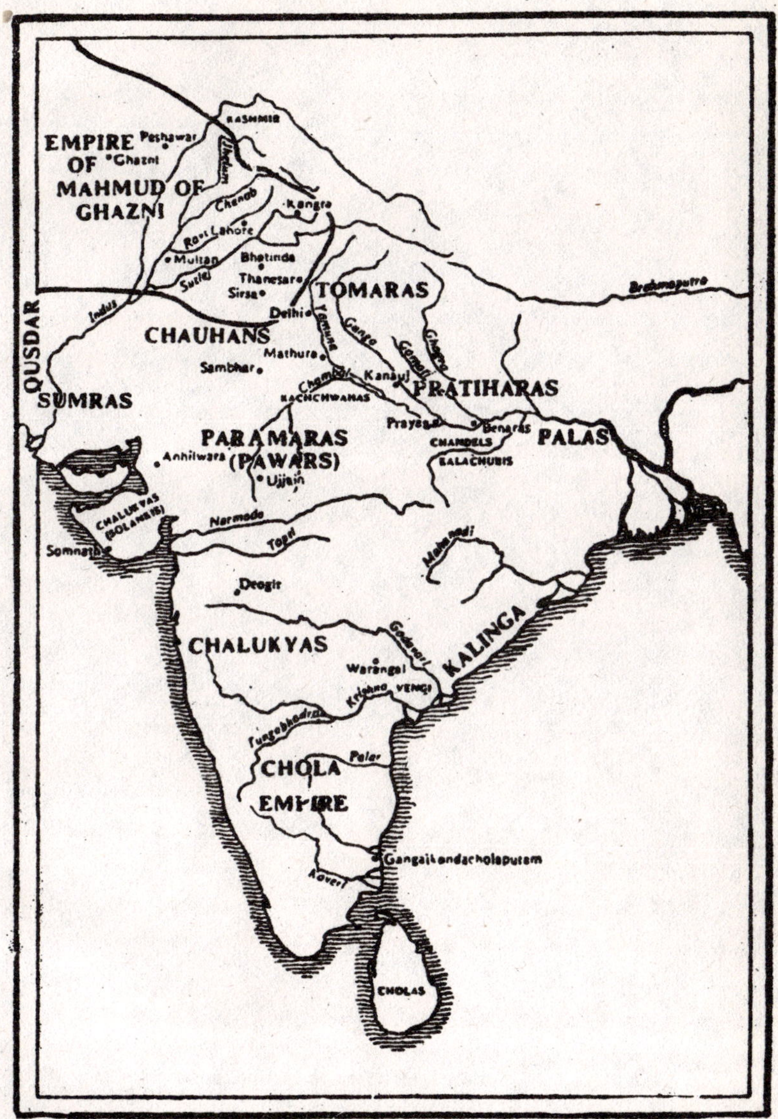

INDIA IN A.D. 1030

An

Accurate Description of

All Categories of Hindu Thought,

As Well Those which are Admissible

As those which must be Rejected.

Composed by

Abu Raihan Muhammad ibn Ahmad

AL-BIRUNI.

PREFACE

In the name of God, the Compassionate, the Merciful

No one will deny that in questions of historic authenticity *hearsay* does not equal *eye-witness;* for in the latter the eye of the observer apprehends the substance of that which is observed, both in the time when and in the place where it exists, whilst hearsay has its peculiar drawbacks. But for these, it would even be preferable to eye-witness: for the object of eye-witness can only be *actual* momentary existence, whilst hearsay comprehends alike the present, the past, and the future, so as to apply in a certain sense both to that which is and to that which is not (i.e., which either has ceased to exist or has not yet come into existence). Written tradition is one of the species of hearsay—we might almost say, the most preferable. How could we know the history of nations but for the everlasting monuments of the pen?

1. On tradition, hearsay and eye-witness
2. The different kinds of reporters
3. Praise of truthfulness

The tradition regarding an event which in itself does not contradict either logical or physical laws will invariably depend for its character as true or false upon the character of the reporters, who are influenced by the divergency of interests and all kinds of animosities and antipathies between the various nations. We must distinguish different classes of reporters.

One of them tells a lie, as intending to further an interest of his own, either *by lauding* his family or nation, because he is one of them, or *by attacking* the family or nation, on the opposite side, thinking that thereby he can gain his ends. In both cases he acts from motives of objectionable cupidity and animosity.

Another one tells a lie regarding a class of people whom he likes, as being under obligations to them, or whom he hates because something disagreeable has happened between them. Such a reporter is near akin to the first-mentioned one, as he too acts from motives of personal predilection and enmity.

Another tells a lie because he is of such a base nature as to aim thereby at some profit, or because he is such a coward as to be afraid of telling the truth.

Another tells a lie because it is his nature to lie, and he cannot do otherwise, which proceeds from the essential meanness of his character and the depravity of his innermost being.

Lastly, a man may tell a lie from ignorance, blindly following others who told him. If, now, reporters of this kind become so numerous as to represent a certain body of tradition, or if in the course of time they even come to form a consecutive series of communities or nations, both the first reporter and his followers form the connecting links between the hearer and the inventor of the lie; and if the connecting links are eliminated, there remains the originator of the story, one of the various kinds of liars we have enumerated, as the only person with whom we have to deal.

That man only is praiseworthy who shrinks from a lie and always adheres to the truth, enjoying credit even among liars, not to mention others.

...When I once called upon the master 'Abu-Sahl 'Abd-Almun'im Ibn 'Ali Ibn Nuh At-tiflisi,[1] may God strengthen him! I found that he blamed the tendency of the author of a book on the Mu'tazila sect[2] to misrepresent their theory. For, according to them, God is omniscient of himself, and this dogma that author had expressed in such a way as to say that *God has no knowledge* (like the knowledge of man), thereby misleading uneducated people to imagine that, according to the Mu'tazilites, *God is ignorant.* Praise

1. On the defects of Muslim works on religious and philosophical doctrines
2. Exemplified with regard to the Hindus. Criticism of the book of Eranshahri
3. Beruni asked to write a book on the subject
4. He states his method

be to God, who is far above all such and similar unworthy descriptions! Thereupon I pointed out to the master that precisely the same method is much in fashion among those who undertake the task of giving an account of religious and philosophical systems from which they slightly differ or to which they are entirely opposed...

In order to illustrate the point of our conversation, one of those present referred to the religions and doctrines of the Hindus by way of an example. Thereupon I drew their attention to the fact that everything which exists on this subject in our literature is second-hand information which one has copied from the other, a farrago of materials never sifted by the sieve of critical examination. Of all authors of this class, I know only one who had proposed to himself to give a simple and exact report of the subiect *sine ira ac studio,* viz. 'Abu-al'abbas Aleranshahri.[3] He himself did not believe in any of the then existing religions, but was the sole believer in a religion invented by himself, which he tried to propagate. He has given a very good account of the doctrines of the Jews and Christians as well as of the contents of both the Thora and the Gospel. Besides, he furnishes us with a most excellent account of the Manichaeans, and of obsolete religions of bygone times which are mentioned in their books. But when he came in his book to speak of the Hindus and the Buddhists, his arrow missed the mark, and in the latter part he went astray through hitting upon the book of *Zarkan,*[4] the contents of which he incorporated in his own work. That, however, which he has not taken from *Zarkan,* he himself has heard from common people among Hindus and Buddhists.

At a subsequent period the master 'Abu-Sahl studied the books in question a second time, and when he found the matter exactly as I have here described it, he incited me to write down what I know about the Hindus as a help to those who want to discuss religious questions with them, and as a repertory of information to those who want to associate with them. In order to please him I have done so, and written this book on the doctrines of the Hindus, never making any unfounded imputations against those, our religious antagonists, and at the same time not considering it inconsistent with my duties as a Muslim to quote their own words at full length when I thought they would contribute to elucidate a subject. If the contents of these quotations happen to be utterly heathenish, and *the followers of the truth* i.e. the Muslims, find them objectionable, we can only say that such is the belief of the Hindus, and that they themselves are best qualified to defend it.

This book is not a *polemical* one. I shall not produce the arguments of our antagonists in order to refute such of them as I believe to be in the wrong. My book is nothing but *a simple historic record of facts.* I shall place before the reader the theories of the Hindus exactly as they are, and I shall mention in connection with them similar theories of the Greeks in order to show the relationship existing between them. For the Greek philosophers, although aiming at truth in the abstract, never in all questions of popular bearing rise much above the customary exoteric expressions and tenets both of their religion and law. Besides Greek ideas we shall only now and then mention those of the Sufis or of some one or other Christian sect, because in their notions regarding the transmigration of souls and the pantheistic doctrine of the unity of God with creation there is much in common between these systems.

I have already translated two books into Arabic, one about the *origines* and a description of all created beings, called *Samkhya,*[5] and another about the emancipation of the soul from the fetters of the body, called *Patanjali*[6] (*Patanjala*?). These two books contain most of the elements of the belief of the Hindus, but not all the single rules derived therefrom. I hope that the present book will enable the reader to dispense with these two earlier ones, and with other books of the same kind; that it will give a sufficient representation of the subject, and will enable him to make himself thoroughly acquainted with it — God willing!

[Al-Biruni's synopsis of the single chapters of the book, *vide* pp. XXIII-XXXIII above, are then given, pp. 9-16.]

CHAPTER I

On The Hindus In General, As An Introduction To Our Account Of Them

Before entering on our exposition, we must form an adequate idea of that which renders it so particularly difficult to penetrate to the essential nature of any Indian subject. The knowledge of these difficulties will either facilitate the progress of our work, or serve as an apology for any shortcomings of ours. For the reader must always bear in mind that the Hindus entirely differ from us in every respect, many a subject appearing intricate and obscure which would be perfectly clear if there were more connection between us. The barriers which separate Muslims and Hindus rest on different causes.

Description of the barriers which separate the Hindus from the Muslims and make it so particularly difficult for a Muslim to study any Indian subject

. . . And here we first mention the language, although the difference of language also exists between other nations. If you want to conquer this difficulty (i.e. to learn Sanskrit), you will not find it easy, because the language is of an enormous range, both in words and inflections, something like the Arabic, calling one and the same thing by various

First reason: Difference of the language and its particular nature names, both original and derived, and using one and the same word for a variety of subjects, which, in order to be properly understood, must be distinguished from each other by various qualifying epithets. For nobody could distinguish between the various meanings of a word unless he understands the context in which it occurs and its relation both to the following and the preceding parts of the sentence. The Hindus, like other people, boast of this enormous range of their language, whilst in reality it is defect.

Further, the language is divided into a neglected vernacular one, only in use among the common people, and a classical one only in use among the upper and educated classes, which is much cultivated, and subject to the rules of grammatical inflection and etymology, and to all the niceties of grammar and rhetoric.

Besides, some of the sounds (consonants) of which the language is composed are neither identical with the sounds of Arabic and Persian, nor resemble them in any way . . . It is very difficult, therefore, to express an Indian word in our writing, for in order to fix the pronunciation we must change our orthographical points and signs, and must pronounce the case endings either according to the common Arabic rules or according to special rules adapted for the purpose.

Add to this that the Indian scribes are careless, and do not take pains to produce correct and well-collated copies. In consequence, the highest results of the author's mental development are lost by their negligence, and his book becomes already in the first or second copy so full of faults, that the text appears as something entirely new, which neither a scholar nor one familiar with the subject, whether Hindu or Muslim, could any longer understand. It will sufficiently illustrate the matter if we tell the reader that we have sometimes written down a word from the mouth of Hindus, taking the greatest pains to fix its pronunciation, and that afterwards when we repeated it to them, they had great difficulty in recognising it.

. . . Besides, the scientific books of the Hindus are composed in various favourite metres, by which they intend, considering that the books soon become corrupted by additions and omissions, to preserve them exactly as they are, in order to facilitate their being learned by heart, because they consider as canonical only that which is known by heart, not that which exists in writing. Now it is well known that in all metrical compositions there is much misty and constrained phraseology merely intended to fill up the metre and serving as a kind of patchwork, and this necessitates a certain amount of verbosity. This is also one of the reasons why a word has sometimes one meaning and sometimes another.

From all this it will appear that the metrical form of literary composition is one of the causes which make the study of Sanskrit literature so particularly difficult.

Secondly, they totally differ from us in religion, as we believe in nothing in which they believe, and *vice versa*. On the whole, there is very little disputing about theological topics among themselves; at the utmost, they fight with words, but they will never stake their soul or body or their property on religious controversy. On the contrary, all their fanaticism is directed against those who do not belong to them—against all foreigners. They call them *mleccha,* i.e. impure, and forbid having any connection with them, be it by intermarriage or any other kind of relationship, or by sitting, eating, and drinking with them, because thereby, they think, they would be polluted. They consider as impure anything which touches the fire and the water of a foreigner; and no household can exist without these two elements. Besides, they never desire that a thing which once has been polluted should be purified and thus recovered; as, under ordinary circumstances, if anybody or anything has become unclean, he or it would strive to regain the state of purity. They are not allowed to receive anybody who does not belong to them, even if he wished it, or was inclined to their religion. This too, renders any connection with them quite impossible, and constitutes the widest gulf between us and them.

Second reason: Their religious prejudices

In the third place, in all manners and usages they differ from us to such a degree as to frighten their children with us, with our dress, and our ways and customs, and as to declare us to be devil's breed, and our doings as the very opposite of all that is good and proper. By the by, we must confess, in order to be just, that a similar deprecation of foreigners not only prevails among us and the Hindus, but is common to all nations towards each other . . .

Third reason: The radical difference of their manners and customs

[Fourthly,] . . . the repugnance of the Hindus against foreigners increased more and more when the Muslims began to make their inroads into their country; for Muhammad Ibn Elkasim Ibn Elmunabbih entered Sindh from the side of Sijistan (Sakastene) and conquered the cities of Bahmanwa and Mulasthana, the former of which he called *Al-mansura,* the latter *Al-ma'mura.* He entered India proper, and penetrated even as far as Kanauj, marched through the country of Gandhara, and on his way back, thorugh the confines of Kashmir, sometimes fighting sword in hand, sometimes gaining his ends by treaties, leaving to the people their ancient belief, except in the case of those who wanted to become Muslims. All these events planted a deeply rooted hatred in their hearts.

Muhammadan conquest of the country by Mahmud

Now in the following times no Muslim conqueror passed beyond the frontier of Kabul and the river Sindh until the days of the Turks, when they seized the power in Ghazna under the Samani dynasty, and the supreme power fell to the lot of Nasiraddaula Sabuktagin. This prince chose the holy war as his calling, and therefore called himself *Al-ghazi* (i.e. *warring on the road of Allah*). In the interest of his successors he constructed, in order to weaken the Indian frontier, those roads on which afterwards his son Yaminaddaula Mahmud marched into India during a period of thirty years and more. God be merciful to both father and son! Mahmud utterly ruined the prosperity of the country, and performed there wonderful exploits, by which the Hindus became like atoms of dust scattered in all directions, and like a tale of old in the mouth of the people. Their scattered remains cherish, of course, the most inveterate aversion towards all Muslims. This is the reason, too, why Hindu sciences have retired far away from those parts of the country conquered by us, and have fled to places which our hand cannot yet reach, to Kashmir, Benares, and other places. And there the antagonism between them and all foreigners receives more and more nourishment both from political and religious sources.

Fifth reason: The self-conceit of the Hindus, and their deprecation of anything foreign

In the fifth place, there are other causes, the mentioning of which sounds like a satire—peculiarities of their national character, deeply rooted in them, but manifest to everybody. We can only say, folly is an illness for which there is no medicine, and the Hindus believe that there is no country but theirs, no nation like theirs, no kings like theirs, no religion like theirs, no science like theirs. They are haughty, foolishly vain, self-conceited, and stolid. They are by nature niggardly in communicating that which they know, and they take the greatest possible care to withhold it from men of another caste among their own people, still much more, of course, from any foreigner. According to their belief, there is no other country on earth but theirs, no other race of man but theirs, and no created beings besides them have any knowledge or science whatsoever. Their haughtiness is such that, if you tell them of any science or scholar in Khurasan and Persis, they will think you to be both an ignoramus and a liar. If they travelled and mixed with other nations, they would soon change their mind, for their ancestors were not as narrow-minded as the present generation is . . .

Now such is the state of things in India. I have found it very hard to work my way into the subject, although I have a great liking for it, in which respect I stand quite alone in my time, and although I do not spare either trouble or money in collecting Sanskrit books from places where I supposed they were likely to be found, and in procuring for myself, even from very remote places, Hindu scholars who understand them and are able to teach me. What scholar, however, has the same favourable opportunities of studying this subject as I have? That would be only the case with one to whom the grace of God accords, what it did not accord to me, a perfectly free disposal of his own doings and goings; for it has never fallen to my lot in my own doings and goings to be perfectly independent, nor to be invested with sufficient power to dispose and to order as I thought best. However, I thank God for that which He has bestowed upon me, and which must be considered as sufficient for the purpose.

Personal relations of the author

The heathen Greeks, before the rise of Christianity, held much the same opinions as the Hindus; their educated classes thought much the same as those of the Hindus; their common people held the same idolatorous views as those of the Hindus . . . The Greeks, however, had philosophers who, living in their country, discovered and worked out for them the elements of science not of popular superstition . . . Think of Socrates when he opposed the crowd of his nation . . . and . . . died faithful to the truth.

The Hindus had no men of this stamp both capable and willing to bring sciences to a classical perfection. Therefore, you mostly find that even the so-called scientific theorems of the Hindus are in a state of utter confusion, devoid of any logical order, and in the last instance always mixed up with the silly notions of the crowd . . . I can only compare their mathematical and astronomical literature, as far as I know it, to a mixture of pearl shells and sour dates, or of pearls and dung or of costly crystals and common pebbles. Both kinds of things are equal in their eyes, since they cannot raise themselves to the methods of a strictly scientific deduction.

In most parts of my work I simply relate without criticising, unless there be a special reason for doing so. I mention the necessary Sanskrit names and technical terms once where the context of our explanation demands it. If the word is an *original* one, the meaning of which can be rendered in Arabic, I only use the corresponding Arabic word; if, however, the Sanskrit word be more practical, we keep this, trying to transliterate it as accurately as possible. If the word is a secondary or *derived* one, but in general use, we also keep it, though there be a corresponding term in Arabic, but before using it we explain its signification. In this way we have tried to facilitate the understanding of the terminology.

Lastly, we observe that we cannot always in our discussions strictly adhere to the geometrical method, only referring to that which precedes and never to that which follows, as we must sometimes introduce in a chapter an unknown factor, the explanation of which can only be given in a later part of the book, God helping us!

CHAPTER II

On The Belief Of The Hindus In God

The belief of educated and uneducated people differs in every nation; for the former strive to conceive abstract ideas and to define general principles, whilst the latter do not pass beyond the apprehension of the senses, and are content with derived rules, without caring for details, especially in questions of religion and law, regarding which opinions and interests are divided. The Hindus believe with regard to God that he is eternal, without beginning and end, acting by free will, almighty, all-wise, living, giving life, ruling, preserving; one who in his sovereignty is unique, beyond all likeness and unlikeness, and that he does not resemble anything nor does anything resemble him. In order to illustrate this we shall produce some extracts from their literature, lest the reader should think that our account is nothing but hearsay.

The nature of God

[Extracts from the *Patanjali*, 'the book *Gita*', a part of the book *Bharata*, from the conversation between Vasudeva and Arjuna', and the book *Samkhya* are quoted. Pp. 27-30.

This is the procedure followed by Al-Biruni in the subsequent chapters too. He first presents a brief summary of the ideas of the Indian philosophers and scientists on a particular topic and then quotes relevant extracts from Indian scientific treatises and/or religious books. Sometimes he draws attention to the similar ideas of Greek thinkers and the Sufis, and quotes from the concerned sources.]

On the notions of the action and the agent

... The Hindus differ among themselves as to the definition of what is *action*. Some who make God the source of action, consider him as the universal cause; for as the existence of the *agents* derives from him, he is the cause of their action, and in consequence it is his own action coming into existence through their intermediation. Others do not derive action from God, but from other sources, considering them as the *particular causes* which in the last instance—according to external observation—produce the action in question.

Philosophical and vulgar notions about the nature of God

... This is what educated people believe about God. They call him *isvara*, i.e. self-sufficing, beneficent, who gives without receiving. They consider the unity of God as absolute, but that everything beside God which may appear as a unity is really a plurality of things. The existence of God they consider as a real existence, because everything that exists, exists through him. It is not impossible to think that the existing beings are *not* and that he *is*, but it is impossible to think that he *is not* and that they *are*.

If we now pass from the ideas of the educated people among the Hindus to those of the common people, we must first state that they present a great variety. Some of them are simply abominable, but similar errors also occur in other religions. Nay, even in Islam we must decidedly disapprove, e.g. of the anthropomorphic doctrines, the teachings of the Jabriyya[8] sect, the prohibition of the discussion of religious topics, and such like. Every religious sentence destined for the people at large must be carefully worded, as the following example shows. Some Hindu scholar calls God *a point*, meaning to say thereby that the qualities of bodies do not apply to him. Now some uneducated man reads this and imagines, God is as small as *a point*, and he does not find out what the word *point* in this sentence was really intended to express. He will not even stop with this offensive comparison but will describe God as much larger, and will say, "He is twelve fingers long and ten fingers broad." Praise be to God, who is far above measure and number! Further, if an uneducated man hears what we have mentioned, that God comprehends the universe so that nothing is concealed from him, he will at once imagine that this comprehending is effected by means of eyesight; that eyesight is only possible by means of an eye, and that two eyes are better than only one; and in consequence he will describe God as having a thousand eyes, meaning to describe his omniscience.

Similar hideous fictions are sometimes met with among the Hindus, especially among those castes who are not allowed to occupy themselves with science, of whom we shall speak hereafter.

CHAPTER III

On The Hindu Belief As To Created Things, Both "Intelligibilia" And "Sensibilia"

Notions of the Greeks and the Sufi philosophers as to the *First Cause*

On this subject the ancient Greeks held nearly the same view as the Hindus, at all events in those times before philosophy rose high among them under the care of the seven so-called *pillars of wisdom,* viz. Solon of Athens, Bias of Priene, Periander of Corinth, Thales of Miletus, Chilon of Lacedaemon, Pittacus of Lesbos, and Cleobulus of Lindos, and their successors. Some of them thought that all things are *one,* and this *one* thing is according to some *to lanthanein,* according to others *he dunamis;* that e.g. man has only this prerogative before a stone and the inanimate world, that he is by one degree nearer than they to the *First Cause.* But this he would not be anything better than they.

Others think that only the *First Cause* has real existence, because it alone is self-sufficing, whilst everything else absolutely requires it; that a thing which for its existence stands in need of something else has only a dream-life, no real life, and that reality is only that *one* and *first* being (the *First Cause*).

This is also the theory of the *Sufis,* i.e. the *sages,* for *suf* means in Greek *wisdom* (*sophia*). Therefore, a philosopher is called *pailasopa* (*philosophos*), i.e. loving wisdom. When in Islam persons adopted something like the doctrines of these *philosophers,* they also adopted their name; but some people did not understand the meaning of the word, and erroneously combined it with the Arabic word *suffa,* as if the *Sufi* (*philosophoi*) were identical with the so-called *Ahl-assuffa* among the companions of Muhammad. In later times the word was corrupted by misspelling, so that finally it was taken for a derivation from *suf,* i.e. *the wool of goats.* Abu-alfath Albusti[9] made a laudable effort to avoid this mistake when he said, "From olden times people have differed as to the meaning of the word *sufi,* and have thought it a derivative from *suf,* i.e. wool. I, for my part, understand by the word a youth who is *safi,* i.e. pure. This *safi* has become *sufi,* and in this form the name of a class of thinkers, the *sufi.*"

Origin of the word Sufi

Further, the same Greeks think that the existing world is only *one* thing; that the *First Cause* appears in it under various shapes; that the power of the *First Cause* is inherent in the parts of the world under different circumstances, which cause a certain difference of the things of the world notwithstanding their original unity.

Others thought that he who turns with his whole being towards the *First Cause*, striving to become as much as possible similar to *it*, will become united with *it* after having passed the intermediate stages, and stripped of all appendages and impediments. Similar views are also held by the *Sufi,* because of the similarity of the dogma.

As to the souls and spirits, the Greeks think that they exist by themselves before they enter bodies; that they exist in certain numbers and groups, which stand in various relations to each other, knowing each other and not knowing; that they, whilst staying in bodies, earn by the actions of their free-will that lot which awaits them after their separation from the bodies, i.e. the faculty of ruling the world in various ways. Therefore, they called them gods, built temples in their names and offered them sacrifices . . .

. . . The Greeks call in general *god* everything that is glorious and noble, and the like usage exists among many nations. They go even so far as to call *gods* the mountains, the seas, &c. Secondly, they apply the term *god* in a special sense to the *First Cause,* to the angels, and to their souls. According to a third usage, Plato calls gods the *Sekinat* (= *mousai*). But on this subject the terms of the interpreters are not perfectly clear; in consequence of which we only know the name, but not what it means.

... There are, however, certain expressions which are offensive according to the notions of one religion, whilst they are admissible according to those of another, which may pass in one language, whilst they are rejected by another. To this class belongs the word *apotheosis,* which has a bad sound in the ears of Muslims. If we consider the use of the word *god* in the Arabic language, we find that all the names by which the *pure truth,* i.e. Allah, has been named, may somehow or other be applied to other beings besides him, except the word Allah, which only applies to *God,* and which has been called his *greatest name.*

Difference of denominating God in Arabic, Hebrew, and Syriac

If we consider the use of the word in Hebrew and Syriac, in which two languages the sacred books before the Koran were revealed, we find that in the Thora and the following books of Prophets which are reckoned with the Thora as one whole, that word *Rabb* corresponds to the word *Allah* in Arabic, insofar as it cannot in a genitive construction be applied to anybody besides God, and you cannot say the *rabb* of the house, the *rabb* of the property (which in Arabic is allowed).

... Passing from the word *God* to those of *father* and *son,* we must state that Islam is not liberal in the use of them; for in Arabic the word *son* means nearly always as much as a *child* in the natural order of things, and from the ideas involved in parentage and birth can never be derived any expression meaning the Eternal Lord of creation. Other languages, however, take much more liberty in this respect; so that if people address a man by *father,* it is nearly the same as if they addressed him by *sir*. As is well known, phrases of this kind have become so prevalent among the Christians, that anybody who does not always use the words *father* and *son* in addressing people would scarcely be considered as one of them. By *the son* they understand most especially Jesus, but apply it also to others besides him.

[Al-Biruni also refers to the anthropomorphic ideas of the Manichaeans, and then comes to the popular religious ideas of Hindus. P. 39.]

... The educated among the Hindus abhor anthropomorphisms of this kind, but the crowd and the members of the single sects use them most extensively. They go even beyond all we have hitherto

Notions of the educated Hindus. All created beings are a unity

mentioned, so as to speak of wife, son, daughter, of the rendering pregnant and other physical processes, all in connection with God. They are even so little pious, that, when speaking of these things, they do not even abstain from silly and unbecoming language. However, nobody minds these classes and their theories, though they be numerous. The main and most essential point of the Hindu world of thought is that which the Brahmans think and believe, for they are specially trained for preserving and maintaining their religion. And this it is which we shall explain, viz. the belief of the Brahmans . . .

Purusha

I. Those Hindus who prefer clear and accurate definitions to vague allusions call the soul *purusha*, which means *man*, because it is the living element in the existing world. Life is the only attribute which they give to it. They describe it as alternately knowing and not knowing, as not knowing *en praxei* (actually), and as knowing *en dunamei* (potentially), gaining knowledge by acquisition. The not-knowing of *purusha* is the cause why action comes into existence, and its knowing is the cause why action ceases.

Avyakta

II. Next follows the general matter, i.e. the abstract *hule,* which they call *avyakta,* i.e. a shapeless thing. It is dead, but has three powers potentially, not actually, which are called *sattva, rajas,* and *tamas.* I have heard that Buddhodana[10] (sic), in speaking to his adherents the Shamanians, calls them *buddha, dharma, sangha,* as it were *intelligence, religion,* and *ignorance* (sic). The first power is rest and goodness, and hence come existing and growing. The second is exertion and fatigue, and hence come firmness and duration. The third is languor and irresolution, and hence come ruin and perishing. Therefore the first power is attributed to the angels, the second to men, the third to the animals. The ideas *before, afterwards,* and *thereupon* may be predicated of all these things only in the sense of a certain sequence and on account of the inadequacy of language, but not so as to indicate any ordinary notions of time.

III. Matter proceeding from *dunamis* into *praxis* under the various shapes and with the *three primary forces* is called *vyakta,* i.e. *having shape,* whilst the union of the *abstract hule* and of the *shaped matter* is called *prakriti.* This term, however, is of no use to us; we do not want

Vyakta and Prakriti

to speak of an *abstract* matter, the term *matter* alone being sufficient for us, since the one does not exist without the other.

Ahankara

IV. Next comes *nature,* which they call *ahankara.* The word is derived from the ideas of *overpowering, developing,* and *self-assertion,* because matter when assuming shape causes things to develop into new forms, and this growing consists in the changing of a foreign element and assimilating it to the growing one. Hence it is as if *nature* were trying to overpower those *other* or foreign elements in this process of changing them, and were subduing that which is changed.

Mahabhuta

V-IX. As a matter of course, each compound presupposes simple elements from which it is compounded and into which it is resolved again. The universal existences in the world are the five elements, i.e. according to the Hindus: heaven, wind, fire, water, and earth. They are called *mahabhuta,* i.e. *having great natures.* They do not think, as other people do, that the fire is a hot dry body near the bottom of the ether. They understand by fire the common fire on earth which comes from an inflammation of smoke.

Panca mataras

X–XIV. As these elements are compound, they presuppose simple ones which are called *panca mataras,* i.e. five mothers. They describe them as the functions of the senses. The simple element of heaven is *sabda* i.e. that which is heard; that of the wind is *sparsa,* i.e. that which is touched; that of the fire is *rupa,* i.e. that which is seen; that of the water is *rasa,* i.e. that which is tasted; and that of the earth is *gandha,* i.e. that which is smelled. With each of these *mahabhuta* elements (earth, water, etc.) they connect, firstly, *one* of the *panca mataras* elements, as we have here shown; and, secondly, all those which have been attributed to the *mahabhuta* elements previously mentioned. So the earth has all five qualities; the water has them *minus* the smelling (= four qualities); the fire has them *minus* the smelling and tasting (i.e. three qualities); the wind has them *minus* smelling, tasting, and seeing (i.e. two qualities); heaven has them *minus* smelling, tasting, seeing, and touching (i.e. one quality).

. . . The result of all these elements which we have enumerated, i.e. a compound of all of them, is the animal. The Hindus consider the plants as a species of animal as Plato also thinks that the plants have a sense, because they have the faculty of distinguishing between that which suits them and that which is detrimental to them. The animal is an animal as distinguished from a stone by virtue of its possession of the senses.

Indriyani

XV–XIX. The senses are five, called *indriyani,* the hearing by the ear, the seeing by the eye, the smelling by the nose, the tasting by the tongue, and the touching by the skin.

Manas

XX. Next follows the will, which directs the senses the exercise of their various functions, and which dwells in the heart. Therefore they call it *manas.*

Karmendriyani

XXI–XXV. The animal nature is rendered perfect by five *necessary functions,* which they call *karmendriyani,* i.e. the senses of action. The former senses bring about learning and knowledge, the latter action and work. We shall call them the *necessaria.* They are:

1) To produce a sound for any of the different wants and wishes a man may have; 2) To throw the hands with force, in order to draw towards or to put away; 3) To walk with the feet, in order to seek something or to fly from it; 4-5) The ejection of the superfluous elements of nourishment by means of the two openings created for the purpose.

Recapitulaion of the twenty-five elements

The whole of these elments are twenty-five, viz.:—

1. The general soul.
2. The abstract *hule.*
3. The shaped matter.
4. The overpowering nature.
5–9. The simple mothers.
10–14. The primary elements.
15–19. The senses of apperception.
20. The directing will.
21–25. The instrumental *necessaria.*

The totality of these elements is called *tattva,* and all knowledge is restricted to them . . .

CHAPTER IV

From What Cause Action Originates, And How The Soul Is Connected With Matter

The soul longing to be united with the body, is so united by intermediary spirits

Voluntary actions cannot originate in the body of any animal, unless the body be living and exist in close contact with that which is living of itself, i.e. the soul. The Hindus maintain that the soul is *en praxei,* not *en dunamei,* ignorant of its own essential nature and of its material substratum, longing to apprehend what it does not know, and believing that it cannot exist unless by matter. As, therefore, it longs for the good which is duration, and wishes to learn that which is hidden from it, it starts off in order to be united with matter. However, substances which are dense and such as are *tenuous,* if they have these qualities in the very highest degree, can mix together only by means of intermediary elements which stand in a certain relation to each of the two. Thus the air is the medium between fire and water, which are opposed to each other by these two qualities, for the air is related to the fire in tenuity and to the water in density, and by either of these qualities it renders the one capable of mixing with the other. Now, there is no greater antithesis than that between *body* and *not body.* Therefore the soul, being what it is, cannot obtain the fulfilment of its wish but by similar media, spirits which derive their existence from the *matres simplices* in the worlds called Bhurloka, Bhuvarloka, and Svarloka. The Hindus call them *tenuous bodies* over which the soul rises like the sun over the earth, in order to distinguish them from the *dense bodies* which derive their existence from the common five elements. The soul, in consequence of this union with the media, uses them as its vehicles. Thus the image of the sun, though he is only *one,* is represented in many mirrors which are placed opposite to him, as also in the water of vessels placed opposite. The sun is seen alike in each mirror and each vessel, and in each of them his warming and light-giving effect is perceived . . .

Such, then, is the supreme highest cause of the soul's starting off into action.

On matter seeking the union with the soul

On the other hand, the *lowest* cause, as proceeding from matter, is this: that matter for its part seeks for perfection, and always prefers that which is better to that which is less good, viz. proceeding from *dunamis* into *praxis.* In consequence of the vain-glory and ambition which are its pith and marrow, matter produces and shows all kinds of possibilities which it contains to its pupil, the soul, and carries it round through all classes of vegetable and animal beings.

On matter as the cause of action according to the Samkhya school of philosophers

. . . The book of Samkhya derives action from matter, for the difference of forms under which matter appears depends upon the *three primary forces,* and upon whether one or two of them gain the supremacy over the remainder. These forces are the *angelic,* the *human,* and the *animal.* The three forces belong only to matter, not to the soul. The task of the soul is to learn the actions of matter like a spectator, resembling a traveller who sits down in a village to repose. Each villager is busy with his own particular work, but he looks at them and considers their doings, disliking some, liking others, and taking an example from them. In this way he is busy without having himself any share in the business going on, and without being the cause which has brought it about . . .

People say the soul resembles the rain-water which comes down from heaven, always the same and of the same nature. However, if it is gathered in vessels placed for the purpose, vessels of different materials, of gold, silver, glass, earthenware. clay, or bitter-salt earth, it begins to differ in appearance, taste, and smell. Thus the soul does not influence matter in any way, except in this, that it gives matter life by being in close contact with it. When, then, matter begins to act, the result is different, in conformity with the one of the *three primary forces* which happens to preponderate, and conformably to the mutual assistance which the other two latent forces afford to the former. This assistance may be given in various ways, as the fresh oil, the dry wick, and the smoking fire help each other to produce light. The soul is in matter like the rider on a carriage, being attended by the senses, who drive the carriage according to the rider's intentions. But the soul for its part is guided by the intelligence with which it is inspired by God. This *intelligence* they describe as that by which the reality of things is apprehended, which shows the way to the knowledge of God, and to such actions as are liked and praised by everybody.

CHAPTER V

On The State Of The Souls, And Their Migrations Through The World In The Metempsychosis

As *the word of confession*, "There is no god but God, Muhammad is his prophet," is the shibboleth of Islam, the Trinity that of Christianity, and the institute of the Sabbath that of Judaism, so metempsychosis is the shibboleth of the Hindu religion. Therefore, he who does not believe in it does not belong to them, and is not reckoned as one of them. For they hold the following belief:

Beginning, development, and ultimate result of metempsychosis

The soul, as long as it has not risen to the highest absolute intelligence, does not comprehend the totality of objects at once, or, as it were, in no time. Therefore it must explore all particular beings and examine all the possibilities of existence; and as their number is, though not unlimited, still an enormous one, the soul wants an enormous space of time in order to finish the contemplation of such a multiplicity of objects. The soul acquires knowledge only by the contemplation of the individuals and the species, and of their peculiar actions and conditions. It gains experience from each object, and gathers thereby new knowledge.

However, these actions differ in the same measure as the three primary forces differ. Besides, the world is not left without some direction, being led, as it were, by a bridle and directed towards a definite scope. Therefore the imperishable souls wander about in perishable bodies conformably to the difference of their actions, as they prove to be good or bad. The object of the migration through the world of *reward* (i.e. heaven) is to direct the attention of the soul to the good, that it should become desirous of acquiring as much of it as possible. The object of its migration through the world of *punishment* (i.e. hell) is to direct its attention to the bad and abominable, that it should strive to keep as far as possible aloof from it.

The migration begins from low stages, and rises to higher and better ones, not the contrary, as we state on purpose, since the one is *a priori* as possible as the other. The difference of these lower and higher stages depends upon the difference of the actions, and this again results from the quantitative and qualitative diversity of the temperaments and the various degrees of combinations in which they appear.

This migration lasts until the object aimed at has been completely attained both for the soul and matter; the *lower* aim being the disappearance of the shape of matter, except any such new formation as may appear desirable; the *higher* aim being the ceasing of the desire of the soul to learn what it did not know before the insight of the soul into the nobility of its own being and its independent existence, its knowing that it can dispense with matter after it has become acquainted with the mean nature of matter and the instability of its shapes, with all that which matter offers to the senses, and with the truth of the tales about its delights. Then the soul turns away from matter; the connecting links are broken, the union is dissolved. Separation and dissolution take place, and the soul returns to its home, carrying with itself as much of the bliss of knowledge as sesame develops grains and blossoms, afterwards never separating from its oil. The intelligent being, intelligence and its object, are united and become one.

It is now our duty to produce from their literature some clear testimonies as to this subject and cognate theories of other nations.

[There follow some quotations from the *Gita* and other Hindu scriptures. Attention is also drawn to the similar views of the Greeks, and Socrates' work *Phaedo* is quoted. Pp. 52–57.]

. . . The same doctrine is professed by those Sufis who teach that this world is a sleeping soul and yonder world a soul awake, and who at the same time admit that God is immanent in certain places—e.g. in heaven—in the *seat* and the *throne* of God (mentioned in the Koran). But then there are others who admit that God is immanent in the whole world, in animals, trees, and the inanimate world, which they call his *universal appearance.* To those who hold this view, the entering of the souls into various beings in the course of metempsychosis is of no consequence.

Sufi doctrine

CHAPTER VI

On The Different Worlds, And On The Places Of Retribution In Paradise And Hell

The three

The Hindus call the world *loka.* Its primary division consists of the upper, the low, and the middle. The upper one is called *svarloka* i.e. paradise; the low, *nagaloka* i.e. the world of the serpents, which is hell; besides they call it *naraloka,* and sometimes also *patala,* i.e. the lowest world. The middle world, that one in which we live, is called *madhyaloka* and *manushyaloka,* i.e. the world of men. In the latter, man has to earn, in the upper to receive his reward; in the low, to receive punishment. A man who deserves to come to *svarloka* or *nagaloka* receives there the full recompense of his deeds during a certain length of time corresponding to the duration of his deeds, but in either of them there is only the soul, the soul free from the body.

For those who do not deserve to rise to heaven and to sink as low as hell there is another world called *tiryagloka,* the irrational world of plants and animals, through the individuals of which the soul has to wander in the metempsychosis until it reaches the human being, rising by degrees from the lowest kinds of the vegetable world to highest classes of the sensitive world. The stay of the soul in this world has one of the following causes: either the award which is due to the soul is not sufficient to raise it into heaven or to sink it into hell, or the soul is in its wanderings on the way back from hell; for they believe that a soul returning to the human world from heaven at once adopts a human body, whilst that one which returns there from hell has first to wander about in plants and animals before it reaches the degree of living in a human body.

Quotation from the Vishnu-Purana

The Hindus speak in their traditions of a large number of hells, of their qualities and their names, and for each kind of sin they have a special hell. The number of hells is 88,000 according to the *Vishnu-Purana*.[11] [Al-Biruni quotes from this book about the different kinds of sins committed by the people and the hells prescribed for them. Among such persons is 'he who bears false witness . . . sheds innocent blood . . . kills cows (and) . . . a Brahman . . . commits adultery with his sister or the wife of his son . . . contemns the Veda and Puranas . . . does not honour the rights of parents' . . . makes swords and knives, rears cocks, cats and pigs, cuts down trees and—worst of all—neglects customs and violates laws. Al-Biruni adds that he was listing these 'only in order to show what kinds of deeds the Hindus abhor as sins.' Pp. 60–61.]

According to some Hindus, the migration through plants and animals takes the place of hell

Some Hindus believe that the middle world, that one for earning, is the human world, and that a man wanders about in it, because he has received a reward which does not lead him into heaven, but at the same time saves him from hell. They consider heaven as a higher stage, where a man lives in a state of bliss which must be of a certain duration on account of the good deeds he has done. On the contrary, they consider the wandering about in plants and animals as a lower stage, where a man dwells for punishment for a certain length of time, which is thought to correspond to the wretched deeds he has done. People who hold this view do not know of another hell, but this kind of degradation below the degree of living as a human being.

Moral principles of metempsychosis

All these degrees of retribution are necessary for this reason, that the seeking for salvation from the fetters of matter frequently does not proceed on the straight line which leads to absolute knowledge, but on lines chosen by guessing or chosen because others had chosen them. Not one action of man shall be lost, not even the last of all; it shall be brought to his account after his good and bad actions have been balanced against each other. The retribution, however, is not according to the deed, but according to the intention which a man had in doing it; and a man will receive his reward either in the form in which he lives on earth, or in that form into which his soul will migrate, or in a kind of intermediary state after he has left his shape and has not yet entered a new one.

Here now the Hindus quit the path of philosophical speculation and turn aside to traditional fables as regards the two places where reward or punishment is given, e.g. that man exists there as an incorporeal being, and that after having received the reward of his actions he again returns to a bodily appearance and human shape, in order to be prepared for his further destiny. Therefore, the author of the book *Samkhya* does not consider the reward of paradise a special gain, because it has an end and is not eternal, and because this kind of life resembles the life of this our world; for it is not free from ambition and envy, having in itself various degrees and classes of existence, whilst cupidity and desire do not cease save where there is perfect equality.

The Samkhya criticises metempsychosis

The Sufi, too, do not consider the stay in paradise a special gain for another reason, because there the soul delights in other things but the Truth, i.e. God, and its thoughts are diverted from the Absolute Good by things which are not the Absolute Good.

Sufi Parallel

We have already said that, according to the belief of the Hindus, the soul exists in these two places without a body. But this is only the view of the educated among them, who understand by the soul an independent being. However, the lower classes, and those who cannot imagine the existence of the soul without a body, hold about this subject verv different views. One is this, that the cause of the agony of death is the soul's waiting for a shape which is to be prepared. It does not quit the body before there has originated a cognate being of similar functions, one of those which nature prepares either as an embryo in a mother's womb or as a seed in the bosom of the earth. Then the soul quits the body in which it has been staying.

On the soul leaving the body, according to popular views

Others hold the more traditional view that the soul does not wait for such a thing, that it quits its shape on account of its weakness whilst another body has been prepared for it out of the elements. This body is called *ativahika,* i.e. *that which grows in haste,* because it does not come into existence by being born. The soul stays in this body a complete year in the greatest agony, no matter whether it has deserved to be rewarded or to be punished. This is like the Barzakh of the Persians, an intermediary stage between the periods of acting and earning and that of receiving award. For this reason the heir of the deceased must, according to Hindus use, fulfil the rites of the year for the deceased, duties which end with the end of the year, for then the soul goes to that place which is prepared for it.

[Extracts from the *Vishnu-Purana* are quoted to illustrate these ideas, Pp. 63–64.]

. . . A theosoph who inclines towards metempsychosis says: "The metempsychosis has four degrees:

1. "The *transferring,* i.e. the procreation as limited to the human species, because it *transfers* existence from one individual to another; the opposite of this is—

Muslim authors on metempsychosis

2. "The *transforming,* which concerns men in particular, since they are *transformed* into monkeys, pigs, and elephants.

3. "A stable condition of existence, like the condition of the plants. This is worse than *transferring,* because it is a stable condition of life, remains as it is through all times, and lasts as long as the mountains."

4. "The *dispersing,* the opposite of number 3, which applies to the plants that are plucked, and to animals immolated as sacrifice, because they vanish without leaving posterity."

Abu-Yakub of Sijistan maintains in his book, called *The disclosing of that which is veiled,* that the species are preserved; that metempsychosis always proceeds in one and the same species, never crossing its limits and passing into another species.

This was also the opinion of the ancient Greeks; . . .

[Extracts from Socrates' *Phaedo* are given; also the views of Plato as stated by Johannes Grammaticus, pp. 65–67.]

CHAPTER VII

On The Nature Of Liberation From The World, And On The Path Leading Thereto

If the soul is bound up with the world, and its being bound up has a certain cause, it cannot be liberated from this bond save by the opposite of this identical cause. Now according to the Hindus, as we have already explained, the reason of the bond is *ignorance,* and therefore it can only be liberated by *knowledge,* by comprehending all things in such a way as to define them both in general and in particular, rendering superfluous any kind of deduction and removing all doubts. For the soul distinguishing between things (*ta onta*) by means of definitions, recognises its own self, and recognises at the same time that it is its noble lot to last for ever, and that it is the vulgar lot of matter to change and to perish in all kinds of shapes. Then it dispenses with matter, and perceives that that which it held to be good and delightful is in reality bad and painful. In this manner it attains real knowledge and turns away from being arrayed in matter. Thereby action ceases, and both matter and soul become free by separáting from each other.

First part:
Moksha in general

. . . The terms of the Sufi as to the *knowing being* and his attaining the *stage of knowledge* come to the same effect, for they maintain that

Sufi parallel

he has two souls—an eternal one, not exposed to change and alteration, by which he knows that which is hidden, the transcendental world, and performs wonders; and another, a human soul, which is liable to being changed and being born.

. . . According to the Hindus, the organs of the senses have been made for acquiring knowledge, and the pleasures which they afford have been created to stimulate people to research and investigation, as the pleasure which eating and drinking afford to the taste has been created to preserve the individual by means of nourishment. So the pleasure of *coitus* serves to preserve the species by giving birth to new individuals. If there was not special pleasure in these two functions, man and animals would not practice them for these purposes.

. . . Further, the Hindus think that a man becomes *knowing* in one of three ways:—

1. By being inspired, not in a certain course of time, but at once, at birth, and in the cradle as, e.g. the sage Kapila, for he was born knowing and wise.

2. By being inspired after a certain time, like the children of Brahman, for they were inspired when they came of age.

3. By learning, and after a certain course of time, like all men who learn when their mind ripens.

Liberation through knowledge can only be obtained by abstaining from *evil.* The branches of evil are many, but we may classify them as *cupidity, wrath,* and *ignorance.* If the roots are cut the branches will wither. And here we have first to consider the rule of the two forces of *cupidity* and *wrath,* which are the greatest and most pernicious enemies of man, deluding him by the pleasure of eating and the delight of revenge, whilst in reality they are much more likely to lead him into pains and crimes. They make a man similar to the wild beasts and the cattle, nay, even to the demons and devils.

Cupidity, wrath, and ignorance are the chief obstacles to Moksha

Next, we have to consider that man must prefer the reasoning force of mind, by which he becomes similar to the highest angels, to the forces of cupidity and wrath; and, lastly, that he must turn away from the actions of the world. He cannot, however, *give up* these actions unless he does away with their causes, which are his lust and ambition. Thereby the second of the *three primary forces* is cut away. However, the abstaining *from action* takes place in two different ways:

1. By laziness, procrastination, and ignorance according to the *third force.* This mode is not desirable, for it will lead to a blamable end.

2. By judicious selection and by preferring that which is better to that which is good, which way leads to a laudable end.

The abstaining from actions is rendered perfect in this way, that a man quits anything that might occupy him and shuts himself up against it. Thereby he will be enabled to restrain his senses from extraneous objects to such a degree that he does not any more know that there exists anything besides himself, and be enabled to stop all motions, and even the breathing. It is evident that a greedy man strains to effect his object, the man who strains becomes tired, and the tired man pants; so the panting is the result of greediness. If this greediness is removed, the breathing becomes like the breathing of a being living at the bottom of the sea, that does not want breath; and then the heart quietly rests on one thing, viz. the search for liberation and for arriving at the absolute unity.

. . . On account of what we have explained, it is necessary that cogitation should be continuous, not in any way to be defined by number; for a number always denotes *repeated times*, and repeated times presuppose a break in the cogitation occurring between two consecutive times. This would interrupt the continuity, and would prevent cogitation becoming united with the object of cogitation. And this is not the object kept in view, which is, on the contrary, *the continuity of cogitation.*

This goal is attained either in a *single shape,* i.e. a single stage of metempsychosis, or *in several shapes,* in this way, that a man perpetually practises virtuous behaviour and accustoms the soul thereto, so that this virtuous behaviour becomes to it a nature and an essential quality.

Virtuous behaviour is that which is described by the religious law. Its principal laws, from which they derive many secondary ones, may be summed up in following nine rules:—

The nine commandments of the Hindu religion

1. A man shall not kill.
2. Nor lie.
3. Nor steal.
4. Nor whore.
5. Nor hoard up treasures.
6. He is perpetually to practise holiness and purity.

7. He is to perform the prescribed fasting without an interruption and to dress poorly.
8. He is to hold fast to the adoration of God with praise and thanks.
9. He is always to have in mind the word *om*, the word of creation, without pronouncing it.

The injunction to abstain from killing as regards animals (No. 1) is only a special part of the general order to *abstain from doing anything hurtful.* Under this head falls also the robbing of another man's goods (No. 3), and the telling lies (No. 2), not to mention the foulness and baseness of so doing.

The abstaining from hoarding up (No. 5) means that a man is to give up toil and fatigue; that he who seeks the bounty of God feels sure that he is provided for; and that, starting from the base slavery of material life, we may, by the noble liberty of cogitation, attain eternal bliss.

Practising purity (No. 6) implies that a man knows the filth of the body, and that he feels called upon to hate it, and to love cleanliness of soul. Tormenting oneself by poor dress (No. 7) means that a man should reduce the body, allay its feverish desires, and sharpen its senses . . .

The holding fast to meditation on God and the angels means a kind of familiar intercourse with them.

Second part: The *practical* path leading to Moksha

. . . In the book of Patanjali we read: "We divide the path of liberation into three parts:—

"I. The *practical one (kriya-yoga),* a process of habituating the senses in a gentle way to detach themselves from the external world, and to concentrate themselves upon the internal one, so that they exclusively occupy themselves with God. This is in general the path of him who does not desire anything save what is sufficient to sustain life."

According to *Patanjali, Vishnu-Dharma,* and the *Gita*

[Relevant extracts from *Vishnu Dharma*[12] and the *Gita* are given. Pp. 77–79.]

. . . II. The second part of the path of liberation is renunciation (the *via omissionis*), based on the knowledge of the evil which exists in the changing things of creation and their vanishing shapes. In consequence the heart shuns them, the longing for them ceases, and a man is raised above the

The path of renunciation as the second part of the path of liberation according to the *Gita three primary forces* which are the cause of actions and of their diversity. For he who accurately understands the affairs of the world knows that the good ones among them are evil in reality, and that the bliss which they afford changes in the course of recompense into pains. Therefore, he avoids everything which might aggravate his condition of being entangled in the world, and which might result in making him stay in the world for a still longer period.

. . . III. The third part of the path of liberation which is to be considered a instrumental to the preceding two is *worship,* for this purpose, that God should help a man to obtain liberation, and deign to consider him worthy of such a shape of existence in the metempsychosis in which he may effect his progress towards beatitude.

Worship as the third part of the path of liberation according to the *Gita*

The author of the book *Gita* distributes the duties of worship among the *body,* the *voice,* and the *heart.*

What the *body* has to do is fasting, prayer, the fulfilment of the law, the service towards the angels and the sages among the Brahmans, keeping clean the body, keeping aloof from killing under all circumstances, and never looking at another man's wife and other's property.

What the *voice* has to do is the reciting of the holy texts, praising God, always to speak the truth, to address people mildly, to guide them, and to order them to do good.

What the *heart* has to do is to have straight, honest intentions, to avoid haughtiness, always to be patient, to keep your senses under control, and to have a cheerful mind.

. . . According to the Hindus, liberation is union with God; for they describe God as a being who can dispense with hoping for a recompense or with fearing opposition, unattainable to thought, because he is sublime beyond all unlikeness which is abhorrent and all likeness which is sympathetic, knowing himself not by a knowledge which comes to him like an accident, regarding something which had not in every phase before been known to him. And this same description the Hindus apply to *the liberated one,* for he is equal to God in all these things except in the matter of beginning, since he has not existed from all eternity, and except this, that before liberation he existed in *the world of entanglement,* knowing the objects of knowledge only by a phantasmagoric kind of knowing which he had acquired by absolute exertion, whilst the object of his knowing is

On the nature of Moksha itself

still covered, as it were, by a veil. On the contrary, in the world of liberation all veils are lifted, all covers taken off, and obstacles removed. There the being is absolutely knowing, not desirous of learning anything unknown, separated from the soiled perceptions of the senses, united with the everlasting ideas. Therefore, in the end of the book of *Patanjali*, after the pupil has asked about the nature of liberation the master says: "If you wish, say Liberation is the cessation of the functions of *the three forces,* and their returning to that home whence they had come. Or if you wish, say, it is the return of the soul as a *knowing* being into its own nature."

Quotations from *Patanjali*

. . . Similar views are also met with among the Sufi. Some Sufi author relates the following story: "A company of Sufi came down unto us, and sat down at some distance from us. Then one of them rose, prayed, and on, having finished his prayer, turned towards me and spoke: 'O master, do you know here a place fit for us *to die,* on?' Now I thought he meant *sleeping,* and so I pointed out to him a place. The man went there, threw himself on the back of his head, and remained motionless. Now I rose, went to him and shook him but lo! he was already cold."

Sufi parallels

The Sufi explains the Koranic verse, "We have made room for him on earth" (Sura 18, 83), in this way: "If he wishes, the earth rolls itself up for him; if he wishes, he can walk on the water and in the air, which offer him sufficient resistance so as to enable him to walk, whilst the mountains do not offer him any resistance when he wants to pass through them."

We next speak of those who, notwithstanding their greatest exertions, do not reach the stage of liberation. There are several classes of them.

On those who do not reach Moksha according to *Samkhya*

[Extracts from the *Samkhya* are given in regard to those who do not attain *moksha* (salvation). Similar ideas of some Greek writers such as Ammonius, Plato and Proculus are referred to, Pp. 83–86.]

The doctrine of *Patanjali* is akin to that of the Sufi regarding being occupied in meditation on *the Truth* (i.e. God), for they say, "As long as you point to something, you cannot be a *monist;* but when *the Truth* seizes upon the object of your pointing and annihilates it, then there is no longer an indicating person nor an object indicated."

There are some passages in their system which show that they believe in the pantheistic union; e.g. one of them, being asked what is *the Truth* (God), gave the following answer: "How should I not know the being which is *I* in essence and *Not-I* in space? If I return once more into existence, thereby I am separated from him; and if I am neglected (i.e. not born anew and sent into the world), thereby I become light and become accustomed to the *union" (sic).* . . .

Abu-Yazid Albistami once being asked how he had attained *his* stage in Sufism, answered: "I cast off my own self as a serpent casts off its skin. Then I considered my own self and found that I was *He,"* i.e. God. . . .

[Al-Biruni concludes the chapter by adding that the Sufis say:] "Between man and God there are a thousand stages of light and darkness. Men exert themselves to pass through darkness to light, and when they have attained to the stations of light, there is no return for them."

CHAPTER VIII

On The Different Classes Of Created Beings, And On Their Names

The subject of this chapter is very difficult to study and understand accurately, since we Muslims look at it from without, and the Hindus themselves do not work it out to scientific perfection. As we, however, want it for the further progress of this treatise, we shall communicate all we have heard of it until the date of the present book. And first we give an extract from the book *Samkhya.*

The various classes of creatures according to *Samkhya*

"The anchorite spoke: 'How many classes and species are there of living bodies?'

"The sage replied: 'There are three classes of them—the spiritual ones in the height, men in the middle, and animals in the depth. Their species are fourteen in number, eight of which belong to the spiritual beings: Brahman, Indra, Prajapati, Saumya, Gandharva, Yaksha, Rakshasa, and Pisaca. Five species are those of the animals—cattle, wild beasts, birds, creeping things, and *growing things, i.e.* the trees. And, lastly, *one* species is represented by man.'"

The author of the same book has in another part of it given the following enumeration with different names: "Brahman, Indra,

Prajapati, Gandharva, Yaksha, Rakshasa, Pitaras, Pisaca."

The Hindus are people who rarely preserve one and the same order of things, and in their enumeration of things there is much that is arbitrary. They use or invent numbers of names, and who is to hinder or to control them?

. . . According to the most popular view of the majority of the Hindus, there are the following eight classes of *spiritual* beings:—

The author enumerates eight classes of spiritual beings

1. The *Deva,* or angels, to whom the north belongs. They specially belong to the Hindus. People say that Zoroaster made enemies of the Shamaniyya or Buddhists by calling the devils by the name of the class of angels which *they* consider the highest, i.e. *Deva.* And this usage has been transmitted from Magian times down to the Persian language of our days.

2. *Daitya, danava,* the demons who live in the south. To them everybody belongs who opposes the religion of the Hindus and persecutes the cows. Notwithstanding the near relationship which exists between them and the Deva, there is, as Hindus maintain, no end of quarrelling and fighting among them.

3. *Gandharva,* the musicians and singers who make music before the Deva. Their harlots are called Apsaras.

4. *Yaksha,* the treasurers or guardians of the Deva.

5. *Rakshasa,* demons of ugly and deformed shapes.

6. *Kinnara,* having human shapes but horses' heads, being the contrary of the centaurs of the Greek, of whom the lower half has the shape of a horse, the upper half that of a man. The latter figure is that of the Zodiacal sign of *Arcitenens.*

7. *Naga,* beings in the shape of serpents.

8. *Vidyadhara,* demon-sorcerers, who exercise a certain witchcraft, but not such a one as to produce permanent results.

If we consider this series of beings, we find the angelic power at the upper end and the demoniac at the lower, and between them there is much interblending. The qualities of these beings are different, inasmuch as they have attained this stage of life in the course of metempsychosis by *action*, and actions are different on account of the *three primary forces.* They live very long, since they have entirely stripped off the bodies, since they are free from all exertion, and are able to do things which are impossible t

Criticisms on this list

man. They serve man in whatever he desires, and are near him in case of need.

However, we can learn from the extract from *Samkhya* that this view is not correct. For Brahman, Indra, and Prajapati are not names of species, but of individuals. Brahman and Prajapati very nearly mean the same, but they bear different names on account of some quality or other. Indra is the ruler of the worlds. Besides, Vasudeva enumerates the Yaksha and Rakshasa together in one and the same class of demons, whilst the Puranas represent the Yaksha as guardian-angels and the servants of guardian-angels.

After all this, we declare that the spiritual beings which we have mentioned, are one category, who have attained their present stage of existence by action during the time when they were human beings. They have left their bodies behind them, for bodies are weights which impair the power and shorten the duration of life. Their qualities and conditions are different, in the same measure as one or other of the *three primary forces* prevails over them. The first force is peculiar to the Deva, or angels who live in quietness and bliss. The predominant faculty of their mind is the comprehending of an idea *without matter,* as it is the predominant faculty of the mind of man to comprehend the idea *in matter.*

On the Devas

The *third force* is peculiar to the Pisaca and Bhuta, whilst the second is peculiar to the classes between them.

The Hindus say that the number of Deva is thirty-three *koti* or crore, of which eleven belong to Mahadeva. Therefore this number is one of his surnames, and his name itself (Mahadeva) points in this direction. The sum of the number of angels just mentioned would be 330,000,000.

Further, they represent the Deva as eating and drinking, cohabiting, living and dying, since they exist within matter, though in the most subtle and most simple kind of it, and since they have attained this by action, not by knowledge. The book *Patanjali* relates that Nandikesvara offered many sacrifices to Mahadeva, and was in consequence transferred into paradise in his human shape; that Indra, the ruler, had intercourse with the wife of Nahusha the Brahmin, and therefore was changed into a serpent by way of punishment.

After the Deva comes the class of the *Pitaras,* the deceased ancestors, and after them the *Bhuta,* human beings who have attached themselves to the *spiritual beings* (Deva), and stand in the middle between them and mankind. He who holds this degree, but without being free from the body, is called either *Rishi, Siddha* or *Muni,* and these differ among themselves according to their qualities. *Siddha* is he who has attained by his action the faculty to do in the world whatever he likes, but who does not aspire further, and does not exert himself on the path leading to liberation. He may ascend to the degree of a Rishi. If a Brahmin attains this degree, he is called *Brahmarshi;* if the Kshatriya attains it, he is called *Rajarshi.* It is not possible for the lower classes to attain this degree. Rishis are the sages who, though they are only human beings, excel the angels on account of their knowledge. Therefore, the angels learn from them, and above them there is none but Brahman.

On the Pitaras and Rishis

After the Brahmarshi and Rajarshi come those classes of the populace which exist also among us, the castes, to whom we shall devote a separate chapter.

All these latter beings are ranged under matter. Now, as regards the notion of that which is above matter, we say that the *hule* is the middle between matter and the spiritual divine ideas that are above matter, and that the *three primary forces* exist in the *hule* dynamically (*en dunamei*). So the *hule* with all that is comprehended in it, is a bridge from above to below.

Vishnu the unity of Brahman, Narayana, and Rudra

Any life which circulates in the *hule* under the exclusive influence of the *First Cause* is called *Brahman, Prajapati,* and by many other names which occur in their religious law and tradition. It is identical with nature insofar as it is active, for all bringing into existence, the creation of the world also, is attributed by them to Brahman.

Any life which circulates in the *hule* under the influence of the *second force* is called *Narayana* in the tradition of the Hindus, which means nature insofar as it has reached the end of its action, and is now striving to preserve that which has been produced. Thus Narayana strives so to arrange the world that it should endure.

Any life which circulates in the *hule* under the influence of the *third force* is called *Mahadeva* and *Samkara,* but his best-known name is *Rudra.* His work is destruction and annihilation, like nature in the last stages of activity, when its power slackens.

These three beings bear different names, as they circulate through the various degrees to above and below, and accordingly their actions are different.

But prior to all these beings there is one source whence everything is derived, and in this unity they comprehend all three things, no more separating one from the other. This unity they call *Vishnu,* a name which more properly designates the *middle force;* but sometimes they do not even make a distinction between this *middle force* and the *first cause* (i.e. they make Narayana the *causa causarum*).

Here there is an analogy between Hindus and Christians, as the latter distinguish between the Three *Persons* and give them separate names, Father, Son, and Holy Ghost, but unite them into one substance.

This is what clearly results from a careful examination of the Hindu doctrines. Of their traditional accounts, which are full of silly notions, we shall speak hereafter in the course of our explanation. You must not wonder if the Hindus, in their stories about the class of the Deva, whom we have explained as *angels,* allow them all sorts of things, unreasonable in themselves, some perhaps not objectionable, others decidedly objectionable both of which the theologians of Islam would declare to be incompatible with the dignity and nature of angels.

Greek parallels. Stories about Zeus

If you compare these traditions with those of the Greeks regarding their own religion, you will cease to find the Hindu system strange . . .

[The stories of Zeus are mentioned. Al-Biruni remarks, as stated above, that compared to the Greek stories those of the Hindus were less strange. Pp. 95–98.]

CHAPTER IX

On The Castes, Called "Colours" (Varna), And On The Classes Below Them

If a new order of things in political or social life is created by a man naturally ambitious of ruling, who by his character and capacity really deserves to be a ruler, a man of firm convictions and unshaken determination, who even in times of reverses is supported by good luck, insofar as people then side with him in recognition of former merits of his, such an order is likely to become consolidated among those for whom it was created, and to continue as firm as the deeply rooted mountains. It will remain among them as a generally recognised rule in all generations through the course of time and the flight of ages. If, then, this new form of state or society rests in some degree on religion, these twins, state and religion, are in perfect harmony, and their union represents the highest development of human society, all that men can possibly desire.

Throne and altar

The kings of antiquity, who were industriously devoted to the duties of their office, spent most of their care on the division of their subjects into different classes and orders, which they tried to preserve from intermixture and disorder. Therefore, they forbade people of different classes to have intercourse with each other, and laid upon each class a particular kind of work or art and handicraft. They did not allow anybody to transgress the limits of his class, and even punished those who would not be content with their class.

Castes of the ancient Persians

All this is well illustrated by the history of the ancient Chosroes (Khusrau), for they had created great institutions of this kind, which could not be broken through by the special merits of any individual nor by bribery. When Ardashir ben Babak restored the Persian empire, he also restored the classes or castes of the population in the following way:—

The first class were the knights and princes.

The second class the monks, the fire-priests, and the lawyers.

The third class the physicians, astronomers, and other men of science.

The fourth class the husbandmen and artisans.

And within these classes there were subdivisions, distinct from each other, like the species within a genus. All institutions of this kind are like a pedigree, as long as their origin is remembered; but when once their origin has been forgotten, they become, as it were, the stable property of the whole nation, nobody any more questioning its origin. And forgetting is the necessary result of any long period of time, of a long succession of centuries and generations.

Among the Hindus institutions of this kind abound. We Muslims, of course, stand entirely on the other side of the question, considering all men as equal, except in piety; and this is the greatest obstacle which prevents any approach or understanding between Hindus and Muslims.

The four castes

The Hindus call their castes *varna,* i.e. *colours,* and from a genealogical point of view they call them *jataka,* i.e. *births.* These castes are from the very beginning only four.

I. The highest caste are the Brahmana, of whom the books of the Hindus tell that they were created from the head of Brahman. And as Brahman is only another name for the force called nature, and the head is the highest part of the animal body, the Brahmana are the choice part of the whole genus. Therefore, the Hindus consider them as the very best of mankind.

II. The next caste are the Kshatriya, who were created, as they say, from the shoulders and hands of Brahman. Their degree is not much below that of the Brahmana.

III. After them follow the Vaisya, who were created from the thigh of Brahman.

IV. The Sudra, who were created from his feet.

Between the latter two classes there is not very great distance. Much, however, as these classes differ from each other, they live together in the same towns and villages, mixed together in the same houses and lodgings.

After the Sudra follow the people called *Antyaja,* who render various kinds of services, who are not reckoned amongst any caste, but only as members of a certain craft or profession. There are eight[13] classes of them, who freely intermarry with each other, except the fuller, shoemaker, and weaver, for no others would condescend to have anything to do with them. These eight guilds are the fuller, shoemaker, juggler, the basket and shield maker, the sailor, fisherman, the hunter of wild animals and of birds, and the weaver. The four castes do not live together with them in one and the same place. These guilds live near the villages and towns of the four castes, but outside them.

Low-caste people

The people called Hadi, Doma (Domba), Candala, and Badhatau (sic) are not reckoned amongst any caste or guild. They are occupied with dirty work, like the cleansing of the villages and other services. They are considered as one sole class, and distinguished only by their occupations. In fact, they are considered like illegitimate children; for according to general opinion they descend from a Sudra father and a Brahmani mother as the children of fornication; therefore they are degraded outcastes.

The Hindus give to every single man of the four castes characteristic names, according to their occupations and modes of life. For example, the Brahmana is in general called by this name as long as he does his work staying at home. When he is busy with the service of one fire, he is called *ishtin;* if he serves three fires, he is called *agnihotrin;* if he besides offers an offering to the fire, he is called *dikshita.* And as it is with the Brahmana, so is it also with the other castes. Of the classes *beneath* the castes, the *Hadi* are the best spoken of, because they keep themselves free from everything unclean. Next follow the Doma, who play on the lute and sing. The still lower classes practise as a trade killing and the inflicting of

Different occupations of the castes and guilds

judicial punishments. The worst of all are the Badhatau, who not only devour the flesh of dead animals, but even of dogs and other beasts.

Each of the four castes, when eating together, must form a group for themselves, one group not being allowed to comprise two men of different castes. If, further, in the group of the Brahmana there are two men who live at enmity with each other, and the seat of the one is by the side of the other, they make a barrier between the two seats by placing a board between them, or by spreading a piece of dress, or in some other way; and if there is only a line drawn between them, they are considered as separated. Since it is forbidden to eat the remains of a meal, every single man must have his own food for himself; for if any one of the party who are eating should take of the food from one and the same plate, that which remains in the plate becomes, after the first eater has taken part, to him who wants to take as the second, *the remains of the meal,* and such is forbidden.

Customs of the Brahmins

Such is the condition of the four castes.

. . . Hindus differ among themselves as to which of these castes is capable of attaining to liberation; for, according to some, only the Brahmana and Kshatriya are capable of it, since the others cannot learn the Veda, whilst according to the Hindu philosophers, liberation is common to all castes and to the whole human race, if their intention of obtaining it is perfect. This veiw is based on the saying of Vyasa: "Learn to know the twenty-five things thoroughly. Then you may follow whatever religion you like; you will no doubt be liberated." This view is also based on the fact that Vasudeva was a descendant of a Sudra family, and also on the following saying of his, which he addressed to Arjuna: "God distributes recompense without injustice and without partiality. He reckons the good as bad if people in doing good forget Him; he reckons the bad as good if people in doing bad remember Him and do not forget Him, whether those people be Vaisya or Sudra or women. How much more will this be the case when they are Brahmana or Kshatriya."

Moksha and the various castes

CHAPTER X

On The Source Of Their Religious And Civil Law, On Prophets, And On The Question Whether Single Laws Can Be Abrogated Or Not

Law and religion among the Greeks founded by their sages

The ancient Greeks received their religious and civil laws from sages among them who were called to the work, and of whom their countrymen believed that they received divine help, like Solon, Draco, Pythagoras, Minos, and others. Also their kings did the same; for Mianos (*sic*), when ruling over the islands of the sea and over the Cretans about two hundred years after Moses, gave them laws, pretending to have received them from Zeus. About the same time also Minos (*sic*) gave his laws . . .

The Rishis, the authors of Hindu law

Such was the case with the Greeks, and it is precisely the same with the Hindus. For they believe that their religious law and its single precepts derive their origin from Rishis, their sages, the pillars of their religion, and not from the prophet, i.e. Narayana, who, when coming into this world, appears in some human figure. But he only comes in order to cut away some evil matter which threatens the world, or to set the world right again when anything has gone wrong. Further, no law can be exchanged or replaced by another, for they use the laws simply as they find them. Therefore they can dispense with prophets, as far as law and worship are concerned, though in other affairs of the creation they sometimes want them.

As for the question of the abrogation of laws, it seems that this is not impossible with the Hindus, for they say that many things which are now forbidden were allowed before the coming of Vasudeva, e.g. the flesh of cows. Such changes are necessitated by the change of the nature of man, and by their being too feeble to bear the whole burden of their duties. To these changes also belong the changes of the *matrimonial system* and of *the theory of descent.* For in former times there were three modes of determining descent or relationship:

Whether laws may be abrogated or not

Different matrimonial systems

1. The child born to a man by his legitimate wife is the child of the father, as is the custom with us and with the Hindus.

2. If man marries a woman and has a child by her; if, further, the marriage-contract stipulates that the children of the woman will belong to *her* father, the child is considered as the child of its grandfather who made that stipulation, and not as the child of its father who engendered it.

3. If a stranger has a child by a married woman, the child belongs to her husband, since the wife being, as it were, the soil in which the child has grown, is the property of the husband, always presupposing that the sowing, i.e. the cohabitation, takes place with his consent.

. . . All these customs have now been abolished and abrogated, and therefore we may infer from their tradition that in principle *the abrogation of a law is allowable.*

As regards unnatural kinds of marriage, we must state that such exist still in our time, as they also existed in the times of Arab heathendom; for the people inhabiting the mountains stretching from the region of Panchir into the neighbourhood of Kashmir live under the rule that several brothers have one wife in common. Among the heathen Arabs, too, marriage was of different kinds:—

Various kinds of marriage with Tibetans and Arabs

1. An Arab ordered his wife to be sent to a certain man to demand sexual intercourse with him; then he abstained from her during the whole time of her pregnancy, since he wished to have from her a generous offspring. This is identical with the third kind of marriage

among the Hindus.

2. A second kind was this, that the one Arab said to the other, "Cede me your wife, and I will cede you mine," and thus they exchanged their wives.

3. A third kind is this, that several men cohabited with one wife. When, then, she gave birth to a child, she declared who was the father; and if she did not know it, the fortune-tellers had to know it.

4. The *Nikah-elmakt* (= *matrimonium exosum*), i.e. when a man married the widow of his father or of his son, the child of such a marriage was called *daizan*. This is nearly the same as a certain Jewish marriage, for the Jews have the law that a man must marry the widow of his brother, if the latter has not left children, and create a line of descent for his deceased brother; and the offspring is considered as that of the deceased man, not as that of the real father. Thereby they want to prevent his memory dying out in the world. In Hebrew they call a man who is married in this way *Yabham*.

[A similar institution among the Magians is referred to. Pp. 109–110.]

We have here given an account of these things in order that the reader may learn by the comparative treatment of the subject how much superior the institutions of Islam are, and how much more plainly this contrast brings out all customs and usages, differing from those of Islam, in their essential foulness.

CHAPTER XI

About The Beginning Of Idol-Worship, And A Description Of The Individual Idols

It is well known that the popular mind leans towards the sensible world, and has an aversion to the world of abstract thought which is only understood by highly educated people, of whom in every time and every place there are only few. And as common people will only acquiesce in pictorial representations, many of the leaders of religious communities have so far deviated from the right path as to give such imagery in their books and houses of worship, like the Jews and Christians, and, more than all, the Manichaeans. These words of mine would at once receive a sufficient illustration if, for example, a picture of the Prophet were made, or of Mekka and the Ka'ba, and were shown to an uneducated man or woman. Their joy in looking at the thing would bring them to kiss the picture, to rub their cheeks against it, and to roll themselves in the dust before it, as if they were seeing not the picture, but the original, and were in this way, as if they were present in the holy places, performing the rites of pilgrimage, the great and the small ones.

Origin of idol-worship in the nature of man

This is the cause which leads to the manufacture of idols,

monuments in honour of certain much venerated persons, prophets, sages, angels, destined to keep alive their memory when they are absent or dead, to create for them a lasting place of grateful veneration in the hearts of men when they die. But when much time passes by after the setting up of the monument, generations and centuries, its origin is forgotten, it becomes a matter of custom, and its veneration a rule for general practice. This being deeply rooted in the nature of man, the legislators of antiquity tried to influence them from this weak point of theirs. Therefore they made the veneration of pictures and similar monuments obligatory on them, as is recounted in historic records, both for the times before and after the Deluge. Some people even pretend to know that all mankind, before God sent them his prophets, were one large idolatrous body . . .

Since, however, here we have to explain the system and the theories of the Hindus on the subject, we shall now mention their ludicrous views; but we declare at once that they are held only by the common uneducated people. For those who march on the path to liberation, or those who study philosophy and theology, and who desire abstract truth which they call *sara,* are entirely free from worshipping anything but God alone, and would never dream of worshipping an image manufactured to represent Him.

Idol-worship as restricted to the low classes of people

[There follows the story of King Ambrisha who after a successful reign had taken exclusively to meditation and worship. Thereupon Indra appeared before him and, in answer to a question by Ambrisha, instructed him that if he was 'ever overpowered by human forgetfulness' he should make for himself an image like that in which Indra had appeared before him and offer to it perfume and flower. Thus he would always remember him'. Pp. 113–15.]

. . . From that time, the Hindus say, people make idols, some with four hands like the appearance we have described, others with two hands, as the story and description require, and conformably to the being which is to be represented.

. . . A famous idol of theirs was that of Multan, dedicated to the sun, and therefore called *Aditya.* It was of wood and covered with red Cordovan leather; in its two eyes were two red rubies. It is said to have been made in the last Kritayuga. Suppose that it was made in the very end of Kritayuga, the time which has

The idol of Multan called Aditya

since elapsed amounts to 216,432 years. When Muhammad Ibn Alkasim Ibn Almunabbih conquered Multan, he inquired how the town had become so very flourishing and so many treasures had there been accumulated, and then he found out that this idol was the cause, for there came pilgrims from all sides to visit it. Therefore, he thought it best to have the idol where it was, but he hung a piece of cow's flesh on its neck by way of mockery. On the same place a mosque was built. When then the Karmatians[14] occupied Multan, Jalam Ibn Shaiban, the usurper, broke the idol into pieces and killed its priests. He made his mansion, which was a castle built of brick on an elevated place, the mosque instead of the old mosque, which he ordered to be shut from hatred against anything that had been done under the dynasty of the Caliphs of the house of 'Umayya. When afterwards the blessed Prince Mahmud swept away their rule from those countries, he made again the old mosque the place of the Friday-worship, and the second one was left to decay. At present it is only a barn-floor, where bunches of Hinna *(Lawsonia inermis)* are bound together . . .

The idol of Taneshar called Cakrasvamin

The city of Taneshar is highly venerated by the Hindus. The idol of that place is called *Cakrasvamin,* i.e. the owner of the *cakra,* a weapon . . . It is of bronze, and is nearly the size of a man. It is now lying in the hippodrome in Ghazna, together with the *Lord of Somanath,* which is a representation of the *penis* of Mahadeva, called *Linga.* Of Somanath we shall hereafter speak in the proper place. This Cakrasvamin is said to have been made in the time of Bharata as a memorial of wars connected with this name.

The idol Sarada in Kashmir

In Inner Kashmir, about two or three days' journey from the capital in the direction towards the mountains of Bolor, there is a wooden idol called *Sarada,* which is much venerated and frequented by pilgrims.

Quotation from the *Samhita* of Varahamihira

We shall now communicate a whole chapter from the book *Samhita* relating to the construction of idols, which will help the student thoroughly to comprehend the present subject.

Varahamihira[15] says: "If the figure is made to represent Rama the son of Dasaratha, or Bali the son of Virocana, give it the height of 120 digits," i.e. of idol *digits,* which must be reduced by one-tenth to become *common digits,* in this case 108.

"To the idol of Vishnu give eight hands, or four, or two, and on the left side under the breast give him the figure of the woman Sri. If you give him eight hands, place in the right hands a sword, a club of gold or iron, an arrow, and make the fourth hand as if it were drawing water; in the left hands give him a shield, a bow, a *cakra,* and a conch.

"If you give him two hands, let the right hand be drawing water, the left holding a conch.

"If the figure is to represent Baladeva, the brother of Narayana, put earrings into his ears, and give him eyes of a drunken man.

"If you make both figures, Narayana and Baladeva, join with them their sister *Bhagavati* (Durga = Ekanansa), her left hand resting on her hip a little away from the side, and her right hand holding a lotus.

"If you make her four-handed, place in the right hands a rosary and a hand drawing water; in the left hands, a book and a lotus.

"If you make her eight-handed, place in the left hands the *kamandalu,* i.e. a pot, a lotus, bow and book; in the right hands, a rosary, a mirror, an arrow, and a water-drawing hand . . .

"The idol of Brahman has four faces towards the four sides, and is seated on a lotus.

"The idol of Skanda, the son of Mahadeva, is a boy riding on a peacock, his hands holding a *sakti,* a weapon like a double-edged sword, which has in the middle a pestle like that of a mortar.

"The idol Indra holds in its hand a weapon called *vajra* of diamond. It has a similar handle to the *sakti,* but on each side it has two swords which join at the handle. On his front place a third eye and make him ride on a white elephant with four tusks.

"Likewise make on the front of the idol of Mahadeva a third eye right above, on his head a crescent, in his hand a weapon called *sula*, similar to the club but with three branches, and a sword; and let his left hand hold his wife Gauri, the daughter of Himavant, whom he presses to his bosom from the side."

"To the idol Jina, *i.e.* Buddha, give a face and limbs as beautiful as possible, make the lines in the palms of his hands and feet like a lotus, and represent him seated on a lotus; give him grey hair, and represent him with a placid expression, as if he were the father of creation . . .

"The idol of Kubera, the teasurer, wears a crown, has a big stomach and wide hips, and is riding on a man.

"The idol of the sun has a red face like the pith of the red lotus, beams like a diamond, has protruding limbs, rings in the ears, the neck adorned with pearls which hang down over the breast, wears a crown of several compartments, holds in his hands two lotuses, and is clad in the dress of the Northerners which reaches down to the ankle.

"If you represent the Seven Mothers, represent several of them together in one figure, Brahmani with four faces towards the four directions, Kaumari with six faces, Vaishnavi with four hands, Varahi with a hog's head on a human body, Indrani with many eyes and a club in her hand, Bhagavati (Durga) sitting as people generally sit, Camunda ugly, with protruding teeth and a slim waist. Further join with them the sons of Mahadeva, Kshetrapala with bristling hair, a sour face, and an ugly figure, but Vinayaka with an elephant's head on a human body, with four hands, as we have heretofore described."

The worshippers of these idols kill sheep and buffaloes with axes *(kutara)*, that they may nourish themselves with their blood. All idols are constructed according to certain measures determined by *idol-fingers* for every single limb, but sometimes they differ regarding the measure of a limb. If the artist keeps the right measure and does not make anything too large nor too small, he is free from sin, and is sure that the being which he represented will not visit him with any mishap.

. . . The Hindus honour their idols on account of those who erected them, not on account of the material of which they are made. We have already mentioned that the idol of Multan was of wood, e.g. the *linga* which Rama erected when he had finished the war with the demons was of sand, which he had heaped up with his own hand. But then it became pertified all at once, since the astrologically correct moment for the erecting of the monument fell before the moment when the workmen had finished the cutting of the stone monument which Rama originally had ordered. Regarding the building of the temple and its peristyle, the cutting of the trees of four different kinds, the astrological determination of the favourable moment for the erection, the celebration of the rites due on such an occasion, regarding all this Rama gave very long and tedious instructions. Further, he ordered that servants and priests to minister to the idols should be nominated from different classes of the people. "To the idol of Vishnu are devoted the class called Bhagavata; to the idol of the Sun, the Maga, i.e. the Magians; to the idol of Mahadeva, a class of saints, anchorites with long hair, who cover their skin with ashes, hang on their persons the bones of dead people, and swim in the pools. The Brahmana are devoted to the Eight Mothers, the Shamanians, to Buddha, to Arhant the class called *Nagna.* On the whole, to each idol certain people are devoted who constructed it, for those know best how to serve it."

Our object in mentioning all this mad raving was to teach the reader the accurate description of an idol, if he happens to see one and to illustrate what we have said before, that such idols are erected only for uneducated low-class people of little understanding; that the Hindus never made an idol of any supernatural being, much less of God; and, lastly, to show how the crowd is kept in thraldom by all kinds of priestly tricks and deceits.

Quotations from the *Gita* showing that God is not to be confounded with the idols

[An extract from the *Gita* is quoted to show that God is not to be confounded with the idols. Pp. 122–24.]

. . . It is evident that the first cause of idolatry was the desire of commemorating the dead and of consoling the living; but on this basis it has developed, and has finally become a foul and pernicious abuse.

The former view, that idols are only memorials, was also held by the Caliph Muawiya regarding the idols of Sicily. When, in the summer of A.H. 53, Sicily was conquered, and the conquerors sent him golden idols adorned with crowns and diamonds which had been captured there, he ordered them to be sent to Sind, that they should be sold there to the princes of the country; for he thought it best to sell them as objects costing sums of so-and-so many denars, not having the slightest scruple on account of their being objects of abominable idolatry, but simply considering the matter from a political, not from a religious point of view.

CHAPTER XII

On The Veda, The Puranas, And Other Kinds Of Their National Literature

Veda means knowledge of that which was before unknown. It is a religious system which, according to the Hindus, comes from God, and was promulgated by the mouth of Brahman. The Brahmins recite the Veda without understanding its meaning and in the same way they learn it by heart, the one receiving it from the other. Only few of them learn its explantation, and still less is the number of those who master the contents of the Veda and their interpretation to such a degree as to be able to hold a theological disputation.

Sundry notes relating to the Veda

The Brahmins teach the Veda to the Kshatriyas. The latter learn it, but are not allowed to teach it, not even to a Brahmin. The Vaisya and Sudra are not allowed to hear it, much less to pronounce and recite it. If such a thing can be proved against one of them, the Brahmins drag him before the magistrate, and he is punished by having his tongue cut off.

The Veda contains commandments and prohibitions, detailed statements about reward and punishment intended to encourage and to deter; but most of it contains hymns of praise, and treats of the various kinds of sacrifices to the fire, which are so numerous and difficult that you could hardly count them.

The Veda transmitted by memory

They do not allow the Veda to be committed to writing, because it is recited according to certain modulations, and they therefore avoid the use of the pen, since it is liable to cause some error, and may occasion an addition or a defect in the written text. In consequence it has happened that they have several times forgotten the Veda and lost it . . .

Further, the Hindus maintain that the Veda, together with all the rites of their religion and country, had been obliterated in the last Dvapara yuga, a period of time of which we shall speak at the proper place, until it was renewed by Vyasa, the son of Parasara . . .

Vasukra commits the Veda to writing

This is the reason why, not long before our time, Vasukra, a native of Kashmir, a famous Brahmin, has of his own account undertaken the task of explaining the Veda and committing it to writing.[16] He has taken on himself a task from which everybody else would have recoiled, but he carried it out because he was afraid that the Veda might be forgotten and entirely vanish out of the memories of men, since he observed that the characters of men grew worse and worse, and that they did not care much for virtue, nor even for duty.

There are certain passages in the Veda which, as they maintain, must not be recited within dwellings, since they fear that they would cause an abortion both to women and the cattle. Therefore, they step out into the open field to recite them there. There is hardly a single verse free from such and similar minatory injunctions.

As we have already mentioned, the books of the Hindus are metrical compositions like the Rajaz poems of the Arabs. Most of them are composed in a metre called *sloka.* The reason of this has already been explained . . .

The Veda, however, is not composed in this common metre, sloka, but in another. Some Hindus say that no one could compose anything in the same metre. However, their scholars maintain that this is possible indeed, but that they refrain from trying it merely from veneration for the Veda.

The four pupils of Vyasa and the four Vedas

According to their tradition, Vyasa divided it into four parts: *Rigveda, Yajurveda, Samaveda,* and *Atharvanaveda* . . .

Each of the four parts has a peculiar kind of recitation. The first is Rigveda, consisting of metrical compositions called *ric,* which are of different lengths. It is called Rigveda as being the totality of the *ric.* It treats of the sacrifices to the fire, and is recited in three different ways. First, in a uniform manner of reading, just as every other book is read. Secondly, in such a way that a pause is made after every single word. Thirdly, in a method which is the most meritorious, and for which plenty of reward in heaven is promised. First you read a short passage, each word of which is distinctly pronounced; then you repeat it together with a part of that which has not yet been recited. Next you recite the added portion alone, and then you repeat it together with the next part of that which has not yet been recited, etc., etc. Continuing to do so till the end, you will have read the whole text twice.

On the Rigveda

The Yajurveda is composed of *kandin.* The word is a derivative noun, and means *the totality of the kandin.* The difference between this and the Rigveda is that it may be read as a text connected by the rules of Samdhi, which is not allowed in the case of Rigveda. The one as well as the other treats of works connected with the fire and the sacrifices.

On the Yajurveda

. . . The Samaveda treats of the sacrifices, commandments and prohibitions. It is recited in a tone like a chant, and hence its name is derived because *saman* means *the sweetness of recitation.*

Samaveda and Atharvanaveda

. . . The Atharvanaveda is as a text connected by the rules of Samdhi. It does not consist of the same compositions as the Rig and Yajur Vedas, but of a third kind called *bhara.* It is recited according to a melody with a nasal tone. This Veda is less in favour with the Hindus than the others. It likewise treats of the sacrifices to the fire, and contains injunctions regarding the dead and what is to be done with them.

As to the Puranas, we first mention that the word means *first, eternal.* There are eighteen Puranas, most of them called by the names of animals, human or angelic beings, because they contain stories about them, or because the contents of the book refer in some way to them, or because the book consists of answers which the creature whose name forms the title of the book

List of the Puranas

has given to certain questions.

The Puranas[16A] are of human origin, composed by the so-called Rishis. In the following I give a list of their names, as I have heard them, and committed them to writing from dictation:—

1. *Adi-purana,* i.e. the first.
2. *Matsya-purana,* i.e. the fish.
3. *Kurma-purana,* i.e. the tortoise.
4. *Varaha-purana,* i.e. the boar.
5. *Narasimha-purana,* i.e. a human being with a lion's head.
6. *Vamana-purana,* i.e. the dwarf.
7. *Vayu-purana,* i.e. the wind.
8. *Nanda-purana,* i.e. servant of Mahadeva.
9. *Skanda-purana,* i.e. a son of Mahadeva.
10. *Aditya-purana,* i.e. the sun.
11. *Soma-purana,* i.e. the moon.
12. *Samba-purana,* i.e. the son of Vishnu.
13. *Brahmanda-purana,* i.e. heaven.
14. *Markandeya-purana*, i.e. a great Rishi.
15. *Tarkshya-purana,* i.e. the bird Garuda.
16. *Vishnu-purana,* i.e. Narayana.
17. *Brahma-purana,* i.e. the nature charged with the preservation of the world.
18. *Bhavishya-purana,* i.e. future things.

Of all this literature I have only seen portions of the Matsya, Aditya, and Vayu Puranas....

A list of Smriti books

The book *Smriti*[17] is derived from the Veda. It contains commandments and prohibitions, and is composed by the following twenty sons of Brahman:—

1. Apastamba, 2. Parasara, 3. Satatapa, 4. Samvarta, 5. Daksha, 6. Vasishtha, 7. Angiras, 8. Yama, 9. Vishnu, 10. Manu, 11. Yajnavalkya, 12. Atri, 13. Harita, 14. Likhita, 15. Sankha, 16. Gautama, 17. Vrihaspati, 18. Katyayana, 19. Vyasa, 20. Usanas.

Besides, the Hindus have books about the jurisprudence of their religion, on theosophy, on ascetics, on the process of becoming god and seeking liberation from the world, as, e.g. the book composed by Gauda the anchorite,[17A] which goes by his name; the book *Samkhya,* composed by Kapila, on divine subjects; the book of Patanjali, on the search for liberation and for the union of the soul with the object of its meditation; the book *Nyayabhasha*[18] composed by Kapila on the Veda and its interpretation, also showing that it has been created and distinguishing within the Veda between such injunctions as are obligatory in certain cases, and those which are obligatory in general; further, the book *Mimamsa*[19], composed by Jaimini, on the same subject; the book *Laukayata,*[20] composed by Brihaspati, treating of the subject that in all investigations we must exclusively rely upon the apperception of the senses; the book *Agastyamata,*[20A] composed by Agastya, treating of the subject that in all investigations we must use the apperception of the senses as well as tradition; and the book *Vishnu dharma.* The word *dharma* means reward, but in general it is used for religion; so that this title means *The Religion of God,* which in this case is understood to be Narayana. Further, there are the books of the six pupils of Vyasa, viz. Devala, Sukra, Bhargava, Vrihaspati, Yagnavalkya, and Manu. The Hindus have numerous books about all the branches of science. How could anybody know the titles of all of them, more especially if he is not a Hindu, but a foreigner?

Mahabharata

Besides, they have a book which they hold in such veneration that they firmly assert that everything which occurs in other books is found also in this book, but not all which occurs in this book is found in other books. It is called *Bharata,* and composed by Vyasa the son of Parasara at the time of the great war between the children of Pandu and those of Kuru. The title itself gives an indication of those times. The book has 100,000 slokas in eighteen parts, each of which is called *Parvan.* Here we give the list of them.

1. *Sabha-parva,* i.e. the king's dwelling.
2. *Aranya,* i.e. going out into the open field, meaning the exodus of the children of Pandu.
3. *Virata,* i.e. the name of a king in whose realm they dwelt during the time of their concealment.
4. *Udyoga,* i.e. the preparing for battle.
5. *Bhishma.*
6. *Drona,* the Brahmin.
7. *Karna,* the son of the Sun.
8. *Salya,* the brother of Duryodhana, some of the greatest heroes who did the fighting, one *always* coming forward after his predecessor had been killed.
9. *Gada,* i.e. the club.

10. *Sauptika,* i.e. the killing of the sleepers, when Asvatthaman the son of Drona attacked the city of Pancala during the night and killed the inhabitants.
11. *Jalapradanika,* i.e. the successive drawing of water for the dead, after people have washed off the impurity caused by the touching of the dead.
12. *Stri,* i.e. the lamentations of the women.
13. *Santi,* containing 24,000 slokas on eradicating hatred from the heart, in four parts:
    (1) *Rajadharma,* on the reward of the kings.
    (2) *Danadharma,* on the reward for alms-giving.
    (3) *Apaddharma,* on the reward of those who are in need and trouble.
    (4) *Mokshadharma,* on the reward of him who is liberated from the world.
14. *Asvamedha,* i.e. the sacrifice of the horse which is sent out together with an army to wander through the world. Then they proclaim in public that it belongs to the king of the world, and that he who does not agree thereto is to come forward to fight. The Brahmans follow the horse, and celebrate sacrifices to the fire in those places where the horse drops its dung.
15. *Mausala,* i.e. the fighting of the Yadavas, the tribe of Vasudeva, among themselves.
16. *Asramavasa,* i.e. leaving one's own country.
17. *Prasthana,* i.e. quitting the realm to seek liberation.
18. *Svargarohana,* i.e. journeying towards Paradise.

These eighteen parts are followed by another one which is called *Harivamsa-Parvan,* which contains the traditions relating to Vasudeva.

In this book there occur passages which, like riddles, admit of manifold interpretations. As to the reason of this the Hindus relate the following story:—Vyasa asked Brahman to procure him somebody who might write for him the *Bharata* from his dictation. Now he entrusted with this task his son Vinayaka, who is represented as an idol with an elephant's head, and made it obligatory on him never to cease from writing. At the same time Vyasa made it obligatory on him to write only that which he understood. Therefore Vyasa, in the course of his dictation, dictated such sentences as compelled the writer to ponder over them, and thereby Vyasa gained time for resting awhile.

CHAPTER XIII

Their Grammatical And Metrical Literature

The two sciences of grammar and metrics are auxiliary to the other sciences. Of the two, the former, grammar, holds the first place in their estimate, called *vyakarana,* i.e. the law of the correctness of their speech and etymological rules, by means of which they acquire and eloquent and classical style both in writing and reading. We Muslims cannot learn anything of it, since it is a branch coming from a root which is not within our grasp—I mean the language itself. That which I have been told as to titles of books on this science is the following:—

List of books on grammar

1. *Aindra,* attributed to Indra, the head of the angels.
2. *Candra,* composed by Candra, one of the red-robe-wearing sect, the followers of Buddha.
3. *Sakata,* so called by the name of its author. His tribe, too, is called by a name derived from the same word, viz. *Sakatayana.*
4. *Panini*[21], so called from its author.
5. *Katantra,* composed by Sarvavarman.
6. *Sasidevavritti,* composed by Sasideva.
7. *Durgavivritti.*
8. *Sishyahitavritti,* composed by Ugrabhuti.

I have been told that the last-mentioned author was the teacher and instructor of Shah Anandapala, the son of Jayapala, who ruled in our time. After having composed the book he sent it to Kashmir, but the people there did not adopt it, being in such things haughtily conservative. Now he complained of this to the Shah, and the Shah, in accordance with the duty of a pupil towards his master, promised him to make him attain his wish. So he gave orders to send 200,000 *dirham* and presents of a similar value to Kashmir, to be distributed among those who studied the book of his master. The consequence was that they all rushed upon the book, and would not copy any other grammar but this one, showing themselves in the baseness of their avarice. The book became the fashion and highly prized.

Shah Anandapala and his master Ugrabhuti

Of the origin of grammar they give the following account:—One of their kings, called Samalvahana, i.e. in the classical language, Satavahana, was one day in a pond playing with his wives, when he said to one of them *"Maudakam dehi,"* i.e. *do not sprinkle the water on me.* The woman, however, understood it as if he had said *modakam dehi,* i.e. *bring sweetmeats.* So she went away and brought him sweetmeats. And when the king disapproved of her doing so, she gave him an angry reply, and used coarse language towards him. Now he was deeply offended, and, in consequence, as is their custom, he abstained from all food, and concealed himself in some corner until he was called upon by a sage, who consoled him, promising him that he would teach people grammar and the inflexions of the language. Thereupon the sage went off to Mahadeva, praying, praising, and fasting devoutly. Mahadeva appeared to him, and communicated to him some few rules, the like of which Abul'aswad Addu'ali[22] has given for the Arabic language. The god also promised to assist him in further development of this science. Then the sage returned to the king and taught it to him. This was the beginning of the science of grammar.

Tale relating to the origin of grammar

Grammar is followed by another science, called *chandas,* i.e. the metrical form of poetry, corresponding to our metrics—a science indispensable to them, since all their books are in verse. By composing their books in metres they intend to facilitate their being learned by heart, and to

The predilection of the Hindus for metrical compositions

prevent people in all questions of science ever recurring to a *written* text, save in a case of bare necessity. For they think that the mind of man sympathises with everything in which there is symmetry and order, and has an aversion to everything in which there is no order. Therefore, most Hindus are passionately fond of their verses, and always desirous of reciting them, even if they do not understand the meaning of the words, and the audience will snap their fingers in token of joy and applause. They do not want prose compositions, although it is much easier to understand them.

Most of their books are composed in sloka, in which I am now exercising myself, being occupied in composing for the Hindus a translation of the books of Euclid and of the Almagest, and dictating to them a treatise on the construction of the astrolabe, being simply guided herein by the desire of spreading science. If the Hindus happen to get some book which does not yet exist among them, they set at work to change it into *Slokas,* which are rather unintelligible, since the metrical form entails a constrained, affected style, which will become apparent when we shall speak of their method of expressing numbers. And if the verses are not sufficiently affected, their authors meet with frowning faces, as having committed something like mere prose, and then they will feel extremely unhappy. God will do me justice in what I say of them.

Books on metrics

The first who invented this art were Pingala and چَلِت (? *CLT*). The books on the subject are numerous. The most famous of them is is the book *Gaisita* (? G—AI—S—T), so called from its author, famous to such a degree that even the whole science of metrics has been called by this name. Other books are that of Mriga-lanchana, that of Pingala, and that of اوليانَد (? U (Au)—L—Y—A—N—D). I, however, have not seen any of these books, nor do I know much of the chapter of the *Brahma-siddhanta* which treats of metrical calculations, and therefore I have no claim to a thorough knowledge of the laws of their metrics. Nevertheless, I do not think it right to pass by a subject of which I have only a smattering, and I shall not postpone speaking of it until I shall have thoroughly mastered it.

In counting the syllables (*ganachandas*) they use similar figures to those used by Alkhalil Ibn Ahmad and our metricians to denote the *consonant without vowel* and the *consonant with vowel,* viz. these two signs, and >, the former of which is called *laghu,* i.e. light; the

On the meaning of the technical terms *laghu* and *guru*

latter, *guru,* i.e. heavy. In measuring (*matrachandas*), the *guru* is reckoned double of a *laghu,* and its place may be filled by two *laghu*.

Further, they have a syllable which they call long (*dirgha*), the measure or prosody of which is equal to that of a *guru.* This, I think, is a syllable with a long vowel (like *ka, ki, ku*). Here, however, I must confess that up to the present moment I have not been able to gain a clear idea of the nature of both *laghu* and *guru,* so as to be able to illustrate them by similar elements in Arabic. However, I am inclined to think that *laghu* does *not* mean a *consonant without vowel,* nor *guru* a *consonant with vowel,* but that, on the contrary, *laghu* means a consonant with a short vowel (e.g. *ka, ki, ku*), and *guru* means the same with a vowelless consonant (e.g. *kat, kit, kut*), like an element in Arabic metrics called *Sahab* (i.e.—or w, a long syllable the place of which may be taken by two short ones). That which makes me doubt as to the first-mentioned definition of *laghu* is this circumstance, that the Hindus use *many laghu* one after the other in an uninterrupted succession. The Arabs are not capable of pronouncing two vowelless consonants one after the other, but in other languages this is possible.

. . . Further, although it is difficult to pronounce a vowelless consonant at the beginning of a word, most nouns of the Hindus begin, if not exactly with vowelless consonants, still with such consonants as have only a Schwa-like vowel-sound to follow them. If such a consonant stands at the beginning of a verse, they drop it in counting, since the law of the *guru* demands that in it the vowelless consonant shall not *precede* but follow the vowel (*ka-t, ki-t, ku-t*).

Further, as our people have composed out of the *feet* (افاعيل) certain schemes or types, according to which verses are constructed,

Definition of matra

and have invented signs to denote the component parts of a foot, i.e. the consonant *with* and *without* a vowel, in like manner also the Hindus use certain names to denote the feet which are composed of *laghu* and *guru,* either the former preceding and the latter following or *vice versa,* in such a way, however, that the *measure* must always be the same, whilst the *number* of syllables may vary. By these names they denote a certain conventional prosodic unity (i.e. certain *feet*). By *measure,* I mean that *laghu* is reckoned =

one *matra,* i.e. measure, and *guru* = two *matra.* If they represent a foot in writing, they only express the measure of the syllables, not their number, as, e.g. (in Arabic) a double consonant (*kka*) is counted as a consonant *without* vowel *plus* a consonant *with* vowel, and a consonant followed by Tanwin (*kun*) is counted as a consonant with a vowel *plus* a consonant without vowel, whilst in writing both are represented as one and the same thing (i.e. by the sign of the consonant in question).

Names of *laghu* and *guru*

Taken alone by themselves, *laghu* and *guru* are called by various names: the former, *la, kali, rupa, camara,* and *graha;* the latter, *ga nivra,* and a *half amsaka.* The latter name shows that a complete *amsaka* is equal to two *guru* or their equivalent. These names they have invented simply to facilitate the versification of their metrical books. For this purpose they have invented so many names that one may fit into the metre if others will not.

[Al-Biruni describes a single foot, and quotes a lexicographical work by Haribhatta on the arrangement of the feet. Pp. 140–42.]

On the *padas*

As the Arabic verse is divided into two halves or hemistichs by the *arud,* i.e. the last foot of the first hemistich, and the *darb,* i.e. the last foot of the second hemistich, in like manner the verses of the Hindus are divided into two halves, each of which is called *foot* (*pada*) . . .

On the metre Arya

The verse is divided into three, or more commonly into four *pada.* Sometimes they add a fifth *pada* in the middle of the verse. The *padas* have no rhyme, but there is a kind of metre, in which the 1 and 2 *padas* end with the same consonant or syllable as if rhyming on it, and also the *padas* 3 and 4 end with the same consonant or syllable. This kind is called *Arya.* At the end of the *pada* a *laghu* may become a *guru,* though in general this metre ends with a *laghu.*

The different poetical works of the Hindus contain a great number of metres. In the metre of 5 *padas,* the fifth *pada* is placed between *padas* 3 and 4. The names of the metres differ according to the number of syllables, and also according to the verses which follow. For they do not like all the verses of a long poem to belong to one and the same metre. They use many metres in the same poem, in order that it should appear like an embroidered piece of silk.

[The difference between the Arab and Hindu method of the notation of a *pada* is given. P. 144.]

I have already once pleaded as my excuse, and do so here a second time, that my slender knowledge of this science does not enable me to give the reader a complete insight into the subject. Still I take the greatest pains with it, though I am well aware that it is only very little I can give.

On the metre *Vritta*

The name *Vritta* applies to each four-*pada* metre in which the signs of both the prosody and the number of the syllables are like each other, according to a certain correspondence of the *padas* among themselves, so that if you know one *pada,* you know also the other ones, for they are like it. Further, there is a law that a *pada* cannot have less than four syllables, since a *pada* with less does not occur in the Veda. For the same reason the smallest number of the syllables of a *pada* is four, the largest twenty-six. In consequence, there are twenty-three varieties of the *Vritta* metre, which we shall here enumerate:—

[The consequential twenty-three varieties of the *Vritta* metre are enumerated. Pp. 145–46.]

. . . If we here take so much trouble with Indian metrics, we do it for the purpose of fixing the laws of the *Sloka,* since most of their books are composed in it.

Theory of the *Sloka*

The *Sloka* belongs to the four-*pada* metres. Each *pada* has eight syllables, which are different in all four *padas.* The last syllable of each of the four *padas* must be the same, viz. a *guru.* Further, the fifth syllable in each *pada* must always be *laghu,* the sixth syllable *guru.* The seventh syllable must be *laghu* in the second and fourth *padas, guru* in the first and third *padas*. The other syllables are entirely dependent upon accident or the writer's fancy.

[A quotation from Brahmagupta, showing the way in which the Hindus use arithmetic in the metrical system, is given. At the end of the quotation Al-Biruni regrets the fact that he could see only 'a single leaf' of the treatise mentioned above and expresses the hope that he would be able to learn more of the subject later on. Also notes that, 'as far as he could guess', the Greeks used in their poetry similar feet to that of the Hindus. Pp. 147–51.]

CHAPTER XIV

Hindu Literature In The Other Sciences, Astronomy, Astrology, Etc.

The number of sciences is great, and it may be still greater if the public mind is directed towards them at such times as they are in the ascendancy and in general favour with all, when people not only honour science itself, but also its representatives. To do this is, in the first instance, the duty of those who rule over them, of kings and princes. For they alone could free the minds of scholars from the daily anxieties for the necessities of life, and stimulate their energies to earn more fame and favour, the yearning for which is the pith and marrow of human nature.

Times unfavourable to the progress of science

The present times, however, are not of this kind. They are the very opposite, and therefore it is quite impossible that a new science or any new kind of research should arise in our days. What we have of sciences is nothing but the scanty remains of bygone better times.

If a science or an idea has once conquered the whole earth, every nation appropriates part of it. So do also the Hindus. Their belief about the cyclical revolutions of times is nothing very special, but is simply in accordance with the results of scientific observation.

The science of astronomy is the most famous among them, since the affairs of their religion are in various ways connected with it. If a man wants to gain the title of an astronomer, he must not only know scientific or mathematical astronomy, but also astrology. The book known among Muslims as *Sindhind*[23] is called by them *Siddhanta,* i.e. *straight,* not crooked nor changing. By this name they call every standard book on astronomy, even such books as, according to our opinion, do not come up to the mark of our so called *Zij,* i.e. handbooks of mathematical astronomy. They have five Siddhantas:—

On the Siddhantas

I. *Surya-siddhanta,* i.e. the Siddhanta of the sun, composed by Lata.

II. *Vasishtha-siddhanta,* so called from one of the stars of the Great Bear, composed by Vishnucandra.

III. *Pulisa-siddhanta,* so called from Paulisa,[24] the Greek, from the city of Saintra, which I suppose to be Alexandria, composed by Pulisa.

IV. *Romaka-siddhanta,* so called from the Rum, i.e. the subjects of the Roman Empire, composed by Srishena.

V. *Brahma-siddhanta,* so called from Brahman, composed by Brahmagupta,[25] the son of Jishnu, from the town of Bhillamala between Multan and Anhilwara, 16 *yojana* from the latter place (?).

The authors of these books draw from one and the same source, the book *Paithamaha,* so called from *the first father,* i.e. Brahman.

Varahamihira has composed an astronomical handbook of small compass called *Panca-siddhantika,* which name ought to mean that it contains the pith and marrow of the preceding five Siddhantas. But this is not the case, nor is it so much better than they as to be called the most correct one of the five. So the name does not indicate anything but the fact that the number of Siddhantas is five.

. . . Up to the present time I have not been able to procure any of these books save those of Pulisa and of Brahmagupta. I have commenced translating them, but have not yet finished my work. Meanwhile, I shall give here a table of contents of the *Brahma-siddhanta,* which in any case will be useful and instructive.

Contents of the twenty-four chapters of the *Brahma-siddhanta:—*

1. On the nature of the globe and the figure of heaven and earth.

Contents of the *Brahma-siddhanta*

2. On the revolutions of the planets; on the calculation of time, i.e. how to find the time for different longitudes and latitudes; how to find the mean places of the planets; how to find the

sine of an arc.

3. On the correction of the places of the planets.

4. On three problems: how to find the shadow, the bygone portion of the day and the *ascendens,* and how to derive one from the other.

5. On the planets becoming visible when they leave the rays of the sun, and their becoming invisible when entering them.

6. On the first appearance of the moon, and about her two cusps.

7. On the lunar eclipse.

8. On the solar eclipse.

9. On the shadow of the moon.

10. On the meeting and conjunction of the planets.

11. On the latitudes of the planets.

12. A critical investigation for the purpose of distinguishing between correct and corrupt passages in the texts of astronomical treatises and handbooks.

13. On arithmetic; on plane measure and cognate subjects.

14. Scientific calculation of the mean places of the planets.

15. Scientific calculation of the correction of the places of the planets.

16. Scientific calculation of the three problems (v. chap.4).

17. On the deflection of eclipses.

18. Scientific calculation of the appearance of the new moon and her two cusps.

19. On *Kuttaka,* i.e. the pounding of a thing. The pounding of oil-producing substances is here compared with *the most minute and detailed research.* This chapter treats of algebra and related subjects, and besides it contains other valuable remarks of a more or less arithmetical nature.

20. On the shadow.

21. On the calculation of the measures of poetry and on metrics.

22. On cycles and instruments of observation.

23. On time and the four measures of time, the *solar,* the *civil,* the *lunar,* and the *sidereal.*

24. About numeral notation in the metrical books of this kind.

These, now, are twenty-four chapters, according to his own statement, but there is a twenty-fifth one, called *Dhyana-graha-adhyaya,* in which he tries to solve the problems by speculation, not by mathematical calculation. I have not enumerated it in this list, because the pretensions which he brings forward in this chapter are repudiated by mathematics. I am rather inclined to think that that which he produces is meant to be the *ratio metaphysica* of all astronomical methods, otherwise how could any problem of this science be solved by anything save by mathematics?

On the literature of Tantras and Karanas

Such books as do not reach the standard of a Siddhanta are mostly called *Tantra* or *Karana.* The former means *ruling under a governor,* the latter means *following,* i.e. following behind the Siddhanta. Under *governors* they understand the *Acaryas,* i.e. the sages, anchorites, the followers of Brahman.

There are two famous *Tantras* by *Aryabhata*[26] and *Balabhadra,* besides the *Rasayana-tantra* by *Bhanuyasas* (?). About what Rasayana means we shall give a separate chapter (chap. xvii).

As for *Karanas,* there is one (*lacuna*) called by his name, besides the *Karana-khanda-khadyaka* by Brahmagupta. The last word, *khanda,* means a kind of their sweetmeats. With regard to the reason why he gave his book this title, I have been told the following:—

Sugriva, the Buddhist, had composed an astronomical handbook which he called *Dadhi-sagara,* i.e. the sea of sour-milk; and a pupil of his composed a book of the same kind which he called *Kura-babaya* (?) i.e. a mountain of rice. Afterwards he composed another book which he called *Lavana-mushti,* i.e. a handful of salt. Therefore Brahmagupta called his book the *Sweetmeat-khadyaka*—in order that all kinds of victuals (sour-milk, rice, salt, &c.) should occur in the titles of the books on this science.

The contents of the book *Karana-khanda-khadyaka* represent the doctrine of Aryabhata. Therefore Brahmagupta afterwards composed a second book, which he called *Uttara-khanda-khadyaka,* i.e. the explanation of the *Khanda-khadyaka.* And this book is again followed by another one called *Khanda-khadyaka-tippa* (*sic*), of which I do not know whether it is composed by Brahmagupta or somebody else. It explains the reasons and the nature of the calculations employed in the *Khanda-khadyaka.* I suppose it is a work of Balabhadra.

Further, there is an astronomical handbook composed by Vijayanandin, the commentator, in the city of Benares, entitled *Karana-tilaka,* i.e. the blaze on the front of the Karanas; another one by Vittesvara the son of Bhadatta (? Mihdatta), of the city of Nagarapura, called *Karana-sara,* i.e. that which has been derived from the Karana; another one, by Bhanuyasas (?), is called *Karana-para-tilaka,* which shows, as I am told, how the corrected places of the stars are derived from one another.

There is a book by Utpala the Kashmirian called *Rahunrakarana* (?), i.e. breaking the Karanas; and another called *Karana-pata,* i.e. killing the Karanas. Besides there is a book called *Karana-cudamani* of which I do not know the author.

There are more books of the same kind with other titles, e.g. the great *Manasa,* composed by Manu, and the commentary by Utpala; the small *Manasa,* an epitome of the former by Puncala (?), from the southern country; *Dasagitika,* by Aryabhata; *Aryashtasata,* by the same; *Lokananda,* so called from the name of the author; *Bhattila* (?), so called from its author, the Brahman Bhattila. The books of this kind are nearly innumerable.

As for astrological literature, each one of the following authors has composed a so-called *Samhita,* viz:—

On astrological literature, the so-called Samhitas

Mandavya.	Balabhadra.
Parasera.	Divyatattva.
Garga.	Varahamihira.
Brahman	

Samhita means that *which is collected,* books containing something of everything, e.g. forewarnings relating to a journey derived from meteorological occurrences; prophecies regarding the fate of dynasties; the knowledge of lucky and unlucky things; prophesying from the lines of the hand; interpretation of dreams, and taking auguries from the flight or cries of birds. For Hindu scholars believe in such things. It is the custom of their astronomers to propound in their Samhitas also the whole science of meteorology and cosmology.

Each one of the following authors has composed a book, *Jataka,* i.e. book of nativities. viz.:—

The Jatakas, i.e. books on nativities

Parasara.	Jivasarman.
Satya.	Mau, the Greek.
Manittha.	

Varahamihira has composed two Jatakas, a small and a large one. The latter of these has been explained by Balabhadra, and the former I have translated into Arabic . . . Of Varahamihira there are several small books, e.g. *Shat-Pancasika,* fifty-six chapters on astrology; *Hora Panca-hotriya* (?) on the same subject.

Travelling is treated of in the book *Yogayatra* and the book *Tikani* (?) *-yatra,* marriage and marrying in the book *Vivaha-patala,* architecture in the book (*lacuna*).

The art of taking auguries from the flight or cries of birds, and of the foretelling by means of piercing a needle into a book, is propounded in the work called *Srudhava* (? *srotavya*), which exists in three different copies . . .

Medicine belongs to the same class of sciences as astronomy, but there is this difference, that the latter stands in close relation to the religion of the Hindus. They have a book called by the name of its author, i.e. *Caraka,*[27] which they consider as the best of their whole literature on medicine. According to their belief, Caraka was a Rishi in the last Dvapara-yuga, when his name was Agnivesa, but afterwards he was called Caraka, i.e. the intelligent one, after the first elements of medicine had been laid down by certain Rishis, the children of *Sutra.* These latter had received them from Indra, Indra from Asvin, one of the two physicians of the Devas, and Asvin had received them from Prajapati, i.e. Brahman, *the first father.* This book has been translated into Arabic for the princes of the house of the Barmecides.[28]

Medical literature

The Hindus cultivate numerous other branches of science and literature, and have a nearly boundless literature. I, however, could not comprehend it with my knowledge. I wish I could translate the book *Pancatantra,* known among us as the book of Kalila and Dimna.[29] It is far spread in various languages, in Persian, Hindi, and Arabic—in translations of people who are not free from the suspicion of having altered the text. For instance, Abdullah Ibn Almukaffa[30] has added in his Arabic version the chapter about Barzoya, with the intention of raising doubts in the minds of people of feeble religious belief, and to gain and prepare them for the propagation of the doctrines of the Manichaeans. And if he is open to suspicion insofar as he has added something to the text which he had simply to translate, he is hardly free from suspicion in his capacity as translator.

On Pancatantra

CHAPTER XV

Notes On Hindu Metrology, Intended To Facilitate The Understanding Of All Kinds Of Measurements Which Occur In This Book

Counting is innate to man. The measure of a thing becomes known by its being compared with another thing which belongs to the same species and is assumed as a unit by general consent. Thereby the difference between the object and this standard becomes known.

The Hindu system of weights

By weighing, people determine the amount of gravity of heavy bodies, when the tongue of the scales stands at right angles on the horizontal plane. Hindus want the scales very little, because their *dirhams* are determined by number, not by weight, and their fractions, too, are simply counted as so-and-so many *fulus.* The coinage of both *dirhams* and *fulus* is different according to towns and districts. They weigh gold with the scales only when it is in its natural state or such as has been worked, e.g. for ornaments, but not coined. They use as a weight of gold the *suvarna* = 1⅓ *tola.* They use the *tola* as frequently as we use the *mithkal.* According to what I have been able to learn from them it corresponds to three of our *dirhams,* of which 10 equal 7 *mithkal.*

Therefore 1 *tola* = 2 1/10 of our *mithkal.*

The greatest fraction of a *tola* is 1/12, called *masha.*

Therefore 16 *masha* = 1 *suvarna.*

Further,

1 *masha* = 4 *andi (eranda),* i.e. the seed of a tree called Gaura.

1 *andi* = 4 *yava.*

1 *yava* = 6 *kala.*

1 *kala* = 4 *pada.*

1 *pada* = 4 *mdri* (?).

. . . Since, the unit of measure is not a natural unit, but a conventional one assumed by general consent, it admits of both practical and imaginary division. Its subdivisions or fractions are different in different places at one and the same time, and at different periods in one and the same country. Their names, too, are different according to places and times; changes which are produced either by the organic development of languages or by accident.

A man from the neighbourhood of Somnath told me that their *mithkal* is equal to ours: that

1 *mithkal* = 8 *ruvu;* 1 *ruvu* = 2 *pali;* 1 *pali* = 16 *yava,* i.e., barley-corn.

Accordingly, 1 *mithkal* = 8 *ruvu* = 16 *pali* = 256 *yava.*

[Varahamihira and Caraka are quoted. The scale given by the former based on the measurements which he prescribes for the construction of idols, is given. Pp. 162–64.]

The balances with which the Hindus weigh things are *charistiones,* of which the weights are immovable, whilst the scales move on certain marks and lines. Therefore, the balance is called *tula.* The first lines mean the units of the weight from 1 to 5, and farther on to 10; the following lines mean the tenths, 10, 20, 30, &c . . .

The Hindu balance

The Hindus have a weight called *bhara,* which is mentioned in the books about the conquest of Sindh. It is equal to 2000 *pala;* for they explain it by 100 × 200 *pala,* and as nearly equal to the weight of an ox. This is all I have lighted on as regards Hindu weights.

By measuring (with dry measures) people determine the body and the bulk of a thing, if it fills up a certain measure which has been gauged as containing a certain quantity of it, it being understood that the way in which the things are laid out in the measure, the way in which their surface is determined, and the way

Dry measures

in which, on the whole, they are arranged within the measure, are in every case identical. If two objects which are to be weighed belong to the same species, they then prove to be equal, not only in bulk, but also in weight; but if they do not belong to the same species, their bodily extent is equal, but not their weight.

They have a measure called *bisi* (? *sibi*) which is mentioned by every man from Kanauj and Somnath.

According to the people of Kanauj—4 *bisi* = 1 *prastha*, ¼ *bisi* = 1 *kudava*.

According to the people of Somnath—16 *bisi* = 1 *panti*, 12 *panti* =1 *moru*. . . .

Mensuration is the determination of distances by lines and of superficies by planes. A plane ought to be measured by part of a plane, but the mensuration by means of lines effects the same purpose, as lines determine the limits of planes.

Measures of distances

[Varahamihira is quoted in regard to the units for measuring distances. These are as follows:]

8 barley-corns put together = 1 *angula*, i.e. finger.
4 fingers = 1 *rama* (?), i.e. the fist.
24 fingers = 1 *hattha*, i.e. yard, also called *dasta*.
4 yards = 1 *dhanu*, i.e. arc = a fathom.
40 arcs = 1 *nalva*.
25 *nalva* = 1 *krosa*.

Hence it follows that 1 *kroh* = 4000 yards; and as our mile has just so many yards, 1 mile = 1 *kroh*. Pulisa, the Greek, also mentions in his Siddhanta that 1 *kroh* = 4000 yards.

The *yard* is equal to 2 *mikyas* or 24 fingers; for the Hindus determine the *sanku*, i.e. *mikyas*, by idol-fingers. They do not call the twelfth part of a *mikyas a finger* in general, as *we* do, but their *mikyas* is always a *span*. The span, i.e. the distance between the ends of the thumb and the small finger at their widest possible stretching, is called *vitasti* and also *kishku*.

The distance between the ends of the fourth or ring-finger and the thumb, both being stretched out, is called *gokarna*.

The distance between the ends of the index-finger and of the thumb is called *karabha*, and is reckoned as equal to two-thirds of a span.

The distance between the tops of the middle finger and of the thumb is called *tala*. The Hindus maintain that the height of a man is eight times his *tala*, whether he be tall or small; as people say with regard to the foot, that it is one-seventh of the height of a man. . . .

After the measure of the *krosa* has been fixed and found to be equal to our *mile,* the reader must learn that they have a measure of distances, called *yojana,* which is equal to 8 miles or to 32,000 yards.

The relation between *yojana,* mile and *farsakh.*

Perhaps somebody might believe that 1 *kroh* is = ¼ *farsakh,* and maintain that the *farsakhs* of the Hindus are 16,000 yards long. But such is not the case. On the contrary, 1 *kroh* = ½ *yojana.* In the terms of this measure, Alfazari has determined the circumference of the earth in his astronomical handbook. He calls it *jun*, in the plural *'ajwan.*

The elements of the calculations of the Hindus on the circumference of the circle rest on the assumption that it is *thrice its diameter.*

Relation between circumference and diameter

So the *Matsya-Purana* says, after it has mentioned the diameters of the sun and moon in *yojanas:* "The circumference is thrice the diameter."

[Extracts from the *Matsya-Purana, Aditya-Purana* and the *Vayu-Purana* are quoted. Pp. 168–69.]

CHAPTER XVI

Notes On The Writing Of The Hindus, On Their Arithmetic And Related Subjects, And On Certain Strange Manners And Customs Of Theirs

On various kinds of writing materials

The tongue communicates the thought of the speaker to the hearer. Its action has therefore, as it were, a momentary life only, and it would have been impossible to deliver by oral tradition the accounts of the events of the past to later generations, more particularly if they are separated from them by long periods of time. This has become possible only by a new discovery of the human mind, by the art of writing, which spreads news over space as the winds spread, and over time as the spirits of the deceased spread. Praise therefore be unto Him who has arranged creation and created everything for the best!

The Hindus are not in the habit of writing on hides, like the Greeks in ancient times. Socrates, on being asked why he did not compose books, gave this reply: "I do not transfer knowledge from the living hearts of men to the *dead* hides of sheep." Muslims, too, used in the early times of Islam to write on hides, e.g. the treaty between the Prophet and the Jews of Khaibar and his letter to Kisra. The copies of the Koran were written on the hides of gazelles, as are still nowadays the copies of the Thora. There occurs this passage in the Koran (Sura vi. 91): "They make it *karatis*." i.e. *tomaria*. The *kirtas* (or *charta*) is made in Egypt, being cut out of the papyrus stalk. Written on this material, the orders of the Khalifs went out into all the world until shortly before our time. Papyrus has this advantage over vellum, that you can neither rub out nor change anything on it, because thereby it would be destroyed. It was in China that paper was first manufactured. Chinese prisoners introduced the fabrication of paper into Samarkand, and thereupon it was made in various places, so as to meet the existing want.

The Hindus have in the south of their country a slender tree like the date and cocoa-nut palms, bearing edible fruits and leaves of the length of one yard, and as broad as three fingers one put beside the other. They call these leaves *tari* (*tala* or *tar-Borassus flabelliformis*), and write on them. They bind a book of these leaves together by a cord on which they are arranged, the cord going through all the leaves by a hole in the middle of each.

In Central and Northern India people use the bark of the *tuz* tree, one kind of which is used as a cover for bows. It is called *bhurja*. They take a piece one yard long and as broad as the outstretched fingers of the hand, or somewhat less, and prepare it in various ways. They oil and polish it so as to make it hard and smooth, and then they write on it. The proper order of the single leaves is marked by numbers. The whole book is wrapped up in a piece of cloth and fastened between two tablets of the same size. Such a book is called *puthi* (cf. *pusta*, *pustaka*). Their letters, and whatever else they have to write, they write on the bark of the *tuz* tree.

On the Hindu alphabet

As to the writing or alphabet of the Hindus, we have already mentioned that it once had been lost and forgotten; that nobody cared for it, and that in consequence people became illiterate, sunken into gross ignorance, and entirely estranged from science. But then Vyasa, the son of Parasara, redisovered their alphabet of fifty letters by an inspiration of God. A letter is called *akshara*.

Some people say that originally the number of their letters was less, and that it increased only by degrees. This is possible, or I should even say necessary. . . .

The great number of the letters of the Hindu alphabet is explained, firstly, by the fact that they express every letter by a separate sign if it is followed by a vowel or a diphthong or a *hamza (visarga),* or a small extension of the sound beyond the measure of the vowel, and, secondly, by the fact that they have consonants which are not found together in any other language, though they may be found scattered through different languages—sounds of such a nature that *our* tongues, not being familiar with them, can scarcely pronounce them, and that *our* ears are frequently not able to distinguish between many a cognate pair of them.

The Hindus write from the left to the right like the Greeks. They do not write on the basis of a line, above which the heads of the letters rise whilst their tails go down below, as in Arabic writing. On the contrary, their ground-line is above, a straight line above every single character, and from this line the letter hangs down and is written under it. Any sign *above* the line is nothing but a grammatical mark to denote the pronunciation of the character above which it stands.

On the local alphabets of the Hindus

The most generally known alphabet is called *Siddhamatrika,* which is by some considered as originating from Kashmir, for the people of Kashmir use it. But it is also used in Varanasi. This town and Kashmir are the high schools of Hindu sciences. The same writing is used in Madhyadesa, i.e. the middle country, the country all around Kanauj, which is also called Aryavarta.

In Malava there is another alphabet called *Nagara,* which differs from the former only in the shape of the characters.

Next comes an alphabet called *Ardhanagari,* i.e. *half-nagara,* so called because it is compounded of the former two. It is used in Bhatiya and some parts of Sindh.

Other alphabets are the *Malwari,* used in Malwashau, in southern Sind, towards the sea-coast; the *Saindhava,* used in Bahmanwa or Almansura; the *Karnata,* used in Karnatadesa, whence those troops come which in the armies are known as *Kannara;* the *Andhri,* used in Andhradesa; the *Dirwari (Dravidi),* used in Dirwaradesa (Dravida-desa); the *Lari,* used in Laradesa (Latadesa); the *Gauri (Gaudi),* used in Purvadesa, i.e. the Eastern country; the *Bhaikshuki,* used in Udunpur[30A] in Purvadesa. This last is the writing of Buddha.

On the word Om

The Hindus begin their books with *Om,* the word of creation, as we begin with "In the name of God". The figure of the word *Om* is ॐ . This figure does not consist of letters;

it is simply an image invented to represent this word, which people use, believing that it will bring them a blessing, and meaning thereby a confession of the unity of God. . . .

The Hindus do not use the letters of their alphabet for numerical notation, as we use the Arabic letters in the order of the Hebrew alphabet. As in different parts of India the letters have different shapes, the numeral signs, too, which are called *anka*, differ. The numeral signs which we use are derived from the finest forms of the Hindu signs. Signs and figures are of no use if people do not know what they mean, but the people of Kashmir mark the single leaves of their books with figures which look like drawings or like the Chinese characters, the meaning of which can only be learned by a very long practice. However, they do not use them when reckoning in the sand.

On their numeral signs

In arithmetic all nations agree that all the *orders* of numbers (e.g. one, ten, hundred, thousand) stand in a certain relation to the ten; that each order is the tenth part of the following and the ten-fold of the preceding. I have studied the names of the *orders* of the numbers in various languages with all kinds of people with whom I have been in contact, and have found that no nation goes beyond the thousand. The Arabs, too, stop with the thousand, which is certainly the most correct and the most natural thing to do. I have written a separate treatise on this subject.

Those, however, who go beyond the thousand in their numeral system are the Hindus, at least in their arithmetical technical terms, which have been either freely invented or derived according to certain etymologies, whilst in others both methods are blended together. They extend the names of the *orders* of numbers until the 18th *order* for religious reasons, the mathematicians being assisted by the grammarians with all kinds of etymologies.

The 18th *order* is called *Parardha,* i.e. the half of heaven, or more accurately, *the half of that which is above. . . .*

The following are the names of the eighteen *orders* of numbers:—

The eighteen orders of numeration

1. *Ekam* 2. *Dasam* 3. *Satam*
4. *Sahasram* 5. *Ayuta* 6. *Laksha*
7. *Prayuta* 8. *Koti* 9. *Nyarbuda*
10. *Padma* 11. *Kharva* 12. *Nikharva*
13. *Mahapadma* 14. *Sanku* 15. *Samudra* 16. *Madhya* 17. *Antya*
18. *Parardha.*

I shall now mention some of their differences of opinion relating to this system.

Variations occurring in the eighteen orders

Some Hindus maintain that *there is a 19th order beyond the Parardha, called Bhuri, and that this is the limit of reckoning.* But in reality *reckoning* is unlimited; it has only a technical limit, which is conventionally adopted as the last of the *orders* of numbers. By the word *reckoning* in the sentence above they seem to mean *nomenclature,* as if they meant to say that the language has no *name* for any reckoning beyond the 19th *order.* It is known that the unit of this *order*, i.e. one *bhuri,* is equal to one-fifth of the *greatest day,* but on this subject they have no tradition. In their tradition there are only traces of combinations of the *greatest day,* as we shall hereafter explain. Therefore this 19th *order* is an addition of an artificial and hyper-accurate nature.

According to others, the limit of reckoning is *koti;* and starting from *koti* the succession of the *orders* of numbers would be *koti,* thousands, hundreds, tenths; for the number of Devas is expressed in *kotis.* According to their belief there are thirty-three *kotis* of Devas, eleven of which belong to each of the three beings, Brahman, Narayana, and Mahadeva.

The names of the *orders* beyond that of the 18th have been invented by the grammarians, as we have said already (p. 82).

Further, we observe that the popular name of the 5th *order* is *Dasa sahasra,* that of the 7th *order, Dasa laksha;* for the two names which we have mentioned in the list above (*Ayuta, Prayuta*) are rarely used.

The book of Aryabhatta of Kusumapura gives the following names of the *orders* from the ten till 10 *koti*:—

Ayutam	*Koti padma*
Niyutam	*Para padma*
Prayutam	

Further, it is noteworthy that some people establish a kind of etymological relationship between the different names; so they call the 6th *order Niyuta,* according to the analogy of the 5th, which is called *Ayuta.* Further, they call the 8th *order Arbuda,* according to the analogy of the 9th, which is called *Nyarbuda.*

There is a similar relation between *Nikharva* and *Kharva,* the names of the 12th and 11th *orders,* and between *Sanku* and *Mahasanku,* the names of the 13th and 14th *orders.* According to this analogy *Mahapadma* ought to follow immediately after *Padma,* but this latter is the name of the 10th, the former the name of the 13th *order*.

These are differences of theirs which can be traced back to certain reasons; but besides, there are many differences without any reason, which simply arise from people dictating these names without observing any fixed order, or from the fact that they hate to avow their ignorance by a frank *I do not know,*—a word which is difficult to them in any connection whatsoever. . . .

The Hindus use the numeral signs in arithmetic in the same way as we do. I have composed a treatise showing how far, possibly, the Hindus are ahead of us in this subject. We have already explained that the Hindus compose their books in Slokas. If, now, they wish, in their astronomical handbooks,to express some numbers of the various *orders,* they express them by words used to denote certain numbers either in one *order* alone or at the same time in two *orders* (e.g. a word meaning either 20 or both 20 and 200). For each number they have appropriated quite a great quantity of words. Hence, if one word does not suit the metre, you may easily exchange it for a synonym which suits. Brahmagupta says: "If you want to write *one,* express it by everything which is unique, as *the earth, the moon; two* by everything which is double, as, e.g. *black* and *white; three* by everything which is threefold; the *nought by heaven,* the *twelve* by the names of the sun."

Numeral notation

I have united in the following table all the expressions for the numbers which I used to hear from them; for the knowledge of these things is most essential for deciphering their astronomical handbooks. Whenever I shall come to know all the meanings of these words, I will add them, if God permits! [The various sets of words used for the different numbers from 0 to 25 are listed, Pp. 178–79.]

. . . We shall now speak of certain strange manners and customs of the Hindus. The strangeness of a thing evidently rests on the fact that it occurs but rarely, and that we seldom have the opportunity of witnessing it. If such strangeness reaches a high degree, the thing becomes a curiosity, or even something like a miracle, which is no longer in accordance with the ordinary laws of nature, and which seems chimerical as long as it has not been witnessed. Many Hindu customs differ from those of our country and of our time to such a degree as to appear to us simply monstrous. One might almost think that they had intentionally changed them

Strange manners and customs of the Hindus

into the opposite, for *our* customs do not resemble theirs, but are the very reverse; and if ever a custom of *theirs* resembles one of *ours*, it has certainly just the opposite meaning.

They do not cut any of the hair of the body. Originally they went naked in consequence of the heat, and by not cutting the hair of the head they intended to prevent sunstroke.

They divide the moustache into single plaits in order to preserve it. As regards their not cutting the hair of the genitals, they try to make people believe that the cutting of it incites to lust and increases carnal desire. Therefore such of them as feel a strong desire for cohabitation never cut the hair of the genitals.

They let the nails grow long, glorying in their idleness, since they do not use them for any business or work, but only, while living a *dolce far niente* life, they scratch their heads with them and examine the hair for lice.

The Hindus eat singly, one by one, on a tablecloth of dung. They do not make use of the remainder of a meal, and the plates from which they have eaten are thrown away if they are earthen.

They have red teeth in consequence of chewing arecanuts with betel-leaves and chalk.

They drink wine before having eaten anything, then they take their meal. They sip the stall of cows, but they do not eat their meat.

They beat the cymbals with a stick.

They use turbans for trousers. Those who want little dress are content to dress in a rag of two fingers' breadth, which they bind over their loins with two cords; but those who like much dress, wear trousers lined with so much cotton as would suffice to make a number of counterpanes and saddle-rugs. These trousers have no (visible) openings, and they are so huge that the feet are not visible. The string by which the trousers are fastened is at the back.

Their *sidar* (a piece of dress covering the head and the upper part of breast and neck) is similar to the trousers, being also fastened at the back by buttons.

The lappets of the *Kurtakas* (short shirts from the shoulders to the middle of the body with sleeves, a female dress) have slashes both on the right and left sides.

They keep the shoes tight till they begin to put them on. They are turned down from the calf before walking (?).

In washing they begin with the feet, and then wash the face. They wash themselves before cohabiting with their wives. . . .

On festive days they besmear their bodies with dung instead of perfumes.

The men wear articles of female dress; they use cosmetics, wear earrings, arm-rings, golden seal-rings on the ring-finger as well as on the toes of the feet. . . .

They ride without a saddle, but if they put on a saddle, they mount the horse from its right side. In travelling they like to have somebody riding behind them.

They fasten the *kuthara,* i.e. the dagger, at the waist on the right side.

They wear a girdle called *Yajnopavita,* passing from the left shoulder to the right side of the waist.

In all consultations and emergencies they take the advice of the women.

When a child is born people show particular attention to the man, not to the woman.

Of two children they give the preference to the younger, particularly in the eastern parts of the country; for they maintain that the elder owes his birth to predominant lust, whilst the younger owes his origin to mature reflection and a calm proceeding.

In shaking hands they grasp the hand of a man from the convex side.

They do not ask permission to enter a house, but when they leave it they ask permission to do so.

In their meetings they sit cross-legged.

They spit out and blow their noses without any respect for the elder ones present, and they crack their lice before them. They consider the *crepitus ventris* as a good omen, sneezing as a bad omen.

They consider as unclean the weaver, but as clean the cupper and the flayer, who kills dying animals for money either by drowning or by burning.

They use black tablets for the children in the schools, and write upon them along the long side, not the broad side, writing with a white material from the left to the right. One would think that the author of the following verses had meant the Hindus:—

"How many a writer uses paper as black as charcoal,
Whilst his pen writes on it with white colour.
By writing he places a bright day in a dark night,
Weaving like a weaver, but without adding a woof."

They write the title of a book at the end of it, not at the beginning.

They magnify the nouns of their language by giving them the feminine gender, as the Arabs magnify them by the diminutive form.

If one of them hands over a thing to another, he expects that it should be thrown to him as we throw a thing to the dogs.

If two men play at *Nard* (backgammon), a third one throws the dice between them.

They like the juice which flows over the cheeks of the rutting elephant, which in reality has the most horrid smell.

On the Indian chess

In playing chess they move the elephant straight on, not to the other sides, one square at a time, like the pawn, and to the four corners also one square at time, like the queen (*firzan*). They say that these five squares (i.e. the one straight forward and the others at the corners) are the places occupied by the trunk and the four feet of the elephant.

They play chess—four persons at a time—with a pair of dice. Their arrangement of the figures on the chess-board is the following:—

Tower (rukh)	Horse	Elephant	King			Pawn	Tower
Pawn	Pawn	Pawn	Pawn			Pawn	Horse
						Pawn	Elephant
						Pawn	King
King	Pawn						
Elephant	Pawn						
Horse	Pawn			Pawn	Pawn	Pawn	Pawn
Tower	Pawn			King	Elephant	Horse	Tower

As this kind of chess is not among us, I shall here explain what I know of it.

The four persons playing together sit so as to form a square round a chess-board, and throw the two dice alternately. Of the numbers of the dice the five and six are blank (i.e. do not count as such). In that case, if the dice shows five or six, the player takes one instead of the five, and four instead of the six, because the figures of these two numerals are drawn in the following manner:—

6			5
4	3	2	1

so as to exhibit a certain likeness of form to 4 and 1, viz. in the Indian signs.

The name *Shah* or *king* applies here to the queen (*firzan*).

Each number of the dice causes a move of one of the figures.

The 1 moves either the pawn or the king. Their moves are the same as in the common chess. The king may be taken, but is not required to leave his place.

The 2 moves the tower (*rukh*). It moves to the third square in the direction of the diagonal, as the elephant moves in *our* chess.

The 3 moves the horse. Its move is the generally known one to the third square in oblique direction.

The 4 moves the elphant. It moves in a straight line, as the tower does in our chess, unless it be prevented from moving on. If this is the case, as sometimes happens, one of the dice removes the obstacle, and enables it to move on. Its smallest move is one square, the greatest fifteen squares, because the dice sometimes show two 4, or two 6, or a 4 and a 6. In consequence of one of these numbers, the elephant moves along the whole side of the margin on the chess-board; in consequence of the other number, it moves along the other side on the other margin of the board, in case there is no impediment in its way. In consequence of these two numbers, the elephant, in the course of his moves, occupies the two ends of the diagonal.

The pieces have certain values, according to which the player gets his share of the stake, for the pieces are taken and pass into the hands of the player. The value of the king is 5, that of the elephant 4, of the horse 3, of the tower 2, and of the pawn 1. He who takes a king gets 5. For two kings he gets 10, for three kings 15, if the winner is no longer in possession of his own king. But if he has still his own king, and takes all three kings, he gets 54, a number which represents a progression based on general consent, not on an algebraic principle.

[Al-Biruni concludes this account of the Hindu manners and customs by remarking that the Hindus claimed to be different from the Muslims and to be 'something better' than them, but adds that this attitude of self-adulation was adopted by the Muslims too. In the context of the 'strange' manners and customs of the Hindus he also recalls some of the immoral practices prevalent among the Arabs before the rise of Islam. He expresses satisfaction over the fact that with the rise of Islam these evils had been abolished in Arabia and 'those parts of India the people of which have become Muhammadans.' Pp. 185–86.]

CHAPTER XVII

On Hindu Sciences Which Prey On The Ignorance Of People

We understand by witchcraft, making by some kind of delusion a thing appear to the senses as something different from what it is in reality. Taken in this sense, it is far spread among people. Understood, however, as common people understand it, as the producing of something which is impossible, it is a thing which does not lie within the limits of reality. For as that which is impossible cannot be produced, the whole affair is nothing but a gross deception. Therefore witchcraft in this sense has nothing whatever to do with science.

On alchemy among the Hindus in general

One of the species of witchcraft is alchemy, though it is generally not called by this name. But if a man takes a bit of cotton and makes it appear as a bit of gold, what would you call this but a piece of witchcraft? It is quite the same as if he were to take a bit of silver and make it appear as gold, only with this difference, that the latter is a generally-known process, i.e. the gilding of silver, the former is not.

The Hindus do not pay particular attention to alchemy, but no nation is entirely free from it, and one nation has more bias for it than another, which must not be construed as proving intelligence or ignorance; for we find that many intelligent people are entirely given to alchemy, whilst ignorant people ridicule the art and its adepts. Those intelligent people, though boisterously exulting over their make-believe science, are not to be blamed for occupying themselves with alchemy, for their motive is simply excessive eagerness for acquiring fortune and for avoiding misfortune. Once a sage was asked why scholars always flock to the doors of the rich, whilst the rich are not inclined to call at the doors of scholars. "The scholars," he answered, "are well aware of the use of money, but the rich are ignorant of the nobility of science." On the other hand, ignorant people are not to be praised, although they behave quite quietly, simply because they abstain from alchemy, for their motives are objectionable ones, rather practical results of innate ignorance and stupidity than anything else.

The adepts in this art try to keep it concealed, and shrink back from intercourse with those who do not belong to them. Therefore I have not been able to learn from the Hindus which methods they follow in this science, and what element they principally use, whether a mineral or an animal or a vegetabe one. I only heard them speaking of the process of *sublimation,* of *calcination*, of *analysis*, and of the *waxing of talc,* which they call in their language *talaka,* and so I guess that they incline towards the mineralogical method of alchemy.

They have a science similar to alchemy which is quite peculiar to them. They call it *Rasayana*, a word composed with *rasa,* i.e. gold. It means an art which is restricted to certain operations, drugs, and compound medicines, most of which are taken from plants. Its principles restore the health of those who were ill beyond hope, and give back youth to fading old age, so that people become again what they were in the age near puberty; white hair become black again, the keenness of the senses is restored as well as the capacity for juvenile agility, and even for cohabitation, and the life of people in this world is even extended to a long period.

The science of Rasayana

[Incredulous stories about some adepts in the 'science of Rasayana', such as Nagarjuna of the 'fort Dihak near Somnath', Vyadi who lived in Ujjain during the reign of Vikramaditya, an unnamed person who lived in Dhar, capital of Malwa, and an indigent fruit-seller called Ranka and King Vallabha of the city of Vallabhi are mentioned. Some of them had accidentally discovered the secret formula and acquired supernatural powers as a result of it. Others had met with tragic ends. Pp. 189–93.]

The greediness of the ignorant Hindu princes for gold-making does not know any limit. If any one of them wanted to carry out a scheme of gold-making, and people advised him to kill a number of fine little children, the monster would not refrain from such a crime; he would throw them into the fire. If this precious science of Rasayana were banished to the utmost limits of the world, where it is unattainable to anybody, it would be the best. . . .

On the bird Garuda

As regards charms and incantations, the Hindus have a firm belief in them, and they, as a rule, are much inclined towards them. The book which treats of those things is considered as a work of Garuda, a bird on which Narayana rode. . . .

The effect of charms on the bite of serpents

Most of their charms are intended for those who have been bitten by serpents.

[Some stories about the effectiveness of charms are mentioned. P. 194.]

Hunting practices

I myself have witnessed that in hunting gazelles they caught them with the hand. One Hindu even went so far as to assert that he, without catching the gazelle, would drive it before him and lead it straight into the kitchen. This, however, rests, as I believe I have found out, simply on the device of slowly and constantly accustoming the animals to one and the same melody. . . .

The shooters of Kata-birds have a custom of beating copper-vessels during the night with one and the same kind of beat, and they manage to catch them with the hand. If, however, the beat is changed, the birds fly off in all directions.

All these things are peculiar customs which have nothing whatsoever to do with charms. Sometimes the Hindus are considered as sorcerers because of their playing with balls on raised beams or on tight ropes, but tricks of this kind are common to all nations.

CHAPTER XVIII

Various Notes On Their Country, Their Rivers, And Their Ocean. Itineraries Of The Distances Between Their Several Kingdoms, And Between The Boundaries Of Their Country

The reader is to imagine the inhabitable world, *he oikoumene,* as lying in the northern half of the earth, and more accurately in one-half of this half—i.e. in one of the quarters of the earth. It is surrounded by a sea, which both in west and east is called the *comprehending one;* the Greeks call its western part near their country *okeanos.* This sea separates the inhabitable world from whatever continents or inhabitable islands there may be beyond it, both towards west and east; for it is not navigable on account of the darkness of the air and the thickness of the water, because there is no more any road to be traced, and because the risk is enormous, whilst the profit is nothing. Therefore people of olden times have fixed marks both on the sea and its shores which are intended to deter from entering it.

The inhabitable world and the ocean

The inhabitable world does not reach the north on account of the cold, except in certain places where it penetrates into the north in the shape, as it were, of tongues and bays. In the south it reaches as far as the coast of the ocean, which in west and east is connected with the *comprehending ocean.* This southern ocean is navigable. It does not form the utmost southern limit of the inhabitable world. On the contrary, the latter stretches still more southward in the shape of large and small islands which fill the ocean. In this southern region land and water dispute with each other their position, so that in one place the continent protrudes into the sea, whilst in another the sea penetrates deeply into the continent.

The continent protrudes far into the sea in the western half of the earth, and extends its shores far into the south. On the plains of this continent live the western Negroes, whence the slaves are brought; and there are the Mountains of the Moon, and on them are sources of the Nile. On its coast, and the islands before the coast, live the various tribes of the Zanj. There are several bays or gulfs which penetrate into the continent on this western half of the earth—the bay of Berbera, that of Klysma (the Red Sea), and that of Persia (the Persian Gulf); and between these gulfs the western continent protrudes more or less into the ocean.

In the eastern half of the earth the sea penetrates as deeply into the northern continent as the continent in the western half protrudes into the southern sea, and in many places it has formed bays and estuaries which run far into the continent—bays being parts of the sea, estuaries being the outlets of rivers towards the sea. This sea is mostly called from some island in it or from the coast which borders it. Here, however, we are concerned only with that part of the sea which is bordered by the continent of India, and therefore is called the *Indian Ocean.*

As to the orographic configuration of the inhabitable world, imagine a range of towering mountains like the vertebrae of a pine stretching through the middle latitude of the earth, and in longitude from east to west, passing through China, Tibet, the country of the Turks, Kabul, Badhakhshan, Tokharistan, Bamiyan Elghor, Khurasan, Media, Adharbaijan, Armenia, the Roman Empire, the country of the Franks, and of the Jalalika (Gallicians). Long as this range is, it has also a considerable breadth, and, besides, many windings which enclose inhabited plains watered by streams which descend from the mountains both towards north and south. One of these plains is India, limited in the south by the above

The orographic system of Asia and Europe

mentioned Indian Ocean, and on all three other sides by the lofty mountains, the waters of which flow down to it. But if you have seen the soil of India with your own eyes and meditate on its nature—if you consider the rounded stones found in the earth however deeply you dig, stones that are huge near the mountains and where the rivers have a violent current; stones that are of smaller size at greater distance from the mountains, and where the streams flow more slowly; stones that appear pulverised in the shape of sand where the streams begin to stagnate near their mouths and near the sea—if you consider all this, you could scarcely help thinking that India has once been a sea which by degrees has been filled up by the alluvium of the streams.

India, a recent alluvial formation

The middle of India is the country round Kanoj (Kanauj), which they call *Madhyadesa,* i.e. the middle of the realms. It is the middle or centre from a geographical point of view, insofar as it lies half way between the sea and the mountains, in the midst between the hot and the cold provinces, and also between the eastern and western frontiers of India. But it is a political centre too, because in former times it was the residence of their most famous heroes and kings.

First orientation regarding Madhyadesa, Kanoj, Mahura, and Taneshar

The country of Sindh lies to the west of Kanoj. In marching from our country to Sindh we start from the country of Nimroz, i.e. the country of Sijistan, whilst marching to *Hind* or India proper we start from the side of Kabul. This, however, is not the only possible road. You may march into India from all sides, supposing that you can remove the obstacles in the way. In the mountains which form the frontier of India towards the west there are tribes of the Hindus, or of people near akin to them—rebellious savage races—which extend as far as the farthermost frontiers of the Hindu race.

Kanoj lies to the west of the Ganges, a very large town, but most of it is now in ruins and desolate since the capital has been transferred thence to the city of Bari[31], east of the Ganges. Between the two towns there is a distance of three to four days' marches.

As Kanoj *(Kanyakubja)* has become famous by the children of Pandu, the city of Mahura *(Mathura)* has become famous by Vasudeva. It lies east of the river Jaun *(Yamuna)*. The distance between Mahura and Kanoj is 28 *farsakh.*[32]

Taneshar *(Sthanesvara)* lies between the two rivers to the north both of Kanoj and Mahura, at a distance of nearly 80 *farsakh* from Kanoj, and nearly 50 *farsakh* from Mahura.

The river Ganges rises in the mountains which have already been mentioned. Its source is called *Ganga-dvara.* Most of the other rivers of the country also rise in the same mountains, as we have already mentioned in the proper place.

Hindu method of determining distances

As for the distances between the various parts of India, those who have not themselves actually seen them must rely upon tradition; but unfortunately it is of such a nature that already Ptolemy incessantly complains of its transmitters and their bias towards story-telling. Fortunately I have found out a certain rule by which to control their lies. The Hindus frequently estimate the burden an ox could bear at 2000 and 3000 *mana* (which is infinitely more than an ox could carry *at once*). In consequence they are compelled to let the caravan make the same march to and fro during many days—in fact, so long until the ox has carried the whole load assigned to it from one end of the route to the other, and then they reckon as the distance between the two places *a march of such a number of days* as the caravan has altogether spent in marching to and fro. It is only with the greatest exertion and caution that we can to some extent correct the statements of the Hindus. However, we could not make up our mind to suppress that which we know on account of that which we do not know. We ask the readers's pardon where there is anything wrong, and now we continue.

From Kanoj to the Tree of Prayaga (Allahabad) and to the eastern coast

A man marching from Kanoj to the south between the two rivers Jaun and Ganges passes the following well known places:—*Jajjamau,* 12 *farsakh* from Kanoj, each *farsakh* being equal to four miles or one *kuroh; Abhapuri,* 8 *farsakh; Kuraha,* 8 *farsakh; Barhamshil,* 8 *farsakh;* the *Tree of Prayaga,* 12 *farsakh,* the place where the water of the Jaun joins the Ganges, where the Hindus torment themselves with various kinds of tortures, which are described in the books about religious sects. The distance from Prayaga to the place where the Ganges flows into the sea is 12 *farsakh (sic).*

Other tracts of country extend from the Tree of Prayaga southward towards the coast. *Arku-tirtha,* 12 *farsakh* from Prayaga; the realm *Uwaryahar,* 40 *farsakh; Urdabishau* on the coast, 50 *farsakh.*

Thence along the coast towards the east there are countries which are now under the sway of *Jaur;* first *Daraur,* 40 *farsakh* from Urdabishau; *Kanji,* 30 *farsakh; Malaya,* 40 *farsakh; Kunk,* 30 *farsakh,* which is the last of Jaur's possessions in this direction.

From Bari to the mouth of the Ganges

Marching from Bari along the Ganges on its eastern side, you pass the following stations:—*Ajodaha* (Ayodhya, Oudh), 25 *farsakh* from Bari; the famous *Banarasi,* 20 *farsakh.*

Thence changing the direction, and marching eastward instead of southward, you come to *Sharwar,* 35 *farsakh* from Banarasi; *Pataliputra,* 20 *farsakh; Mungiri,* 15 *farsakh; Janpa,* 30 *farsakh; Dugumpur,* 50 *farsakh; Gangasayara,* 30 *farsakh,* where the Ganges flows into the sea.

Kanoj through Nepal to Bhoteshar

Marching from Kanoj towards the east, you come to *Bari,* 10 *farsakh; Dugum,* 45 *farsakh;* the empire of *Shilahat,* 10 *farsakh;* the town *Bihat,* 12 *farsakh.* Farther on the country to the right is called *Tilwat,* the inhabitants *Taru,* people of very black colour and flat-nosed like the Turks. Thence you come to the mountains of Kamru, which stretch away as far as the sea.

Opposite Tilwat the country to the left is the realm of Naipal. A man who had travelled in those countries gave me the following report:—"When in Tanwat, he left the easterly direction and turned to the left. He marched to Naipal, a distance of 20 *farsakh,* most of which was ascending country. From Naipal he came to Bhoteshar in thirty days, a distance of nearly 80 *farsakh,* in which there is more ascending than descending country. And there is a water which is several times crossed on bridges consisting of planks tied with cords to two canes, which stretch from rock to rock, and are fastened to milestones constructed on either side. People carry the burdens on their shoulders over such a bridge, whilst below, at a depth of 100 yards, the water foams as white as snow, threatening to shatter the rocks. On the other side of the bridges, the burdens are transported on the back of goats. . . ."

"Bhoteshar is the first frontier of Tibet. There the language changes as well as the costumes and the anthropological character of the people. Thence the distance to the top of the highest peak is 20 *farsakh.* From the height of this mountain, India appears as a black expanse below the mist, the mountains lying below this peak like small hills, and Tibet and China appear as red. The descent towards Tibet and China is less than one *farsakh.*"

Marching from Kanoj towards the south-east, on the western side of the Ganges, you come to the realm of *Jajahuti*, 30 *farsakh* from Kanoj. The capital of the country is *Kajuraha*. Between this town and Kanoj there are two of the most famous fortresses of India, Gwaliyar (Gwalior) and Kalanjar. *Dahala* [—*farsakh*], a country the capital of which is Tiauri, and the ruler of which is now Gangeya.

From Kanoj to Banavas

The realm of *Kannakara*, 20 *farsakh*, *Apsur*, *Banavas*, on the seacoast.

Marching from Kanoj towards the south-west, you come to *Asi*, 18 *farsakh* from Kanoj; *Sahanya*, 17 *farsakh*; *Jandra*, 18 *farsakh*; *Rajauri*, 15 *farsakh*; *Bazana*, the capital of Guzarat, 20 *farsakh*. This town is called *Narayan* by our people. After it had fallen into decay the inhabitants migrated to another place called Jadura (?)

From Kanoj to Bazana

The distance between Mahura and Kanoj is the same as that between Kanoj and Bazana, viz. 28 *farsakh*. If a man travels from Mahura to Ujain, he passes through villages which are only five *farsakh* and less distant from each other. At the end of a march of 35 *farsakh*, he comes to a large village called *Dudahi*; thence to *Bamahur*, 17 *farsakh* from Dudahi; *Bhailsan*, 5 *farsakh*, a place most famous among the Hindus. The name of the town is identical with that of the idol worshipped there. Thence to *Ardin*, 9 *farsakh*. The idol worshipped there is called *Mahakala*. *Dhar*, 7 *farsakh*.

From Mahura to Dhar

Marching from Bazana southward, you come to *Maiwar*, 25 *farsakh* from Bazana. This is a kingdom the capital of which is *Jattaraur*. From this town to Malava and its capital, *Dhar*, the distance is 20 *farsakh*. The city of Ujain lies 7 *farsakh* to the east of Dhar.

From Bazana to Mandagir

From Ujain to Bhailasan, which likewise belongs to Malava, the distance is 10 *farsakh*.

Marching from Dhar southward, you come to *Bhumihara*, 20 *farsakh* from Dhar; *Kand*, 20 *farsakh*; *Namavur*, on the banks of the Narmada (Nerbudda), 10 *farsakh*; *Alispur*, 20 *farsakh*; *Mandagir*, on the banks of the river Godavar, 60 *farsakh*.

Again marching from Dhar southward, you come to the valley of *Namiyya*, 7 *farsakh* from Dhar; *Mahratta-Desh*, 18 *farsakh*; the province of *Kunkan*,

From Dhar to Tana

and its capital, Tana, on the sea-coast, 25 *farsakh*. . . .

The *ganda* exists in large numbers in India, more particularly about the Ganges. It is of the build of a buffalo, has a black scaly skin, and dewlaps hanging down under the chin. It has three yellow hoofs on each foot, the biggest one forward, the others on both sides. The tail is not long; the eyes lie low, farther down the cheek than is the case with all other animals. On the top of the nose there is a single horn which is bent upwards. The Brahmins have the privilege of eating the flesh of the *ganda.* I have myself witnessed how an elephant coming across a young *ganda* was attacked by it. The *ganda* wounded with its horn a forefoot of the elephant, and threw it down on its face.

Notes about various animals of India

I thought that the *ganda* was the rhinoceros (or *karkadann*), but a man who had visited Sufala, in the country of the Negroes, told me that the *kark,* which the Negroes call *impila,* the horn of which furnishes the material for the handles of our knives, comes nearer this description than the rhinoceros.

There are crocodiles in the rivers of India as in the Nile, a fact which led simple Aljahiz, in his ignorance of the courses of the rivers and the configuration of the ocean, to think that the river of Muhran (the river Sindh) was a branch of the Nile. Besides, there are other marvellous animals in the rivers of India of the crocodile tribe, *makara,* curious kinds of fishes, and an animal like a leather-bag, which appears to the ships and plays in swimming. It is called *burlu* (porpoise ?). I suppose it to be the dolphin or a kind of dolphin. People say that it has a hole on the head for taking breath like the dolphin. . . .

After this digression we return to our subject.

From Bazana to Somanath

Marching from Bazana towards the south-west, you come to *Anhilvara,* 60 *farsakh* from Bazana; *Somanath,* on the sea-coast, 50 *farsakh.*

Marching from Anhilvara southward, you come to *Lardesh,* to the two capitals of the country, *Bihroj* and *Rihanjur,* 42 *farsakh* from Anhilvara. Both are on the sea-coast to the east of Tana.

From Anhilvara to Loharani

Marching from Bazana towards the west, you come to *Multan,* 50 *farsakh* from Bazana; *Bhati,* 15 *farsakh.*

Marching from Bhati towards the south-west, you come to *Aror,*

15 *farsakh* from Bhati, a township between two arms of the Sindh river; *Bamhanwa Almansura,* 20 *farsakh; Loharani,* at the mouth of the Sindh river, 30 *farsakh.*

From Kanoj to Kashmir

Marching from Kanoj towards the north-north-west, you come to *Shirsharaha,* 50 *farsakh* from Kanoj; *Pinjaur,* 18 *farsakh,* situated on the mountains, whilst opposite it in the plain there lies the city of Taneshar; *Dahmala,* the capital of Jalandhar, at the foot of the mountains, 18 *farsakh; Ballawar,* 10 *farsakh;* thence marching westward, you come to *Ladda,* 13 *farsakh;* the fortress *Rajagiri,* 8 *farsakh;* thence marching northward, you come to *Kashmir,* 25 *farsakh.*

From Kanoj to Ghazna

Marching from Kanoj towards the west, you come to *Diyamau,* 10 *farsakh* from Kanoj; *Kuti,* 10 *farsakh; Anar,* 10 *farsakh; Mirat,* 10 *farsakh; Panipat,* 10 *farsakh.* Between the latter two places flows the river *Jaun; Kawital,* 10 *farsakh; Sunnam,* 10 *farsakh.*

Thence marching towards the north-west, you come to *Adittahaur,* 9 *farsakh; Jajjanir,* 6 *farsakh; Mandahukur,* the capital of Lauhawur, east of the river Irawa, 8 *farsakh;* the river *Candraha,* 12 *farsakh;* the river *Jailam,* west of the river Biyatta, 8 *farsakh; Waihind,* the capital of Kandhar, west of the river Sindh, 20 *farsakh; Purshawar,* 14 *farsakh; Dunpur,* 15 *farsakh; Kabul,* 12 *farsakh; Ghazna,* 17 *farsakh.*

Notes about Kashmir

Kashmir lies on a plateau surrounded by high inaccessible mountains. The south and east of the country belongs to the Hindus, the west to various kings, the Bolar-Shah and the Shugnan-Shah and the more remote parts up to the frontiers of Badhakhshan, to the Wakhan-Shah. The north and part of the east of the country belong to the Turks of Khoten and Tibet. The distance from the peak of Bhoteshar to Kashmir through Tibet amounts to nearly 300 *farsakh.*

The inhabitants of Kashmir are pedestrians, they have no riding animals nor elephants. The noble among them ride in palankins called *katt,* carried on the shoulders of men. They are particularly anxious about the natural strength of their country, and therefore take always much care to keep a strong hold upon the entrances and roads leading into it. In consequence, it is very difficult to have any commerce with them. In former times they used to allow one or two foreigners to enter their country, particularly Jews, but at present they do not allow any Hındu whom they do not know personally to enter, much less other people.

. . . The city of Kashmir covers a space of four *farsakh* being built along both banks of the river Jailam, which are connected with each other by bridges and ferry-boats. The Jailam rises in the mountains Haramakot, where also the Ganges rises, cold, impenetrable regions where the snow never melts nor disappears. Behind them there is *Mahacin*, i.e. Great China. . . .

This is the frontier of India from the north.

In the western frontier mountains of India there live various tribes of the Afghans, and extend up to the neighbourhood of the Sindh Valley.

The western and southern frontiers of India

The southern frontier of India is formed by the ocean. The coast of India begins with Tiz, the capital of Makran, and extends thence in a south-eastern direction towards the region of Al-daibal, over a distance of 40 *farsakh*. Between the two places lies the Gulf of Turan. . . .

After the above-mentioned gulf follow the small Munha, the great Munha, then the Bawarij, i.e. the pirates of Kacch and Somanath. They are thus called because they commit their robberies on sea in ships called *bira*. The places on the coast are:—*Tawalleshar*, 50 *farsakh* from Daibal; *Loharani*, 12 *farsakh*; *Baga*, 12 *farsakh*; *Kacch*, where the *mukl*-tree grows, and *Baroi*, 6 *farsakh*; *Somanath*, 14 *farsakh*; *Kanbayat*, 30 *farsakh*; *Asawil*, 2 days; *Bihroj*, 30 *farsakh* (?); *Sandan*, 50 *farsakh*; *Subara*, 6 *farsakh*; *Tana*, 5 *farsakh*.

Thence the coast-line comes to the country *Laran*, in which lies tne city of *Jimur*, then to *Vallabha*, *Kanji*, *Darvad*. Next follows a great bay in which *Singaldib* lies, i.e. the island Sarandib (Ceylon). Round the bay lies the city of *Panjayavar (sic)*. When this city had fallen into ruins, the king, Jaur, built instead of it, on the coast towards the west, a new city which he called *Padnar*.

The next place on the coast is Ummalnara, then *Ramsher* (Rameshar?) opposite Sarandib; the distance of the sea between them is 12 *farsakh*. The distance from Panjayavar to Ramsher is 40 *farsakh*, that between Ramsher and *Setubandha* 2 *farsakh*. Setubandha means *bridge of the ocean*. It is the dike of Rama, the son of Dasaratha, which he built from the continent to the castle Lanka. At present it consists of isolated mountains between which the ocean flows. Sixteen *farsakh* from Setubandha towards the east is *Kihkind*. the mountains of the monkeys. Every day the king of monkeys comes out of the thicket together with his hosts, and settles down in particular seats prepared for them. The inhabitants of that region prepare for them cooked rice, and bring it to them on leaves. After having eaten it they return into the thicket, but in case they are neglected, this would be the ruin of the country, as they are not only numerous but also savage and aggressive. According to the popular belief, they are a race of men changed into monkeys on account of the help which they had afforded to Rama when making war against the demons; he is believed to have bequeathed those villages to them as a legacy. When a man happens to fall in with them, and he recites to them the poetry of Rama and pronounces the incantations of Rama, they will quietly listen to him; they will even lead on the right path him who has gone astray and give him meat and drink. At all events, thus the matter stands according to popular belief.

Islands in the Indian and Chinese Seas

The eastern islands in this ocean, which are nearer to China than to India, are the islands of the *Zabaj,* called by the Hindus *Suvarna-dvipa,* i.e. the gold islands. The western islands in this ocean are those of the Zanj (Negroes), and those in the middle are the islands *Ramm* and the Diva islands (Malediva, Laccadiva), to which belong also the Kumair islands. It is peculiar to the Diva islands that they rise slowly; first there appears a sandy tract above the surface of the ocean; it rises more and more and extends in all directions, till at last it becomes a firm soil, whilst at the same time another island falls into decay and melts away, finally is submerged and disappears in the ocean. As soon as the inhabitants become aware of this process, they search for a new island of increasing fertility, transport there their cocoanut palms, date palms, cereals, and household goods, and emigrate to it. These islands are, according to their products, divided into two classes, the *Diva-kudha,* i.e. the Diva of the kauri-shells, because there they gather kauri-shells from the branches of the cocoanut palms which they plant in the sea, and *Divakanbar,* i.e. the Diva of the cords twisted from cocoanut fibres, and used for fastening together the planks of the ships.

. . . In former times there were pearl-banks in the bay of Sarandib (Ceylon), but at present they have been abandoned. Since the Sarandib pearls have disappeared, other pearls have been found at Sufala in the country of the Zanj, so that people say the pearls of

Sarandib have migrated to Sufala.

On the rainfall in India

India has the tropical rains in summer, which is called *varshakala,* and these rains are the more copious and last the longer the more northward the situation of a province of India is, and the less it is intersected by ranges of mountains. The people of Multan used to tell me that they have no *varshakala,* but the more northern provinces nearer the mountains have the *varshakala.* In Bhatal and Indravedi it begins with the month of Ashadha, and it rains continually for four months as though water-buckets were poured out. In provinces still farther northward, round the mountains of Kashmir up to the peak of *Judari* between Dunpur and Barshawar, copious rain falls during two and a half months, beginning with the month Sravana. However, on the other side of this peak there is no rainfall; for the clouds in the north are very heavy, and do not rise much above the surface. When, then, they reach the mountains, the mountain-sides strike against them, and the clouds are pressed like olives or grapes, in consequence of which the rain pours down, and the clouds never pass beyond the mountains. Therefore, Kashmir has no *varshakala,* but continual snowfall during two and a half months, beginning with Magha, and shortly after the middle of Caitra continual rain sets in for a few days, melting the snow and cleansing the earth. This rule seldom has an exception; however, certain amount of extraordinary meteorological occurrences is peculiar to every province of India.

CHAPTER XIX

On The Names Of The Planets, The Signs Of The Zodiac, The Lunar Stations, And Related Subjects

We have already mentioned, near the beginning of the book that the language of the Hindus is extremely rich in nouns, both original and derivative, so that in some instances they call *one* thing by a multitude of different names. So I have heard them saying that they have a thousand names all meaning *sun*; and no doubt, each planet has quite as many, or nearly as many names, since they could not do with less (for the purposes of versification).

The names of the days of the week

The names of the week-days are the best known names of the planets connected with the word *bara,* which follows after the planet's name, as in Persian the word *shambih* follows after the number of the week-day (*dushambih, sihshambih,* & c.).

So tney say:

Aditya bara, i.e. Sunday.
Soma bara i.e. Monday.
Mangala bara, i.e. Tuesday.
Budha bara, i.e. Wednesday.
Brihaspati bara, i.e. Thursday.
Sukra bara, i.e. Friday.
Sanaiscara bara, i.e. Saturday.

And thus they go on counting, beginning anew with Sunday,

Monday, & c. . . .

It is a custom of the Hindus to enumerate the planets in the order of the week-days. They will persist in using it in their astronomical handbooks, as well as in other books, and they decline to use any other order, though it be much more correct.

Order of the planets and their notation

The Greeks mark the planets with figures, to fix thereby their limits on the *astrolabe* in an easily intelligible manner, images which are not letters of the alphabet. The Hindus use a similar system of abridgement; however, *their* figures are not images invented for the purpose, but the initial characters of the names of the planets, e.g. a = *Aditya,* or the sun; *c* = *Candra,* or the moon; *b* = *Budha,* or Mercury.

The following table exhibits the commonest names of the seven planets:—

The Planets	*Their Names in the Indian Language.*
Sun	Aditya, surya, bhanu, arka, divakara, ravi, bibata (?), heli.
Moon	Soma, candra, indu, himagu, sitarasmi, himarasmi, sitamsu, sitadidhiti, himamayukha.
Mars	Mangala, bhaumya, kuja, ara, vakra, avaneya, maheya, krurakshi (?), rakta.
Mercury	Budha, saumya, candra, jna, bodhana, vitta (?), hemna.
Jupiter	Vrihaspati, guru, jiva, devejya, devapurohita, devamantrin, angiras, suri, devapita.
Venus	Sukra, bhrigu, sita, bhargava, asbati (?), danavaguru, bhriguputra, asphujit (?).
Saturn	Sanaiscara, manda, asita, kona, adityaputra, saura, arki, suryaputra.

On the twelve suns

The multiplicity of names of the sun as exhibited in the previous table was the cause which led the theologians to assume also a multiplicity of *suns,* so that according to them there are twelve suns, each of which rises in a particular month. . . .

The moon too, the companion of the sun, has many names, e.g. *Soma,* because she is *lucky,* and everything lucky is called *somagraha,*

Names of the moon

whilst all that is unlucky is called *papagraha.* Further, *Nisesa,* i.e. lord of the night, *Nakshatranatha,* i.e. lord of the lunar stations, *Dvijesvara,* i.e. lord of the Brahmins, *Sitamsu,* i.e. having a cold ray, because the moon's globe is *watery,* which is a blessing to the earth. When the solar ray meets the moon, the ray becomes as cool as the moon herself, then, being reflected, it illuminates the darkness, makes the night cool and extinguishes any hurtful kind of combustion wrought by the sun. Similarly, the moon is also called *Candra,* which means the *left eye of Narayana,* as the sun is his right eye. . . .

If the names of the month given in the following table differ in some respects from those used heretofore, the reader must know that the names which we have hitherto used are the vernacular or vulgar ones, whilst those given in this table are the classical :—

The Months	*The Lunar Stations*	*The Months*	*The Lunar Stations*
Karttika	3 Krittika*	Vaisakha	16 Visakha*
	4 Rohini		17 Anuradha
Margasirsha	5 Mrigasirsha*	Jyaiṣhtha	18 Jyeshtha*
	6 Ardra		19 Mula
Pausha	7 Punarvasu	Ashadha	20 Purvashadha*
	8 Pushya*		21 Uttarashadha
Magha	9 Aslesha	Sravana	22 Sravana*
	10 Magha*		23 Dhanishta
Phalguna	11 Purva-phalguni*	Bhadrapada	24 Satabhishaj
	12 Uttara-phalguni		25 Purva-bhadra-pada*
	13 Hasta		
Caitr	14 Citra*		26 Uttara-bhadra-pada*
	15 Svati		
		Asvayuja	27 Revati
			1 Asvini*
			2 Bharani

On the names of signs of the Zodiac

The signs of the zodiac have names corresponding to the images which they represent, and which are the same among the Hindus as among all other nations. The third sign is called *Mithuna,* which means a pair consisting of a boy and a girl; in fact, the same as *the Twins,* the well-known image of this sign.

[Varahamihira is quoted in regard to these signs. It is pointed out that besides the common names Varahamihira also mentions 'certain Indian names of the signs which are not generally known'. A consolidated table showing both these sets of names is given. Pp. 219–20.]

CHAPTER XX

On The Brahmanda

Brahmanda means *the egg of Brahman,* and applies in reality to the whole of heaven (*aither*), on account of its being round, and of the particular kind of its motion. It applies even to the whole world, insofar as it is divided into an upper and an under part. When they enumerate the heavens, they call the sum of them Brahmanda. The Hindus, however, are devoid of training in astronomy, and have no correct astronomical notions. In consequence, they believe that the earth is at rest, more particularly as they, when describing the bliss of paradise as something like worldly happiness, make the earth the dwelling-place of the different classes of gods, angels, &c., to whom they attribute locomotion from the upper worlds to the lower.

The egg of Brahman, its coming forth from the water

According to the enigmatic expressions of their tradition, the water was before every other thing, and it filled the space of the whole world. This was, as I understand them, at the beginning of the day of the soul (*purushahoratra,* p. 153), and the beginning of formation and combination. Further, they say the water was rolling and foaming. Then something white came forth from the water, of which the Creator created the egg of Brahman. Now, according to some, the egg broke; Brahman came forth from it, the one half became the heaven, the other the earth, and the broken bits between the two halves became the rains. If they said *mountains* instead of *rains,* the matter would be somewhat more plausible. According to others, God spoke to Brahman: "I create an egg, which I make for thy dwelling in it." He had created it of the above mentioned foam of the water, but when the water sank and was absorbed, the egg broke into two halves. . . .

Water the first element of creation. The egg of Brahman broken in two halves

The theory of the Hindus, that the water existed before all creation, rests on this, that it is the cause of the cohesion of the atoms of everything, the cause of the growing of everything, and of the duration of life in every animated being. Thus the water is an instrument in the hand of the Creator when he wants to create something out of matter. . . .

The theory of the division of the egg into two halves proves that its originator was the contrary of a scientific man, one who did not know that the heaven comprehends the earth, as the shell of the egg of Brahman comprehends its yolk. He imagined the earth to be below and the heaven in only one of the six directions from the earth, i.e. above it. If he had known the truth, he might have spared himself the theory of the breaking of the egg. However, he wished by his theory to describe one half of the egg as spread out for the earth, and the other half as placed upon it for cupola, trying to outvie Ptolemy in the planispheric representation of a globe, but without success.

[The views of several Indian writers—Brahmagupta, Pulisa, Balabhadra and Aryabhatta—are quoted, and criticised. Pp. 223–27.]

CHAPTER XXI

Descriptions Of Earth And Heaven According To The Religious Views Of The Hindus, Based Upon Their Traditional Literature

On the seven earths

The people of whom we have spoken in the preceding chapter, think that the earths are seven like seven covers one above the other, and the upper one they divide into seven parts, differing from our astronomers, who divide it into *klimatia,* and from the Persians, who divide it into *Kishvar.* We shall afterwards give a clear explanation of their theories derived from the first authorities of their religious law, to expose the matter to fair criticism. If something in it appears strange to us, so as to require a commentary, or if we perceive some coincidence with others, even if both parties missed the mark, we shall simply put the case before the reader, not with the intention of attacking or reviling the Hindus, but solely in order to sharpen the minds of those who study these theories.

Differences in the sequence of the earths explained as resulting from the copiousness of the language

They do not differ among themselves as to the number of earths nor as to the number of the parts of the upper earth, but they differ regarding their names and the order of these names. I am inclined to derive this difference from the great verbosity of their language, for they call one and the same thing by a multitude of names. For instance, they call the sun by a thousand different names according to their own statement, just as the Arabs call the lion by nearly as many. Some of these names are original, while others are derived from the changing conditions of his life or his actions and faculties. The Hindus and their like boast of this copiousness, whilst in reality it is one of the greatest faults of the language. For it is the task of language to give a name to everything in creation and to its effects, a name based on general consent, so that everybody, when hearing this name pronounced by another man, understands what he means. If therefore one and the same name or word means a variety of things, it betrays a defect of the language and compels the hearer to ask the speaker what he means by the word. And thus the word in question must be dropped in order to be replaced either by a similar one of a sufficiently clear meaning, or by an epithet describing what is really meant. If one and the same thing is called by many names, and this is not occasioned by the fact that every tribe or class of people uses a separate one of them, and if, in fact, one single name would be sufficient, all the other names save this one are to be classified as mere nonsense, as a means of keeping people in the dark, and throwing an air of mystery about the subject. And in any case this copiousness offers painful difficulties to those who want to learn the whole of the language, for it is entirely useless, and only results in a sheer waste of time.

Frequently it has crossed my mind that the authors of books and the transmitters of tradition have an aversion to mentioning the earths in a definite arrangement, and limit themselves to mentioning their names, or that the copyists of the books have arbitrarily altered the text. For those men who explained and translated the text to me were well versed in the language, and were not known as persons who would commit a wanton fraud.

The earths according to the *Aditya-Purana*

The following table exhibits the names of the earths, as far as I know them. We rely chiefly on that list, which has been taken from the *Aditya-Purana,* because it follows a certain rule, combining every single earth and heaven with a single member of the members of the sun. The heavens are combined with the members from the skull to the womb, the earths with the members from the navel to the foot. This mode of comparison illustrates their sequence and preserves it from confusion:—

The number of the Earths	*Aditya-Purana*		*Vishnu-Purana*	*Vayu-Purana*		Vernacular names
	What members of the Sun they represent	Their names		Their names	Their Epithets	
I.	The navel.	Tala.	Atala.	Abhastala.	Krishna-bhumi, the dark earth.	Amsu (?)
II.	The thighs.	Sutala.	Vitala.	Ila (?)	Sukla-bhumi, the bright earth.	Ambaratala.
III.	The knees.	Patala.	Nitala.	Nitala.	Rakta-bhumi, the red earth.	Sarkara (?) (Sakkaru)
IV.	Under the knees.	Asala (?)	Gabhasti-mat.	Gabhastala	Pita-bhumi, the yellow earth.	Gabhastimat.
V.	The calves.	Visala (?)	Mahakhya (?)	Mahatala.	Pashana-bhumi, the earth of marble.	Mahatala.
VI.	The ankles.	Mrittala.	Sutala.	Sutala.	Silatala, the earth of brick	Sutala.
VII.	The feet	Rasatala.	Jagara (?)	Patala.	Suvarna-varna, the gold-coloured earth.	Rasatala.

. . . After the earths follow the heavens, consisting of seven stories, one above the other. They are called *loka,* which means "*gathering-place*".

. . . The names of the *lokas* do not differ like those of the earths. There is a difference of opinion only regarding their order. We exhibit the names of the *lokas* in a table similar to the former (p. 211).

The number of the Heavens	What members of the Sun they represent according to the *Aditya-Purana*	Their names according to the *Aditya, Vayu* and *Vishnu Puranas*
I.	The stomach.	Bhurloka.
II.	The breast.	Bhuvarloka.
III.	The mouth.	Svarloka.
IV.	The eyebrow.	Maharloka.
V.	The forehead.	Janaloka.
VI.	Above the forehead.	Tapoloka.
VII.	The skull.	Satyaloka.

. . . So much about the seven earths and the seven heavens. We shall now speak of the division of the surface of the uppermost earth and of related subjects.

Dip (dvipa) is the Indian word for *island.* Hence the words *Sangaladip* (Simhaladvipa), which we call Serendib, and the *Dibajat* (Maledives, Laccadives). The latter are numerous islands, which become, so to speak, decrepit, are dissolved and flattened, and finally disappear below the water, whilst at the same time other formations of the same kind begin to appear above the water like a streak of sand which continually grows and rises and extends. The inhabitants of the former island leave their homes, settle on the new one and colonise it.

The system of Dvipas and seas

According to the religious traditions of the Hindus, the earth on which we live is round and surrounded by a sea. On the sea lies an earth like a collar, and on this earth lies again a round sea like a collar. The number of dry collars, called *islands,* is seven, and likewise that of the seas. The size of both *dvipas* and seas rises in such a progression that each *dvipa* is the double of the preceding *dvipa,* each sea the double of the preceding sea, i.e. in the progression of the powers of two. If the middle earth is reckoned as one, the size of all seven earths represented as collars is 127. If the sea surrounding the middle earth is counted as one, the size of all seven seas represented as collars is 127. The total size of both earths and seas is 254.

[The commentator of Patanjali and the *Vayu-Purana* are quoted regarding the size of the dvipas and the seas. Also the former on the determining of 'the dimension of the world'. Pp. 234–38.]

CHAPTER XXII

Traditions Relating To The Pole

The origin of the South Pole. and the story of Somadatta

The pole, in the language of the Hindus, is called *dhruva,* and the axis *salaka.* The Hindus, with the exception of their astronomers, speak always only of *one* pole, the reason of which is their belief in *the dome of heaven,* as we have heretofore explained. According to *Vayu-Purana,* heaven revolves round the pole like a potter's wheel, and the pole revolves round itself, without changing its own place. This revolution is finished in 30 *muhurta,* i.e. in one *nychthemeron.*

[Regarding the South Pole, Al-Biruni refers to a tradition about a king, Somadatta, who by his noble deeds had come to earn the Paradise, but who wanted to enter it with his body. He approached Rishi Vashishtha for this favour but was told that it was impossible. Further, he was scoffed by Vashishtha's children. Then he went to Rishi Visvamitra who was pleased by him and began making a 'new Paradise' for the king. The Rishi 'began to make the pole and the Great Bear in the south', but Indra requested him not to do so. Visvamitra agreed on condition that Somadatta was to be admitted into Paradise *with his body,* and it was done. The Rishi thereupon desisted from making 'a second world, but that which he had already made up to that moment remained.' Pp. 239–40.]

It is well known that the North Pole with us is called the Great Bear; the South Pole Canopus. But some of our people (Muslims) who do not rise above the uneducated mass, maintain that in the south of heaven too there is a Great Bear of the same shape as the northern, which revolves round the southern pole.

Such a thing would not be impossible nor even strange, if the report about it came from a trustworthy man, who had made long sea-voyages. Certainly in southern regions stars are seen which we do not know in our latitudes. . .

When Brahman wanted to create mankind, he divided himself into two halves, of which the right one was called *Viraj,* the left one *Manu.* The latter one is the being from whom the period of time called *Manvantara* has received its name. Manu had two sons, Priyavrata and Uttanapada, the bow-legged king. The latter had a son called *Dhruva,* who was slighted by one of the wives of his father. On account of this, he was presented with the power to turn round all the stars as he pleased. He appeared in the Manvantara of Svayambhuva, the first of all Manvantaras, and he has for ever remained in his place, . . .

The story of Dhruva

CHAPTER XXIII

On Mount Meru According To The Belief Of The Authors Of The Puranas And Of Others

We begin with the description of this mountain, since it is the centre of the *dvipas* and seas, and, at the same time, the centre of Jambu-Dvipa. Brahmagupta says: "Manifold are the opinions of people relating to the description of the earth and to Mount Meru, particularly among those who study the Puranas and the religious literature. Some describe this mountain as rising above the surface of the earth to an excessive height. It is situated under the pole, and the stars revolve round its foot, so that rising and setting depends upon Meru. It is called Meru because of its having the faculty of doing this, and because it depends alone upon the influence of its head that sun and moon become visible. The day of the angels who inhabit Meru lasts six months, and their night also six months."

Brahmagupta on the earth and Mount Meru

[The views of Balabhadra on this topic are criticised. Also, those of Aryabhatta as quoted by the former. Pp. 243–46. In regard to the latter Al-Biruni points out that there were two persons named Aryabhatta; one known as 'Aryabhatta the elder' and the other as 'Aryabhatta of Kusumpura'. Al-Biruni writes, 'In the book of

Aryabhatta of Kusumpura we read that the mountain Meru is in Himavant, the cold zone, not higher than a *yojana.* In the translation however, it has been rendered so as to express that it is not higher than Himavant by more than a *yojana.*

This author is not identical with the elder Aryabhatta, but he belongs to his followers, for he quotes him and follows his example. I do not know which of these two names is meant by Balabhadra.' See also Pp. 172.]

In general, what we know of the conditions of the place of this mountain we know only by ratiocination. About the mountain itself they have many traditions. Some give it the height of one *yojana,* others more; some consider it as quadrangular, others as an octagon. We shall now lay before the reader what the Rishis teach regarding this mountain. . . .

[Extracts from some of the Puranas and the views of the commentator of Patanjali are given. Pp. 247–49.]

This is all I could find of Hindu traditions regarding Meru; and as I have never found a Buddhistic book, and never knew a Buddhist from whom I might have learned their theories on this subject, all I relate of them I can only relate on the authority of Aleranshahri, though, according to my mind, his report has no claim to scientific exactness, nor is it the report of a man who has a scientific knowledge of the subject. According to him, the Buddhists believe that Meru lies between four worlds in the four cardinal directions; that it is square at the bottom and round at the top; that it has the length of 80,000 *yojana,* one half of which rises into heaven, whilst the other half goes down in the earth. That side which is next to our world consists of blue sapphires, which is the reason why heaven appears to us blue; the other sides are of rubies, yellow and white gems. Thus Meru is the centre of the earth. . . .

Buddhistic views

CHAPTER XXIV

Traditions Of The Puranas Regarding Each Of The Seven Dvipas

We must ask the reader not to take any offence if he finds all the words and meanings which occur in the present chapter to be totally different from anything corresponding in Arabic. As for the difference of words, it is easily accounted for by the difference of languages in general; and as regards the difference of the meanings, we mention them only either in order to draw attention to an idea which might seem acceptable even to a Muslim, or to point out the irrational nature of a thing which has no foundation in itself.

Description of the Dvipas according to the *Matsya* and *Vishnu Puranas*

We have already spoken of the central Dvipa when describing the environs of the mountain in its centre. It is called Jambu-Dvipa, from a tree growing in it, the branches of which extend over a space of 100 *yojana.* In a latter chapter, devoted to the description of the inhabitable world and its division, we shall finish the description of Jambu-Dvipa. Next, however. we shall describe the other *dvipas* which surround it, following, as regards the order of the names, the authority of *Matsya-Purana*. . . .

1. Jambu-Dvipa

[There follow brief descriptions of the six *dvipas*, based mainly on the *Matsya* and the *Vishnu-Puranas*. The account contains some mythological stories and some incredible particulars, such as the inhabitants of some of the *dvipas* living up to the ages of 3000 or 11,000 years. In the extracts reproduced below such portions have been omitted. Only the geographical particulars as also those relating to the social organisation of the inhabitants of the various *dvipas* have been included. Pp. 252–56.]

2. Saka-Dvipa

. . . We shall now describe Saka-Dvipa. It has . . . seven great rivers,one of which equals the Ganges in purity. [In it] there are seven mountains adorned with jewels, some of which are inhabited by Devas, others by demons. One of them is a golden lofty mountain, whence the clouds rise which bring us the rain. Another contains all the medicines. . . .

. . . The inhabitants of the Saka-Dvipa are pious, long-lived beings, who can dispense with the rule of the kings, since they do not know envy nor ambition . . . The four colours are among them, i.e. the different castes, which do not intermarry nor mix with each other . . . the names of their castes are Aryaka, Kurura, Vivimas (Vivamsa), and Bhavin (?), and they worship Vasudeva.

3. Kusa-Dvipa

The third *dvipa* is Kusa-Dvipa. [It] has seven mountains containing jewels, fruits, flowers, odoriferous plants and cereals . . . [It] has seven kingdoms and innumerable rivers flowing to the sea, which are then changed by Indira into rain. To the greatest rivers belong *Jaunu* (Yamuna), which purifies all sins . . . the inhabitants are pious, sinless people . . . They worship *Janardana,* and the names of their castes are Damin, Sushmin, Sneha, and Mandeha.

4. Kraunca-Dvipa

The fourth, or Kraunca-Dvipa has . . . mountains containing jewels, rivers which are branches of the Ganges, and kingdoms the people of which have a white colour and are pious and pure. According to the *Vishnu-Purana* the people there live in one and the same place without any distinction among members of the community but afterwards it says that the names of their castes are Pushkara. Pushkala. Dhanva. and Tishya (?). They worship *Janardana.*

The fifth, or Salmala-Dvipa, has mountains and rivers. Its inhabitants are pure, long-lived, mild, and never angry. They never suffer from drought or dearth, for their food comes to them simply in answer to their wishes, without their sowing or toiling. They do not require the rule of kings, since they do not know the desire for property. The climate of this Dvipa

5. Salmala-Dvipa

never alters in cold or heat, so they are not bound to protect themselves against either. They have no rain, but the water bubbles up for them out of the earth and drops down from the mountains. This is also the case with the following *dvipas*. . . .

They have beautiful faces and worship *Bhagavat.* They bring offerings to the fire. . . The names of their castes are Kapila, Aruna, Pita, and Krishna.

The sixth, or Gomeda-Dvipa, has two great mountains, the deep-black *Sumanas,* which encompasses the greatest part of the Dvipa, and the *Kumuda,* of golden colour and

6. Gomeda-Dvipa

very lofty; the latter one contains all the medicines. This Dvipa has two kingdoms.

According to the *Vishnu-Purana* the inhabitants are pious and without sin and worship Vishnu. The names of their castes are Mriga, Magadha, Manasa and Mandaga. The climate of this *dvipa* is so healthy and pleasant that the inhabitants of paradise now and then visit it on account of the fragrancy of its air.

The seventh, or Pushkara-Dvipa, has according to *Matsya-Purana* in its eastern part the mountain *Citrasala,* i.e. having a variegated roof with horns of jewels. Its height is

7. Pushkara-Dvipa

34,000 *yojana,* and its circumference 25,000 *yojana.* In the west lies the mountain Manasa, shining like the full moon; its height is 35,000 *yojana.* In the east of this *dvipa* are two kingdoms. . . . The water bubbles up for them out of the earth, and drops down from the mountains. They have no rains and no flowing river; they know neither summer nor winter. They are of one kind, without any distinction of caste. They never suffer from dearth, and do not get old . . . It is as if they were in a suburb of paradise... So there is no service, nor rule, no sin, no envy, no opposition, no debating, no toiling in agriculture and diligence in trading . . .

According to the *Vishnu-Purana* the inhabitants are equal among each other, not claiming any superiority. . . . In this *dvipa* there is only a single mountain, called *Manasottama,* which rises in a round form on the round *dvipa.* From its top all other *dvipas* are visible, for its height is 50,000 *yojanas,* and the breadth the same.

CHAPTER XXV

On The Rivers Of India, Their Sources And Courses

. . . The *Matsya-Purana* and *Vayu-Purana* mention the rivers flowing in Jambu-Dvipa, and say that they rise in the mountains of Himavant. In the following table we simply enumerate them without following any particular principle of arrangement. The reader must imagine that the mountains form the boundaries of India. The northern mountains are the snowy Himavant. In their centre lies Kashmir, and they are connected with the country of the Turks. This mountain region becomes colder and colder till the end of the inhabitable world and Mount Meru. Because this mountain has its chief extension in longitude, the rivers rising on its northside flow through the countries of the Turks, Tibetans, Khazars, and Slavonians, and fall into the sea of Jurjan (the Caspian Sea), or the sea of Khwarism (the Aral Sea), or the Sea Pontus (the Black Sea), or the northern sea of the Slavonians (the Baltic); whilst the rivers rising on the southern slopes flow through India and fall into the great ocean, some reaching it single, others combined.

The rivers of Europe and Asia rising in the Himalaya and its extensions to west and east

The rivers of India come either from the cold mountains in the north or from the eastern mountains, both of which in reality form one and the same chain, extending towards the east, and then turning towards the south until they reach the great ocean, where parts of it penetrate into the sea at the place called the *Dike of Rama.* Of course, these mountains differ very much in cold and heat.

Rivers of India

We exhibit the names of the rivers in the following table:

Sindh or the river of Vaihand	Biyatta or Jailam	Candrabhaga or Candaraha	Biyaha to the west of Lahore	Iravati to the east of Lahore	S'atarudra or Shataldar
Sarsat, flowing through the country Sarsat	Jaun	Ganga	Sarayu or Sarwa	Devika	Kuhu
Gomati	Dhutapapa	Visala	Bahudasa (!)	Kausiki	Niscira
Gandaki	Lohita	Drishadvati	Tamra Aruna	Parnasa	Vedasmriti
Vidasini	Candana	Kawana	Para	Carman-vati	Vidisa
Venumati	S'ipra, rises in the Pariyatra and passes Ujain	Karatoya	Shamahina		

. . . The river Biyatta known as Jailam, from the city of this name on its western banks, and the river Candaraha join each other nearly fifty miles above Jahravar, and pass along west of Multan.

Rivers of the Punjab

The river Biyaha flows east of Multan, and joins afterwards the Biyatta and Candaraha.

The river Irava is joined by the river Kaj, which rises in Nagarkot in the mountains of Bhatul. Thereupon follows as the fifth the river

Shatladar (Satlej).

After these five rivers have united below Multan at a place called *Pancanada,* i.e. the meeting place of the five rivers, they form an enormous watercourse. In flood-times it sometimes swells to such a degree as to cover nearly a space of ten *farsakh,* and to rise above the tree of the plains, so that afterwards the rubbish carried by the floods is found in their highest branches like birds-nests.

The Muslims call the river, after it has passed the Sindhi city Aror, as a united stream, *the river of Mihran.* Thus it extends, flowing straight on, becoming broader and broader, and gaining in purity of water, enclosing in its course places like islands, until it reaches Almansura, situated between several of its arms, and flows into the ocean at two places, near the city Loharani, and more eastward in the province of Kacch at a place called *Sindhu-sagara,* i.e. *the Sindh Sea.* . . .

The river Sarsati falls into the sea at the distance of a bowshot east of Somanath.

The river Jaun joins the Ganges below Kanoj, which lies west of it. The united stream falls into the great ocean near Gangasagara.

Various rivers of India

Between the mouths of the rivers Sarsati and Ganges is the mouth of the river Narmada, which descends from the eastern mountains, takes its course in a south-western direction, and falls into the sea near the town Bahroj, nearly sixty *yojana* east of Somanath.

Behind the Ganges flow the rivers Rahab and Kawini, which join the river Sarwa near the city of Bari. . . .

The river Ganges, which is the middle and main stream, flows through the Gandharva, the musicians, Kimnara, Yakshas, Rakshasa, Vidyadhara, Uraga, i.e. those who creep on their breasts, the serpents, Kalapagrama, i.e. the city of the most virtuous, Kimpurusha, Khasa (?), the mountaineers, Kirata, Pulinda, the hunters in the plains, robbers, Kuru, Bharata, Pancala, Kaushka (?), Matsya, Magadha, Brahmottara, and Tamalipta. These are the good and bad beings through whose territories the Ganges flows. Afterwards it enters into branches of the mountain Vindhya, where the elephants live, and then it falls into the southern ocean.

Of the eastern Ganges arms, the Hradini flows through the countries Nishaba, Upakana, Dhivara, Prishaka, Nilamukha, Kikara, Ushtrakarna, i.e. people whose lips are turned like their ears, Kirata, Kalidara, Vivarna, i.e. the colourless people, so called on account of their intense blackness, Kushikana, and Svargabhumi, i.e. a country like Paradise. Finally it falls into the eastern ocean. ...

CHAPTER XXVI

On The Shape Of Heaven And Earth According To The Hindu Astronomers

This and similar questions have received at the hands of the Hindus a treatment and solution totally different from that which they have received among us Muslims. The sentences of the Koran on these and other subjects necessary for man to know are not such as to require a strained interpretation in order to become positive certainties in the minds of the hearers, and the same may be said regarding the holy codes revealed before the Koran. The sentences of the Koran on the subjects necessary for man to know are in perfect harmony with the other religious codes, and at the same time they are perfectly clear, without any ambiguity. . . .

The Koran, a certain and clear basis of all research

The religious books of the Hindus and their codes of tradition, the Puranas, contain sentences about the shape of the world which stand in direct opposition to scientific truth as known to their astronomers. By these books people are guided in fulfilling the rites of their religion, and by means of them the great mass of the nation have been wheedled into a predilection for astronomical

Veneration of the Hindus for their astronomers

calculation and astrological predictions and warnings. The consequence is, that they show much affection to their astronomers declaring that they are excellent men, that it is a good omen to meet them, and firmly believing that all of them come into Paradise and none into hell. For this the astronomers requite them by accepting their popular notions as truth, by conforming themselves to them, however far from truth most of them may be, and by presenting them with such spiritual stuff as they stand in need of. This is the reason why the two theories, the vulgar and the scientific, have become intermingled in the course of time, why the doctrines of the astronomers have been disturbed and confused, in particular the doctrines of those authors—and they are the majority—who simply copy their predecessors, who take the basis of their science from tradition and do not make them the objects of independent scientific research.

Astronomers admit popular notions into their doctrines

We shall now explain the views of Hindu astronomers regarding the present subject, viz. the shape of heaven and earth. According to them, heaven as well as the whole world is round, and the earth has a globular shape, the northern half being dry land, the southern half being covered with water. The dimension of the earth is larger according to them than it is according to the Greeks and modern observations, and in their calculations to find this dimension they have entirely given up any mention of the traditional seas and *Dvipas,* and of the enormous sums of *yojana* attributed to each of them. The astronomers follow the theologians in everything which does not encroach upon their science, e.g. they adopt the theory of Mount Meru being under the North Pole, and that of the island Vadavamukha lying under the South Pole. Now, it is entirely irrelevant whether Meru is there or not, as it is only required for the explanation of the particular mill-like rotation, which is necessitated by the fact that to each spot on the plane of the earth corresponds a spot in the sky as its zenith. Also, the fable of the southern island Vadavamukha does no harm to their science, although it is possible nay, even likely, that each pair of quarters of the earth forms a coherent, uninterrupted unity, the one as a continent, the other as an ocean (and that in reality there is no such island under the South Pole). Such a disposition of the earth is required by the law of gravitation, for according to them the earth is

General observations on the rotundity of the earth, on Meru and Vadavamukha in the centre of the universe, and everything heavy gravitates towards it. Evidently on account of this law of gravitation they consider heaven, too, as having a globular shape.

We shall now exhibit the opinions of the Hindu astronomers on this subject according to our translation of their works. In case, however, one word or other in our translation should be used in a meaning different from that which it generally has in our sciences, we ask the reader to consider only the original meaning of the word (not the technical one), for this only is meant.

[Extracts from Pulisa's *Siddhanta* and Brahmagupta's *Brahma-Siddhanta* are given. Aryabhatta, Vasishta and Lata are also referred to. Pp. 266–69.]

These are the words of Hindu astronomers regarding the globular shape of heaven and earth, and what is between them, and regarding the fact that the earth, situated in the centre of the globe, is only of a small size in comparison with the visible part of heaven. These thoughts are the elements of astronomy as contained in the first chapter of Ptolemy's *Almagest,* and of similar books, though they are not worked out in that scientific form in which we are accustomed to give them.

Considerations regarding the rotundity of the earth, the balance of gravity between the northern and southern halves, and the attraction of gravitation

(Lacuna,)

for the earth is more heavy than the water, and the water is fluid like the air. The globular form must be to the earth a physical necessity, as long as it does not, by the order of God, take another form. Therefore the earth could not move towards the north, nor the water move towards the south, and in consequence one whole half is not *terra firma,* nor the other half water, unless we suppose that the *terra firma* half be hollow. As far as our observations, based on induction, goes, the *terra firma* must be in one of the two northern quarters, and therefore we guess that the same is the case on the adjacent quarter. We admit the possibility of the existence of the island Vadava-mukha, but we do not maintain it, since all we know of it and of Meru is exclusively based on tradition.

The equatorial line does not, in the quarter of the earth known to us, represent a boundary between *terra firma* and the ocean. For in certain places the continent protrudes far into the ocean, so as to pass beyond the equator, e.g. the plains of the negroes in the west, which protrude far towards the south, even beyond the *mountains of the moon* and the sources of the Nile, in fact, into regions which we do not exactly know. For that continent is desert and impassable, and likewise the sea behind Sufala of the Zanj is unnavigable. No ship which ventured to go there has ever returned to relate what it had witnessed.

Also a great part of India above the province of Sindh deeply protrudes far towards the south, and seems even to pass beyond the equator.

In the midst between both lie Arabia and Yemen, but they do not go so far south as to cross the equator.

Further, as the *terra firma* stretches far out into the ocean, thus the ocean too penetrates into *terra firma,* breaking into it in various places, and forming bays and gulfs. For instance, the sea extends as a tongue along the west side of Arabia as far as the neighbourhood of Central Syria. It is narrowest near Kulzum, whence it is also called *the Sea of Kulzum.*

Another and still larger arm of the sea exists east of Arabia, the so-called *Persian Sea.* Between India and China, also, the sea forms a great curve towards the north.

Hence it is evident that the coast-line of these countries does not correspond to the equator, nor keep an invariable distance from it,

(Lacuna,)

and the explanation relating to the four cities will follow in its proper place.

The difference of the times which has been remarked is one of the results of the rotundity of the earth, and of its occupying the centre of the globe. And if they attribute to the earth, though it be round, inhabitants—for cities cannot be imagined without inhabitants—the existence of men on earth is accounted for by the attraction of everything heavy towards its centre, i.e. the middle of the world.

Much to the same effect are the expressions of *Vayu-Purana,* viz: that noon in Amaravati is sunrise in Vaivasvata, midnight in Sukha, and sunset in Vibha. . . .

In the definition of what is *low* the Hindus agree with us, viz. that it is *the centre of the world,* but their expressions on this head are subtle, more particularly as this is one of the great questions which is only handled by the most eminent of their scholars.

Brahmagupta and Varahamihira on the law of gravitation

So Brahmagupta says: "Scholars have declared that the globe of the earth is in the midst of heaven, and that Mount Meru, the home of the Devas, as well as Vadavamukha below, is the home of their opponents; the Daitya and Danava belong to it. But this *below* is according to them only a relative one. Disregarding this, we say that the earth on all its sides is the same; all people on earth stand upright, and all heavy things fall down to the earth by a law of nature, for it is the nature of the earth to attract and to keep things, as it is the nature of water to flow, that of fire to burn, and that of the wind to set in motion. If a thing wants to go deeper down than the earth, let it try. The earth is the only *low* thing, and seeds always return to it, in whatever direction you may throw them away, and never rise upwards from the earth."

Varahamihira says: "Mountains, seas, rivers, trees, cities, men, and angels, all are around the globe of the earth. And if Yamakoti and Rum are opposite to each other, one could not say that the one is *low* in its relation to the other, since the *low* does not exist. How could one say of one place of the earth that it is low, as it is in every particular identical with any other place on earth, and one place could as little *fall* as any other. . . . For the earth attracts that which is upon her, for it is the *below* towards all directions, and heaven is the *above* towards all directions."

[Balabhadra's definition of the extent which may be reached by the human eye is critically examined; also Pulisa's views on the axis of the earth. Pp. 274–77.]

CHAPTER XXVII

On The First Two Motions Of The Universe (That From East To West According To Ancient Astronomers And The Precession Of The Equinoxes), Both According To Hindu Astronomers And The Authors Of The Puranas

The astronomers of the Hindus hold on this subject mostly the same views as ourselves. We shall give quotations from them, but shall at once confess that that which we are able to give is very scanty indeed.

[Extracts are given from the works of Pulisa, Brahmagupta and Balabhadra. Pp. 278–80.]

This is all I have read in Indian books on the subjects.

Their speaking of the wind as the *motor (supra)* has, I think, only the purpose of bringing the subject near to the understanding of people and to facilitate its study; for people see with their own eyes that the wind, when blowing against instruments with wings and toys of this kind, puts them into motion. But as soon as they come to speak of the *first mover* (God), they at once give up any comparison with the natural

Criticisms of the author. The wind as the motor of the sphere wind, which in all its phases is determined by certain causes. For though it puts things into motion, the *moving* is not its essence; and besides, it cannot move without being in contact with something, because the wind is a body, and is acted upon by external influences or means, its motion being commensurate with their force.

Their saying that the wind does not rest, simply means that the moving power works perpetually, and does not imply rest and motion such as are proper to bodies. Further, their saying that it does *not slacken* means that it is free from all kinds of accidents; for *slackening and weakening* only occur in such bodies or beings which are composed of elements of conflicting qualities.

On the two poles *keeping* the sphere

The expression that the two poles *keep* the sphere of the fixed stars means that they keep or preserve it in its normal state of motion, not that they keep or preserve it from falling down.

[Al-Biruni critically examines the views of Balabhadra and Brahmagupta, as also those contained in the *Puranas,* on the following points: (a) the relative nature of time, (b) the fixed stars, (c) the direction of the heavenly motion, as seen from the different point of the earth. Pp. 281–88.]

CHAPTER XXVIII

On The Definition Of The Ten Directions

The extension of bodies in space is in three directions: *length*, *breadth*, and *depth* or *height*. The path of any real direction, not an imaginary one, is limited; therefore the lines representing these three paths are limited, and their six end-points or limits are the *directions*. If you imagine an animal in the centre of these lines, i.e. where they cut each other, which turns its face towards one of them, the directions with relation to the animal are *before*, *behind*, *right*, *left*, *above*, and *below*.

If these directions are used in relation to the world, they acquire new names. As the rising and setting of the heavenly bodies depend upon the horizon and the *first motion* becomes apparent by the horizon, it is the most covenient to determine the directions by the horizon. The four directions, *east*, *west*, *north*, *south* (corresponding to before, behind, left, and right), are generally known, but the directions which lie between each two of these are less known. These make eight directions, and, together with *above* and *below*, which do not need any further explanation, ten directions. . . .

The Hindus, in giving names to the directions, have not taken any notice of the blowing of a wind; they simply call the four cardinal directions, as well as the secondary directions between them, by separate names. So they have eight directions in the *horizontal* plane, as exhibited by the following diagram:

S.W.		South		S.E.
	Nairrita	Dakshina	Agneya	
West	Pascima	Madhyadesa (i.e. the middle country)	Purva	East
	Vayava	Uttara	Aisana	
N.W.		North		N.E.

Besides there are two directions more for the two poles of the horizontal plane, the *above* and *below,* the former being called *upari,* the second *Adhas* and *Tala*. . . .

The Hindus can never speak of anything, be it an object of the intellect or of imagination, without representing it as a personification, and individual. They at once marry him, make him celebrate marriage, make his wife become pregnant and give birth to something. So, too, in this case. The *Vishnu-Dharma* relates that *Atri,* the star who rules the stars of the Great Bear, married *the directions,* represented as *one* person, though they are eight in number, and that from her the moon was born. . . .

According to their custom, the Hindus attribute certain dominants to the eight directions in the horizontal plane, which we exhibit in the following table:

Their Dominants	The Directions	Their Dominants	The Directions
Indra	East	Varuna	West
The Fire	S.E.	Vayu	N.W.
Yama	South	Kuru	North
Prithu	S.W.	Mahadeva	N.E.

CHAPTER XXIX

Definition Of The Inhabitable Earth According To The Hindus

In the book of the Rishi Bhuvanakosa we read that the inhabitable world stretches from Himavant towards the south, and is called *Bhartavarsha,* so called from a man, Bharata, who ruled over them and provided for them. The inhabitants of this *oikoumene* are those to whom alone reward and punishment in another life are destined. It is divided into nine parts, called *Navakhanda-prathama,* i.e. the primary nine parts. Between each two parts there is a sea, which they traverse from one *khanda* to the other. The breadth of the inhabitable world from north to south is 1000 *yojana.*

The Rishi Bhuvanakosa on the inhabitable world

By Himavant the author means the northern mountains, where the world, in consequence of the cold, ceases to be inhabitable. So all civilisation must of necessity be south of these mountains.

His words, that the inhabitants are subject to *reward and punishment,* indicate that there are other people *not* subject to it. These beings he must either raise from the degree of man to that of angels, who, in consequence of the simplicity of the elements they are composed of and of the purity of their nature, never disobey a divine order, being always willing to worship; or he must degrade them to the degree of irrational animals. According to him, therefore, there are no human beings outside the *oikoumene* (i.e. *Bharatavarsha*).

Bharatavarsha is not India alone, as Hindus think, according to whom *their* country is the world, and their race the only race of mankind; for India is not traversed by an ocean separating one *khanda* from the other. Further, they do not identify these *khanda* with the *dvipas*, for the author says that on those seas people pass from one shore to the other. Further, it follows from his statement that all the inhabitants of the earth and the Hindus are subject to reward and punishment, that they are one great religious community.

The nine parts are called *Prathama*, i.e. *primary* ones, because they also divide India alone into nine parts. So the division of the *oikoumenė* is a *primary* one, but the division of Bharatavarsha a *secondary* one. Besides, there is still a third division into nine parts, as their astrologers divide each country into nine parts when they try to find the lucky and unlucky places in it. . . .

Further, the *Vayu-Purana* mentions the cities and countries which lie in each direction. We shall exhibit them in tables, together with similar information from other sources, for this method renders the study of the subject easier than any other.

Here follows a diagram representing the division of Bharatavarsha into nine parts.

	Nagadvipa	South Gabhastimat	Tamravarna	
West	Saumya	Indradvipa or Madhyadesa, i.e. the middle country	Kaserumat	East
	Gandharva	North	Nagarasamvritta	

On the figure Kurma-cakra

We have already heretofore mentioned that that part of the earth in which the *oikoumenē* lies resembles a tortoise, because its borders are round, because it rises above the water, and is surrounded by the water, and because it has a globular convexity on its surface. However, there is a possibility that the origin of the name is this, that their astronomers and astrologers divide the directions according to the lunar stations. Therefore the country, too, is divided according to the lunar stations, and the figure which represents this division is similar to a tortoise. Therefore it is called *Kurma-cakra,* i.e. the tortoise-circle or the tortoise-shape. . . .

The division of Bharatavarsha according to Varahamihira

Varahamihira calls each of the *Nava-khanda* a *varga.* He says: "By them (the *vargas*) Bharatavarsha, i.e. half of the world, is divided into nine parts, the central one, the eastern, etc." Then he passes to the south, and thus round the whole horizon. That he understands by Bharatavarsha India alone is indicated by his saying that each *varga* has a region, the king of which is killed when some mishap befalls it. So belong

To the 1st or central varga, the region Pancala.

"	2d varga,	......	"	Magadha.
"	3d varga,	......	"	Kalinga.
"	4th varga,	......	"	Avanti, i.e. Ujain.
"	5th varga,	......	"	Ananta.
"	6th varga,	......	"	Sindhu & Sauvira.
"	7th varga,	......	"	Harahaura.
"	8th varga,	......	"	Madura.
"	9th varga,	......	"	Kulinda.

All these countries are parts of India proper.

Most of the names of countries under which they appear in this context are not those by which they are now generally known

On the change of geographical names

Utpala, a native of Kashmir, says in his commentary on the book *Samhita* regarding this subject: "the names of countries change, and particularly in the *yugas.* So Multan was originally called Kasyapapura, then Hamsapura, then Bagapura, then Sambhapura, and then *Mulashthana,* i.e. *the original place,* for *mula* means root, origin, and *tana* means place."

A *yuga* is a long space of time, but names change rapidly, when, for instance, a foreign nation with a different language occupies a country. Their tongues frequently mangle the words, and thus transfer them into their own language, as is, e.g. the custom of the Greeks. Either they keep the original meaning of the names, and try a sort of translation, but then they undergo certain changes. So the city of Shash, which has its name from the Turkish language, where it is called Tash-kand, i.e. *stone-city*, is called *stone-tower* in the book *Geographia.* In this way new names spring up as translations of older ones. Or, secondly, the barbarians adopt and keep the local names, but with such sounds and in such forms as are adapted to their tongues, as the Arabs do in Arabising foreign names, which become disfigured in their mouth: e.g. *Bushaṅg* they call in their books *Fusani* and *Sakilkand* they call in their revenue-books *Farfaza (sic).* However, what is more curious and strange is this, that sometimes one and the same language changes in the mouth of the same people who speak it, in consequence of which strange and uncouth forms of words spring up, not intelligible save to him who discards every rule of the language. And such changes are brought about in few years, without there being any stringent cause or necessity for it. Of course, in all of this the Hindus are actuated by the desire to have as many names as possible, and to practise on them the rules and arts of their etymology, and they glory in the enormous copiousness of their language which they obtain by such means.

The following names of countries, which we have taken from the *Vayu-Purana,* are arranged according to the four directions, whilst the names taken from the *Samhita* are arranged according to the eight directions. All these names are of that kind which we have here described (i.e. they are not the names now in general use). ...

[The names of the 'countries' or regions are listed. Pp. 299–302.]

On Romaka, Yamakoti, and Siddhapura

Hindu astronomers determine the longitude of the inhabitable world by Lanka, which lies in its centre on the equator, whilst Yamakoti lies on its east, Romaka on its west, and Siddhapura on that part of the equator which is diametrically opposed to Lanka. Their remarks on the rising and setting of the heavenly bodies show that Yamakoti and Rum are distant from each other by half a circle. It seems that they assign the countries of the West (i.e. North Africa) to Rum or the Roman Empire, because the Rum or Byzantine Greeks occupy the opposite shores of the same sea (the Mediterranean); for the Roman Empire has much northern latitude and penetrates high into the north. No part of it stretches far southward, and, of course, nowhere does it reach the equator, as the Hindus say with regard to Romaka.

We shall here speak no more of Lanka (as we are going to treat of it in a separate chapter). Yamakoti is, according to Yakub[33] and Alfazari, the country where is the city *Tara* within a sea. I have not found the slightest trace of this name in Indian literature. As *koti* means *castle* and Yama is the angel of death, the word reminds me of Kangdiz, which, according to the Persians, had been built by Kaika'us or Jam in the most remote east, behind the sea. Kaikhusrau traversed the sea to Kangdiz when following the traces of Afrasiab the Turk, and there he went at the time of his anchorite life and expatriation. For *diz* means in Persian *castle,* as *koti* in the Indian language, Abu-Ma'shar of Balkh has based his geographical canon on Kangdiz as the 0° of longitude or first meridian.

How the Hindus came to suppose the existence of Siddhapura I do not know, for they believe, like ourselves, that behind the inhabited half-circle there is nothing but unnavigable seas.

The meridian of Ujain the first meridian

In what way the Hindus determine the latitude of a place has not come to our knowledge. That the longitude of the inhabitable world is a half-circle is a far-spread theory among their astronomers; they differ (from Western astronomers) only as to the point which is to be its beginning. If we explain the theory of the Hindus as far as we understand it, their beginning of longitude is Ujain, which they consider as the eastern limit of one quarter (of the *oikoumenē*), whilst the limit of the second quarter lies in the west at some distance from the end of civilisation, as we shall hereafter explain in the chapter about the difference of the longitudes of two places.

The theory of the Western astronomers on this point is a double one. Some adopt the beginning of longitude the shore of the (Atlantic) ocean. . . . Now, according to this theory, things have been united which have no connection with each other. So Shapurkan and Ujain are placed on the same meridian. . . . Others adopt the *Islands of Happy Ones* as the beginning of longitude. . . . Both these theories are totally different from that of the Hindus. . . .

If I, by the grace of God, shall live long enough, I shall devote a special treatise to the longitude of Nishapur where this subject shall be thoroughly inquired into.

note the number of *yojanas* of its distance from the meridian of Ujain. And the more to the west the position of a place is, the greater is the number of *yojanas;* the more to the east it is, the smaller is this number. They call it *desantara,* i.e. *the difference between the places.* Further, they multiply the *desantara* by the mean daily motion of *the planet* (the sun), and divide the product by 4800. Then the quotient represents that amount of the motion of the star which corresponds to the number of *yojana* in question, i.e. that which must be added to the mean place of the sun, as it has been found for moon or midnight of Ujain, if you want to find the longitude of the place in question.

The number which they use as divisor (4800) is the number of the *yojanas* of the circumference of the earth, for the difference between the spheres of the meridians of the two places stands in the same relation to the whole circumference of the earth as the mean motion of the planet (sun) from one place to the other to its whole daily rotation round the earth. . . .

On the circumference of the earth

[The observations of Pulisa and Brahmagupta on the circumference of the earth are critically examined; also the method of calculating the *desantara.* Aryabhatta's views on the meridian of Ujain are criticised. Pp. 312–16.]

Y'akub Ibn Tarik says in his book entitled *The Composition of the Spheres,* that the latitude of Ujain is 4 3/5 degrees but he does not say whether it lies in the north or the south. . . .

On the other hand, however, all canons of the Hindus agree in this, that the latitude of Ujain is 24 degrees, and that the sun culminates over it at the time of the summer solistice.

I myself have found that the latitude of the fortress Lauhur to be 34° 10′. . . . What other latitudes I have been able to observe myself, I shall enumerate in this place:—Ghazna 33° 35′; Kabul 33° 47′; Kandi, the guard-station of the prince, 33° 55′; Dunpur 34° 20′; Lamghan 34° 43′; Purshavar 34° 44′; Waihind 34° 30′; Jailam 32° 20′; the fortress Nandna 32° 0′. . . . Sialkot 32° 58′; Mandakkakor 31° 50′; Multan 29° 40′. . . .

We ourselves have (in our travels) in their country not passed beyond places which we have mentioned, nor have we learned any more longitudes and latitudes (of places in India) from their literature. It is God alone who helps to reach our objects.

CHAPTER XXXII

On The Notions Of Duration And Time In General, And On The Creation Of The World And Its Destruction

According to the relation of Muhammad Ibn Zakariyya Alrazi,[35] the most ancient philosophers of the Greeks thought that the following five things existed from all eternity, the *creator*, the *universal soul*, the *first hulē*, *space in the abstract*, and *time in the abstract*. On these things Alrazi has founded that theory of his, which is at the bottom of his whole philosophy. Further, he distinguishes between *time* and *duration* in so far as *number* applies to the former, not to the latter; for a thing which can be numbered is finite, whilst duration is infinite. Similarly, philosophers have explained *time* as duration with a beginning and an end, and *eternity* as duration without beginning and end.

On the notion of time according to Alrazi and other philosophers

According to Alrazi, those five things are *necessary postulates* of the actually existing world. For that which the senses perceive in it is the *hulē* acquiring shape by means of combination. Besides, the *hulē* occupies some place, and therefore we must admit the existence of *space*. The changes apparent in the world of sense compel us to assume the existence of time, for some of them are earlier, others later, and the *before* and the *afterwards*, the earlier and the later, and the simultaneous can only be perceived by means of the notion of time, which is a necessary postulate of the existing world.

Further, there are living beings in the existing world. Therefore we must assume the existence of the *soul.* Among these living beings there are *intelligent* ones, capable of carrying the arts to the highest perfection; and this compels us to assume the existence of a Creator, who is wise and intelligent, who establishes and arranges everything in the best possible manner, and inspires people with the force of intelligence for the purpose of liberation.

On the other hand, some sophists consider eternity and time as one and the same thing, and declare the motion which serves to measure time alone to be finite.

Another one declares eternity to be the circular motion. No doubt this motion is indissolubly connected with that being which *moves* by it, and which is of the most sublime nature, since it lasts for ever. Thereupon he rises in his argumentation from the moving being to its mover, and from the moving mover to the first mover who is motionless.

This kind of research is very subtle and obscure. But for this, the opinions would not differ to such an extent that some people declare that there is no time at all, while others declare that time is an independent substance. According to Alexander of Aphrodisias, Aristotle gives in his book *Phusikē Akroasis* the following argumentation: "Everything moving is moved by a mover", and Galenus says on the same subject that he could not understand the notion of time, much less prove it.

The theory of the Hindus on this subject is rather poor in thought and very little developed. Varahamihira says in the opening of his book *Samhita,* when speaking of that which existed from all eternity: "It has been said in the ancient books that the first primeval thing was darkness, which is not identical with the black colour, but a kind of non-existence like the state of a sleeping person. Then God created this world for Brahman as a cupola for him. He made it to consist of two parts, a higher and a lower one, and placed the sun and moon in it." Kapila declares: "God has always existed, and with him the world, with all its substances and bodies. He, however, is a cause to the world, and rises by the subtlety of his nature above the gross nature of the world."

The notions of Hindu philosophers on time

Kumbhaka says: "The primeval one is *Mahabhuta*, i.e. the compound of the five elements. Some declare that the primeval thing is *time*, others *nature*, and still others maintain that the director is *karman*, i.e. action."

In the book *Vishnu-Dharma*, Vajra speaks to Markandeya: "Explain to me the times;" whereupon the latter answers: "Duration is *atmapurusha*," i.e. a *breath*, and *purusha*, which means *the lord of the universe*. Thereupon, he commenced explaining to him the divisions of time and their dominants, just as we have propounded these things in detail in the proper chapters (chap. xxxiii, *et seq.*).

The Hindus have divided duration into two periods, a period of *motion*, which has been determined as *time*, and a period of *rest*, which can be determined only in an imaginary way according to the analogy of that which has first been determined, the period of motion. The Hindus hold the eternity of the *Creator* to be *determinable*, not *measurable*, since it is infinite. We, however, cannot refrain from remarking that it is extremely difficult to imagine a thing which is *determinable* but not *measurable*, and that the whole idea is very far-fetched. We shall here communicate so much as will suffice for the reader of the opinions of the Hindus on this subject, as far as we know them.

The Day of Brahman a period of creation, the Night of Brahman a period of non-creation

The common notion of the Hindus regarding creation is a popular one, for as we have already mentioned, they believe matter to be eternal. Therefore, they do not, by the word *creation* understand a *formation of something out of nothing*. They mean by creation only the working with a piece of clay, working out various combinations and figures in it, and making such arrangements with it as will lead to certain ends and aims which are potentially in it. For this reason they attribute the creation to angels and demons, nay, even to human beings, who create either because they carry out some legal obligation which afterwards proves beneficial for the creation, or because they intend to allay their passions after having become envious and ambitious. So, for instance, they relate that Visvamitra, the Rishi, created the buffaloes for this purpose, that mankind should enjoy all the good and useful things which they afford. . . .

Here in this context we meet with a duration of time which Muslim authors, following the example of the Hindus, call *the years of the world*. People think that at their beginnings and endings creation and destruction take place as kinds of new formations. This, however, is not the belief of the people at large. According to them, this duration is a day of Brahman and a consecutive night of Brahman; for Brahman is entrusted with creating. Further, the coming into existence is a motion in that which grows out of something different from itself, and the most apparent of the causes of this motion are the meteoric motors, i.e. the stars. These, however, will never exercise regular influences on the world below them unless they move and change their shapes in every direction (= their *aspects*). Therefore the coming into existence is limited to the *day of Brahman,* because in it only, as the Hindus believe, the stars are moving and their spheres revolving according to their pre-established order, and in consequence the process of coming into existence is developed on the surface of the earth without any interruption.

On the contrary, during *the night of Brahman* the spheres rest from their motions, and all the stars, as well as their apsides and nodes, stand still in one particular place.

In consequence all the affairs of the earth are in one and the same unchanging condition, therefore the coming into existence has ceased, because he who makes things come into existence rests. So both the processes of acting and of being acted upon are suspended; the elements rest from entering into new metamorphoses and combinations, as they rest now in (*lacuna; perhaps:* the night), and they prepare themselves to belong to new beings, which will come into existence on the following day of Brahman.

In this way existence circulates during *the life of Brahman,* a subject which we shall propound in its proper place.

According to these notions of the Hindus, creation and destruction only refer to the surface of the earth. By such a creation, not

Critical remark of the author

one piece of clay comes into existence which did not exist before, and by such a destruction not one piece of clay which exists ceases to exist. It is quite impossible that the Hindus should have the notion of a creation as long as they believe that *matter* existed from all eternity.

The Hindus represent to their common people the two *durations* here mentioned, the day of Brahman and the night of Brahman, as his *waking* and *sleeping;* and we do not disapprove of these terms, as they denote something which has a beginning and end. Further, the *whole of the life of Brahman,* consisting of a succession of motion and rest in the world during such a period, is considered as applying only to existence, not to non-existence, since during it the piece of clay exists and, besides, also its shape. The *life of Brahman is* only a *day* for that being who is above him, i.e. Purusha (cf. chap. xxxv). When he dies all compounds are dissolved during his *night,* and in consequence of the annihilation of the compounds, that also is suspended which kept him (Brahman) within the laws of nature. This, then, is the rest of Purusha, and of all that is under his control (*lit.* and of his vehicles).

Brahman's waking and sleeping

When common people describe these things, they make the night of Brahman follow after the night of Purusha; and as Purusha is the name for a man, they attribute to him sleeping and waking. They derive destruction from his snoring, in consequence of which all things that hang together break asunder, and everything standing is drowned in the sweat of his forehead. And more of the like they produce, things which the mind declines to accept and the ear refuses to hear.

Vulgar and scientific notions on the sleep of Brahman

Therefore the educated Hindus do not share these opinions (regarding the waking and sleeping of Brahman), for they know the real nature of sleep. They know that the body, a compound of antipathetic *humores*, requires sleep for the purpose of resting, and for this purpose that all which nature requires, after being wasted, should be duly replaced. So, in consequence of the constant dissolution, the body requires food in order to replace that which had been lost by emaciation. Further, it requires cohabitation for the purpose of perpetuating the species by the body, as without cohabitation the species would die out. Besides, the body requires other things, evil ones, but necessary, while simple substances can dispense with them, as also he can who is above them, like to whom there is nothing.

Further, the Hindus maintain that the world will perish in consequence of the conjunction of the twelve suns, which appear one after the other in the different months, ruining the earth by burning and calcining it, and by withering and drying up all moist substances. Further, the world perishes in consequence of the union of the four rains which now come down in the different

Notions regarding the end of the world

seasons of the year; that which has been calcined attracts the water and is thereby dissolved. Lastly, the world perishes by the cessation of light and by the prevalence of darkness and non-existence. By all this the world will be dissolved into atoms and be scattered. . . .

The context of these passages makes it clear that this destruction of the world takes place at the end of a *kalpa,* and hence is derived the theory of Abu Ma'shar that a deluge takes place at the conjunction of the planets, because, in fact, they stand in conjunction at the end of each *caturyuga* and at the beginning of each *kaliyuga.* If this conjunction is not a complete one, the deluge, too, will evidently not attain the highest degree of its destructive power. The farther we advance in the investigation of these subjects, the more light will be shed on all ideas of this kind, and the better the reader will understand all words and terms occurring in this context.

Abu-Ma'shar uses Indian theories

Aleranshahri records a tradition, as representing the belief of the Buddhists, which much resembles the silly tales just mentioned. On the sides of Mount Meru there are four worlds, which are alternately civilised or desert. A world becomes desert when it is overpowered by the fire, in consequence of the rising of seven suns, one after the other, over it, when the water of the fountains dries up, and the burning fire becomes so strong as to penetrate into the world. A world becomes civilised when the fire leaves it and migrates to another world; after it has left, a strong wind rises in the world, drives the clouds, and makes them rain, so that, the world becomes like an ocean. Out of its foam shells are produced, with which the souls are connected, and out of these human beings originate when the water has sunk into the ground. Some Buddhists think that a man comes by accident from the perishing world to the growing world. Since he feels unhappy on account of his being alone, out of his thought there arises a spouse, and from this couple generation commences.

Buddhist notions from Aleranshahri

CHAPTER XXXIII

On The Various Kinds Of The Day Or Nychthemeron, And On Day And Night In Particular

Definition of day and night

According to the general usage of Muslims, Hindus, and others, a *day* or nychthemeron means the duration of one revolution of the sun in a rotation of the universe, in which he starts from the one half of a *great circle* and returns to the same. Apparently it is divided into two halves: the *day* (i.e. the time of the sun's being visible to the inhabitants of a certain place on earth), and the *night* (i.e. the time of his being invisible to them). His being visible and being invisible are relative facts, which differ as the horizons differ. It is well known that the horizon of the equator, which the Hindus call *the country without latitude,* cuts the circles parallel to the meridian in two halves. In consequence, day and night are always equal there. However, the horizons which cut the parallel circles without passing through their pole divide them into two unequal halves, the more so the smaller the parallel circles are. In consequence, there day and night are unequal, except at the times of the two equinoxes, when on the whole earth, except Meru and Vadavamukha, day and night are equal. Then all the places north and south of the line share in this peculiarity of the line, but only at this time, not at any other.

The beginning of the day is the sun's rising above the horizon, the beginning of the night his disappearing below it. The Hindus consider the day as the first, the night as the second, part of the nychthemeron. Therefore they call the former *Savana,* i.e. a day depending on the rising of the sun. Besides, they call it *Manushyahoratra,* i.e. a human day, because, in fact, the great mass of their people do not know any other kind of day but this. Now, assuming the *Savana* to be known to the reader, we shall in the following use it as a standard and gauge, in order thereby to determine all the other kinds of days.

Manushyahoratra

[Al-Biruni describes 'the other kinds of days'. Selected extracts from this description are given below:]

After the human days follows *Pitrinamahoratra,* i.e. the nychthemeron of the forefathers, whose spirits, according to the belief of the Hindus, dwell in the sphere of the moon. Its day and night depend upon light and darkness, not upon the rising and setting in relation to a certain horizon. When the moon stands in the highest parts of the sphere with reference to them, this is a day to them; and when it stands in the lowest parts, it is night to them. Evidently their moon is the time of the *conjunction* or full moon, and their midnight is *opposition,* or new moon. Therefore the nychthemeron of the forefathers is a complete lunar month, the day beginning at the time of half-moon, when the light on the moon's body begins to increase, and the night beginning at the time of half-moon, when her light begins to wane. . . .

Days of the fathers

Next follows the *Divyahoratra,* i.e. the nychthemeron of the angels. It is known that the horizon of the greatest latitude, i.e. that of 90 degrees where the pole stands in the zenith, is the equator, not exactly, but approximately, because it is a little below the visible horizon for that place on earth which is occupied by Mount Meru; for its top and slopes the horizon in question and the equator may be absolutely identical, although the visible horizon lies a little below it (i.e. farther south). Further, it is evident that the zodiac is divided into two halves by being intersected by the equator, the one half lying above the equator (i.e. north of it), the second half below it. As long as the sun marches in the signs of northern

Days of the Devas

declination it revolves like a mill, since the diurnal arcs which he describes are parallel to the horizon, as in the case of the sun-dials. For those who live under the north pole the sun appears above the horizon, therefore they have day. Whilst for those under south pole the sun is concealed below the horizon, and therefore they have night. When, then, the sun migrates to the southern signs, he revolves like a mill below the horizon, (i.e. south of the equator); hence it is night to the people living under the north pole and day to those living under the south pole.

The dwellings of the *Devaka,* i.e. the spiritual beings, are under the two poles; therefore this kind of day is called by their name, i.e. the nychthemeron of *the Deva.*

Aryabhatta of Kusumpura says that the Devas see one half of the solar year, the Danava the other; that the Pitaras see one half of the lunar month, human beings the other. So one revolution of the sun in the zodiac affords day and night both to the Deva and Danava, and their totality is a nychthemeron.

In consequence our year is identical with the nychthemeron of the Deva. In it, however, day and night are not equal (as in the nychthemeron of the forefathers), because the sun moves slowly in the half of the northern declination about its apogee, by which the day becomes a little longer. However, this difference is not equal to the difference between the visible horizon and the real one, for this cannot be observed on the globe of the sun. Besides, according to Hindu notions, the inhabitants of those places are raised above the surface of the earth, dwelling on Mount Meru. Whoever holds this view holds regarding the height of Meru the same opinions as those we have described in the proper place (in chap. xxiii). In consequence of this height of Mount Meru, its horizon must fall a little lower (i.e. more southward than the equator), and in consequence the rate of the day's being longer than the night is lessened (as then the sun does not entirely reach his northern apogee, where he makes the longest days). If this were anything else but simply a religious tradition of the Hindus, besides being one regarding which even they do not agree among themselves, we should try to find, by astronomical calculation, the amount of this depression of the horizon of Mount Meru below the equator, but as there is no use in this subject (Mount Meru being simply an invention), we drop it. . . .

Next follows the *Brahmahoratra,* i.e. the nychthemeron of

Brahman. It is not derived from light and darkness (as that of the forefathers), nor from the appearing or disappearing of a heavenly body (like that of the Devas), but from the physical nature of created things, in consequence of which they *move* in the day and *rest* in the night. The length of the nychthemeron of Brahman is 8,640,000,000 of our years. During one half of it, i.e. during the day, the aether, with all that is in it, is moving, the earth is producing, and the changes of existence and destruction are constantly going on upon the surface of the earth. During the other half, i.e. the night, there occurs the opposite of everything which occurs in the day; the earth is not changing, because those things which produce the changes are resting and all motions are stopped, as nature rests in the night and in the winter, and concentrates itself, preparing for a new existence in the day and in the summer.

Day of Brahman

Each day of Brahman is a *kalpa,* as also each night, and a *kalpa* is that space of time which Muslim authors call *the year of the Sindhind.*

Lastly follows the *Purushahoratra,* i.e. the nychthemeron of the All-soul, which is also called *Mahakalpa,* i.e. the greatest *kalpa.* The Hindus only use it for the purpose of determining duration in general by something like a notion of time, but do not specify it as day and night. I almost feel inclined to think that the day of this nychthemeron means the duration of the soul's being connected with the *hule,* whilst the night means the duration of their being separated from each other, and of the resting of the souls (from the fatigue of being mixed up with the *hule*), and that that condition which necessitates the soul's being connected with the *hule* or its being separated from the *hule* reaches its periodical end at the end of this nychthemeron. The *Vishnu-Dharma* says: "The life of Brahman is the day of Purusha, and the night of Purusha has the same length". . . .

Day of Purusha

CHAPTER XXXIV

On The Division Of The Nychthemeron Into Minor Particles Of Time

The Hindus are foolishly painstaking in inventing the most minute particles of time, but their efforts have not resulted in a universally adopted and uniform system. On the contrary, you hardly ever meet with two books or two men representing the subject identically. In the first instance, the nychthemeron is divided into sixty minutes or *ghati*. . . .

Ghati

Each minute is divided into sixty seconds, called *cashaka* or *cakhaka,* and also *vighatika.*

Cashaka

Each second is divided into six parts or *prana,* i.e. breath. . . .

Prana

It is all the same whether we determine the *prana* according to this rule (one nychthemeron = 21,600 *prana*) or if we divide each *ghati* into 360 parts ($60 \times 360 = 21,600$), or each degree of the sphere into sixty parts ($360 \times 60 = 21,600$).

As far as this all Hindus agree with each other in the matter, though they use different terms. . . .

Vinadi

Other people insert between minute and second a third measure, called *kshana,* which is equal to one-fourth of a minute (or fifteen

Kshana

seconds). Each *kshana* is divided into fifteen *kala,* each of which is equal to one-sixtieth of a minute, and this is the *cashaka,* only called by another name.

Nimesha, lava, truti

Among the lower orders of these fractions of time there occur three names which are always mentioned in the same sequence. The largest is the *nimesha,* i.e. the time during which the eye, in the normal state of things, is open between two consecutive looks. The *lava* is the mean, and the *truti* the smallest part of time, the latter word meaning the cracking of the forefinger against the inside of the thumb, which is with them a gesture expressive of astonishment or admiration. The relation between these three measures varies very much. According to many of the Hindus—

2 *truti* = 1 *lava.*
2 *lava* = 1 *nimehsa*

Further, they differ as to the relation between the *nimesha* and the next higher order of fractions of time, for according to some the latter *(kashtha)* contains fifteen, according to others thirty *nimesha.* Others, again, divide each of these three measures into eighths, so that—

8 *truti* = 1 *lava*
8 *lava* = 1 *nimesha*
8 *nimesha* = 1 *kashtha* (?) . . .

The whole system is represented in the following Table:

The names of the measures of time	*How many times the smaller one is contained in the larger one*	*How many of it are contained in one day*
Ghati, Nadi	60	60
Kshana	4	240
Cashaka, Vinadi, Kala .	15	3,600
Prana	6	21,600
Nimesha	8	172,800
Lava	8	1,382,400
Truti	8	11,059,200
Anu	8	88,473,600

The Hindus have also a popular kind of division of the nychthemeron into eight *prabara,* i.e. changes of the watch, and in some parts of their country they have clepsydrae regulated according to the *ghati,* by which the times of the eight watches are determined. After a watch lasts seven and a half *ghati* has elapsed, they beat the drum and blow a winding shell called *sankha,* in Persian *sped-muhra.* I have seen this in the town of *Purshur.* Pious people have bequeathed for these clepsydrae, and for their administration, legacies and fixed incomes.

Prabara

Further, the day is divided into thirty *muhurtas,* but this division is not free from a certain obscurity; for sometimes you think that the *muhurtas* have always the same length, since they compare them either with the *ghati* and say that two *ghati* are one *muhurta,* or with the *watches*, and say that one *watch* is three and three-quarters *muhurtas.* Here the *muhurtas* are treated as if they were *horoe oequinoctiales* (i.e. so and so many *equal* parts of the nychthemeron). However, the number of such hours of day or of a night differs on every degree of latitude, and this makes us think that the length of a *muhurta* during the day is different from its length during the *night*. . . .

Muhurta

[Pulisa's views as to whether the length of the *muhurta* is variable or invariable is critically examined. Pp. 338–342.]

We represent the dominants of the single *muhurta* in the following Table:

Dominants of the *muhurta*

The number of the muhurta	*The dominants of muhurta in the day*	*The dominants of the muhurta in the night*
1.	Shiva, i.e. Mahadeva	Rudra, i.e. Mahadeva
2.	Bhujaga, i.e. the snake	Aja, i.e. the lord of all cloven-footed animals
3.	Mitra	Ahirbudhnya, the lord of Uttarabhadrapada
4.	Pitri	Pushan, the lord of Revati
5.	Vasu	Dasra, the lord of Asvini
6.	Apas, i.e. the water	Antaka, i.e. the angel of death
7.	Visva	Agni, i.e. the fire
8.	Virincya, i.e. Brahman	Dhatri, i.e. Brahma the preserver

9.	Kesvara(?), i.e. Mahadeva	Soma, the lord of Mrigasirsha
10.	Indragni	Guru, i.e. Jupiter
11.	Indra, the prince	Hari, i.e. Narayana
12.	Nisakara, i.e. the moon	Ravi, i.e. the sun
13.	Varuna, i.e. the lord of the clouds	Yama, the angel of death
14.	Aryaman	Tvashtri, the lord of Citra
15.	Bhageya(?)	Anila, i.e. the wind

On the hours in Hindus astrology

Nobody in India uses *the hours* except the astrologers, for they speak of the *dominants of the hours,* and, in consequence, also of *dominants of the nychthemera.* The dominant of the nychthemeron is at the same time the dominant of the night, for they do not separately establish a dominant for the day, and the night is, in this connection, never mentioned. They arrange the order of the dominants according to the *horoe temporales.*

They call the hour *hora,* and this name seems to indicate that in reality they use the *horoe obliquoe temporales;* for the Hindus call the *media signorum* (the centres of the signs of the Zodiac) *hora,* which we Muslims call *nimbahr* (cf. chap. 1xxx). The reason is this, that in each day and each night always six signs rise above the horizon. If, therefore, the hour is called by the name of the centre of a sign, each day and each night has twelve hours, and in consequence the hours used in the theory of the dominants of the hours are *horoe obliquoe temporales,* as they are used in our country and are inscribed on the astrolabes on account of these dominants. . . .

Names of the twenty-four *horas*

The Hindus give certain names to the *horoe obliquoe,* which we have united in the following Table. We think they are taken from the book *Srudhava.*

The number of the Horas	*Names of the Horas in the day*	*Whether favourable or unlucky*	*Their names in the night*	*Whether favourable or unlucky*
1.	Raudra	Unlucky	Kaḷaratri	Unlucky
2.	Saumya	Lucky	Rodhini	Lucky

3.	Karala	Unlucky	Vairahma(?)	Lucky
4.	Sattra	Lucky	Trasaniya	Unlucky
5	Vega	Lucky	Guḥaniya(?)	Lucky
6.	Visala	Lucky	Maya	Unlucky
7.	Mrityusara	Unlucky	Damariya(?)	Lucky
8.	Subha	Lucky	Jivaharani	Unlucky
9.	Kroda	Lucky	Soshini	Unlucky
10.	Candala	Lucky	Vrishni	Lucky
11.	Krittika	Lucky	Dahariya(?)	The most unlucky of all
12.	Amrita	Lucky	Cantima(?)	Lucky

CHAPTER XXXV

On The Different Kinds Of Months And Years

The *natural* month is the period of the moon's synodical revolution. We call it physical because it develops in the same way as all natural phenomena, rising out of a certain beginning like non-existence, increasing by degrees, and growing, standing still when the climax is attained, then descending, waning away and decreasing, till at last they return to the non-existence whence they came. In the same manner the light develops on the body of the moon, since she appears after the moonless nights as a crescent, then as a young moon (after the third night), and as full moon, and thereafter returns through the same stages to the last night, which is like non-existence, at all events with reference to human senses. It is well known to everybody why the moon continues for some length of time in the moonless nights, but it is not equally known, not even to educated people, why she continues some time as full moon. They must learn how small the body of the moon is in comparison with that of the sun, that in consequence the enlightened portion by far exceeds the dark one, and that this is one of the causes why the moon must necessarily appear as full moon for some length of time.

Definition of the lunar month

That the moon has certain effects on moist substances, that they are apparently subject to her influences that, for instance, increase and decrease in ebb and flow develop periodically and parallel with the moon's phases, all this is well known to the inhabitants of seashores and seafaring people. Likewise physicians are well aware that she affects the *humores* of sick people, and that the fever-days revolve parallel with the moon's course. Physical scholars know that the life of animals and plants depends upon the moon, and experimentalists know that she influences marrow and brain, eggs and the sediments of wine in casks and jugs, that she excites the minds of people who sleep in full moonlight, and that she affects (?) linen clothes which are exposed to it. Peasants know how the moon acts upon fields of cucumbers, melons, cotton, etc., and even make the times for the various kinds of sowing, planting, and grafting, and for the covering of the cattle depend upon the course of the moon. Lastly, astronomers know that meteorologic occurrences depend upon the various phases through which the moon passes in her revolutions. This is the month, and twelve of them are in technical language called *a lunar year.*

Effects of moonlight

The natural year is the period of a revolution of the sun in the ecliptic. We call it the *natural,* because it comprehends all the stages in the process of generation which revolve through the four seasons of the year. In the course of it, the rays of the sun as passing through a window-glass and the shadows of the sundials reassume the same size, position, and direction in which, or from which, they commenced. This is the year, and is called *the solar one,* in antithesis to the *lunar* year. As the lunar month is the twelfth part of the lunar year, the twelfth part of the solar year is a solar month in theory, the calculation being based on the mean rotation of the sun. If, however, the calculation is based on his varying rotation a solar month is the period of his staying in one sign of the zodiac.

Solar month

These are the well-known two kinds of months and years.

The Hindus call the conjunction *amavasya,* the opposition *purnima*, and the two quarters ATVH (?). Some of them use the lunar year with lunar months and days, whilst others use the lunar year but solar months, beginning with 0° of each zodiacal sign. The sun's entering a sign is called *sankranti.* This luni-

On luni-solar calculation

solar calculation is, however, only an approximative one. If they constantly used it, they would soon feel induced to adopt the solar year itself and solar months. In using this mixed system they had only this advantage, that they could dispense with intercalation.

Beginning of the lunar months

Those who use lunar months begin the month with conjunction of new moon, and this method is *the canonical* one, whilst the others begin it with the opposition or full moon. ...

The month counted as two halves

The numeration of the days of the month begins with the new moon and the first lunar day is called *brba,* and again enumeration begins with full noon (i.e. they count twice fifteen days, beginning with new moon and full moon). Each two days which are equidistant from new moon or full moon have the same name (or number). In them, light and darkness on the body of the moon are in corresponding phases of increasing and waning, and the hours of the rising of the moon in one day correspond to the hours of her setting in the other. ...

Various kinds of months

As months are composed of days, there are as many kinds of months as there are kinds of days. Each month has thirty days. We shall here use the *civil* day (*Savana,* v. chap. xxxiii) as a standard. ...

A month has 30 lunar days, for this number is canonical, as the number of 360 is canonical for the number of days of a year. The *solar month* has 30 solar days and

$$30\frac{1,362,987}{3,110,400} \text{ civil days. ...}$$

The solar year has $365\ \frac{827}{3,200}$ civil days. ...

CHAPTER XXXVI

On The Four Measures Of Time Called Mana

Mana and *pramana* mean *measure.* The four kinds of measures are mentioned by Yakub Ibn Tarik in his book *Compositio Sphoerarum,* but he did not know them thoroughly, and besides, the names are misspelled, if this is not the fault of the copyists.

They are—

Saura-mana, i.e. the solar measure.

Savana-mana, i.e. the measure depending upon *the rising* (civil measure).

Candra-mana; i.e. the lunar measure.

Nakshatra-mana i.e. the lunar-station measure (*sidereal* measure).

The *saura-mana* is used in the computation of the years which compose the *kalpa* and the four *yugas* in the *caturyugas,* of the years of the nativities, of the equinoxes and solstices, of the sixth parts of the year or the seasons, and of the difference between day and night in the nychthemeron. All these are computed in solar years, months, and days.

What use is made of the *saura-mana, candra-mana,* and *savana-mana*

The *candra-mana* is used in the computation of the eleven *karana* (v. chap. lxxviii), in the determination of the leap month, in the computation of the sum of days of the *unaratra* (v. chap. li), and of new moon and full moon for lunar and solar eclipses (v. chap. lix).

The *savana-mana* is used in the calculation of the *vara,* i.e. the days of the week, of the *ahargana,* i.e. the sum of the days of an era (v. chap. li); in determining the days of marriage and fasting (v. chap. lxxv); the *sutaka,* i.e. the days of childbed (v. chap. lxix); the days of the uncleanness of the houses and the vessels of the dead (v. chap. lxxii); the *cikitsa,* i.e. certain months and years in which Hindu medical science prescribes the taking of certain medicines; further in determining, the *prayascitta*, i.e. the days of the expiations which the Brahmans make obligatory for those who have committed some sin, times during which they are obliged to fast and to besmear themselves with butter and dung (v. chap. lxxi). All these things are determined according to *savana-mana.*

On the contrary, they do not determine anything by the *nakshatra-mana*, since it is comprehended in the *candra-mana.*

Every measure of time which any class of people may choose by general consent to call a day, may be considered as a *mana.* Some such days have already been mentioned in a preceding chapter (v. chap. xxxiii). However, the four *manas par excellence* are those to the explanation of which. we have limited the present chapter.

CHAPTER XXXVII

On The Parts Of The Month And The Year

As the year is one revolution of the sun in the ecliptic, it is divided in the same way as the ecliptic. The latter is divided into two halves, depending upon the two solstitial points. Correspondingly, the year is divided into two halves, each of which is called *ayana.*

Uttarayana and *dakshinayana*

When the sun leaves the point of the winter solstice, he begins to move towards the north pole. Therefore this part of the year, which is nearly one half, is referred to the north and called *uttarayana,* i.e. the period of the sun's marching through six zodiacal signs beginning with *Caper.* In consequence, this half of the ecliptic is called *makaradi,* i.e. *having Caper as beginning.*

When the sun leaves the point of the summer solstice he begins to move towards the south pole; therefore this second half is referred to the south and called *dakshinayana,* i.e. the period of the sun's marching through six zodiacal signs beginning with *Cancer.* In consequence, this half of the ecliptic is called *karkadi,* i.e. *having Cancer as beginning.*

Uneducated people use only these two divisions or year-halves, because the matter of the two solstices is clear to them from appearance.

observation of their senses.

Further, the ecliptic is divided into two halves, according to its declination from the equator, and this division is a more scientific one, less known to the people at large than the former, because it rests on calculation and speculation. Each half is called *kula*. That which has northern declination is called *uttarakula* or *meshadi*, i.e. *having Aries as beginning;* that which has southern declination is called *dakshakula* or *tuladi*, i.e. *having Libra as beginning.*

Uttarakula and *dakshakula*

Further, the ecliptic is by both these divisions divided into four parts, and the periods during which the sun traverses them are called the *seasons of the year*—spring, summer, autumn, and winter. Accordingly, the zodiacal signs are distributed over the seasons. However, the Hindus do not divide the year into four, but into six parts, and call these six parts *ritu*. Each *ritu* comprehends two solar months, i.e. the period of the sun's marching through two consecutive zodiacal signs. Their names and dominants are represented, according to the most widespread theory, in the following diagram.

The seasons

I have been told that in the region of Somanath people divide the year into three parts, each consisting of four months, the first being *varshakala,* beginning with month *ashadha;* the second, *sitakala,* i.e. the winter; and the third, *ushnakala*, i.e. the summer. . . . The months are divided into two halves from new moon to full moon, and from full moon to new moon. . . .

CHAPTER XXXVIII

On The Various Measures Of Time Composed Of Days, The Life Of Brahman Included

Recapitulation of the single measures of time

The day is called *dimas (dimasu),* in classical language *divasa,* the night *ratri,* and the nychthemeron *ahoratra.* The month is called *masa* and its half *paksha.* The first or *white* half is called *suklapaksha,* because the first parts of its nights have moonlight at times when people do not yet sleep, when the light on the moon's body increases and the dark portion decreases. The other or *black* half is called *krishnapaksha,* because the first parts of its nights are moonless, whilst other parts have moonlight, but only when people sleep. They are the nights when the light on the body of the moon wanes, whilst the dark part increases.

The sum of two months is a *ritu*, but this is only an approximative definition, for the month which has two *paksha* is a lunar month, whilst that one the double of which is a *ritu* is a solar month.

Six *ritu* are a year of mankind, a solar year, which is called *barh* or *barkh* or *barsh,* the three sounds *h, kh,* and *sh* being much confounded in the month of the Hindus (Skr. *varsha*).

Three hundred and sixty years of mankind are one year of the angels, called *dibba-barh (divya-varsh)*, and 12,000 years of the angels are unanimously reckoned as one *caturyuga*. There is a difference of opinion only regarding the four parts of the *caturyuga* and regarding the multiplications of it which form a *manavantara* and a *kalpa*. This subject will be fully explained in the proper place (v. chaps. xli and xliv). . . .

CHAPTER XXXIX

On Measures Of Time Which Are Larger Than The Life Of Brahman

Want of system regarding the greatest measures of time

All that is devoid of order or contradicts the rules laid down in the preceding parts of this book is repulsive to our nature and disagreeable to our ear. But the Hindus are people who mention a number of names, all—as they maintain—referring to the One, the First, or to some one behind him who is only hinted at. When they come to a chapter like this, they repeat the same names as denoting a multitude of beings, measuring out lives for them and inventing huge numbers. The latter is all they want; they indulge in it most freely, and numbers are patient, standing as you place them. Besides, there is not a single subject on which the Hindus themselves agree among each other, and this prevents us on our part adopting the use of it. On the contrary, they disagree on these imaginary measures of time to the same extent as on the divisions of the day which are less than a *prana*.

Sources quoted regarding the calculation of the greatest measure of time as determined by *kalpas* and *trutis*. Pp. 361–363.]

CHAPTER XL

On The Samdhi, The Interval Between Two Periods Of Time, Forming The Connecting Link Between Them

Explanation of the two *samdhis*

The original *samdhi* is the interval between day and night, i.e. morning-dawn, called *samdhi udaya*, i.e. the *samdhi* of the rising, and evening dawn, called *samdhi astamana,* i.e. the *samdhi* of the setting. The Hindus require them for a religious reason, for the Brahmans wash themselves during them, and also at noon in the midst between them for dinner, whence an uninitiated person might infer that there is still a third *samdhi.* However, none who knows the subject properly will count more than two *samdhis.* ...

On the *samdhi* of the year-half and its combination with the precession of the equinoxes. Other kinds of *samdhi*

Besides the two *samdhi* of the natural day, astronomers and other people assume still other *samdhis,* which do not rest on a law of nature nor on observation, but simply on some hypothesis. So they attribute a *samdhi* to each *ayana*, i.e. to each of the year-halves in which the sun ascends and descends (v. chap. xxxvii), a *samdhi* of seven days before its real beginning. On this subject I have an idea which is certainly possible, and even rather likely, viz. that this theory is of recent origin, not of ancient date, and that it has been brought forward about 1300 of Alexander (= A.D. 989), when the Hindus found out that the real solstice precedes the solstice of their calculation. ...

CHAPTER XLI

Definition Of The Terms "Kalpa" And "Caturyuga," And An Explication Of The One By The Other

Twelve thousand *divya years,* the length of which has already been explained (v. chap. xxxv), are one *caturyuga,* and 1,000 *caturyugas* are one *kalpa,* a period at the beginning and end of which there is a conjunction of the seven planets and their apsides and nodes in 0° of Aries. The days of the *kalpa* are called the *kalpa-ahargana,* for *ah* means *day,* and *argana* means *the sun.* Since they are *civil days* derived from the *rising* of the sun, they are also called *days of the earth, for rising* presupposes an horizon, and an horizon is one of the necessary attributes of the earth.

On the measure of a *caturyuga* and a *kalpa*

By the same name, *kalpa-ahargana*, people also call the sum of days of any era up to a certain date.

Our Muslim authors call the days of the *kalpa the days of the Sindhind or the days of the world*, counting them as 1,577,916, 450,000 days (*savana* or civil days), or 4,320,000,000 solar years, or 4,452,775,000 lunar years. . . .

Within the space of a *kalpa* 71 *caturyugas* are equal to 1 *manu,* i.e. *manavantara,* or Manu-period, and 14 *manus* are equal to 1 *kalpa.*

Multiplying 71 by 14, you get 994 *caturyugas* as the period of 14 *manavantaras,* and a remainder of 6 *caturyugas* till the end of the *kalpa.* . . .

Relation between *manavantara* and *kalpa*

All we have said in this chapter rests on the theory of Brahmagupta and on the arguments by which he supports it.

Aryabhatta the elder and Pulisa compose the *manavantara* from 72 *caturyugas,* and the *kalpa* from 14 *manavantaras,* without inserting anywhere *samdhi.* Therefore, according to them, a *kalpa* has 1,008 *caturyugas;* further 12,096,000, *divya years* or 4,354, 560,000 human years. . . .

Theories of Aryabhatta the elder, Pulisa, and Aryabhatta the younger

I have not been able to find anything of the books of Aryabhatta. All I know of him I know through quotations from him given by Brahmagupta. . . .

Aryabhatta of Kusumpura, who belongs to the school of the elder Aryabhatta, says in a small book of his on Al-ntf (?) that "1,008 *caturyugas* are one day of Brahmạn. The first half of 504 *caturyugas* is called *utsarpini,* during which the sun is ascending, and the second half is called *avasrapini,* during which the sun is descending. The midst of this period is called *sama,* i.e. equality, for it is the midst of the day, and the two ends are called *durtama* (?)."

CHAPTER XLII

On The Division Of The Caturyuga Into Yugas, And The Different Opinions Regarding The Latter

The single parts of a *caturyuga* according to *Vishnu-Dharma* Brahma

The author of the *Vishnu-Dharma* says: "Twelve hundred *divya years* are one *yuga,* called *tishya.* The double of it is a *dvapara*, the triple a *treta,* the quadruple a *krita,* and all four *yugas* together are one *caturyuga,* i.e the four *yugas* or *sums.*

"Seventy-one *caturyugas* are one *manavantara,* and 14 *manavantaras,* together with a *samdhi* of the duration of one *kritayuga* between each two of them, are one *kalpa.* Two *kalpas* are a nychthemeron of Brahman, and his life is a hundred years, or one day of Purusha, the first man, of whom neither beginning nor end is known."

[Brahmagupta's view on the subject and his 'offensive' criticism of Aryabhatta's views are stated, pp. 373–376. On the latter point Al-Biruni remarks that:]

Now, it is evident that that which Brahmagupta relates on his authority, and with which he himself agrees is entirely unfounded; but he is blind to this from sheer hatred of Aryabhatta, whom he abuses excessively. And in this respect Aryabhatta and Pulisa are the same to him. I take for witness the passage of Brahmagupta, where he says that Aryabhatta has subtracted something from the cycles of the *Caput Draconis* and of the *apsis* of the moon and thereby rendered confused the computation of the eclipse. He is rude enough to compare Aryabhatta to a worm which, eating the wood, by chance describes certain characters in it, without understanding them and without intending to draw them....In such offensive terms he attacks Aryabhatta and maltreats him. ...

CHAPTER XLIII

A Description Of The Four Yugas, And Of All That Is Expected To Take Place At The End Of The Fourth Yuga

The ancient Greeks held regarding the earth various opinions, of which we shall relate one for the sake of an example.

On natural cataclysms

The disasters which from time to time befall the earth, both from above and from below, differ in quality and quantity. Frequently it has experienced one so incommensurable in quality or in quantity, or in both together, that there was no remedy against it, and that no flight or caution was of any avail. The catastrophe comes on like a deluge or an earthquake, bringing destruction either by the breaking in of the surface, or by drowning with water which breaks forth, or by burning with hot stones and ashes that are thrown out, by thunderstorms, by landslips, and typhoons; further, by contagious and other diseases, by pestilence, and more of the like. Thereby a large region is stripped of its inhabitants; but when after a while, after the disaster and its consequences have passed away, the country begins to recover and to show new signs of life, then different people flock there together like wild animals, who formerly were dwelling in hiding-holes and on the tops of the mountains. They become civilised by assisting each other against common foes, wild beasts or men, and furthering each other in the hope for a life in safety and joy. Thus they increase to great numbers; but then ambition, circling round them with the wings of wrath and envy, begins to disturb the serene bliss of their life.

Sometimes a nation of such a kind derives its pedigree from a person who first settled in the place or distinguished himself by something or other, so that he alone continues to live in the recollection of the succeeding generations, whilst all others beside him are forgotten. . . .

Hindu notions regarding the four ages or *yugas*

The Hindus have similar traditions regarding the *caturyuga,* for according to them, at the beginning of it, i.e. at the beginning of *kritayuga,* there was happiness and safety, fertility and abundance, health and force, ample knowledge and a great number of Brahmans. The good is complete in this age, like four-fourths of a whole, and life lasted 4,000 years alike for all beings during this whole space of time.

Thereupon things began to decrease and to be mixed with opposite elements to such a degree, that at the beginning of *tretayuga* the good was thrice as much as the invading bad, and that bliss was three-quarters of the whole. There were a greater number of Kshatriyas than of Brahmans, and life had the same length as in the preceding age. So it is represented by the *Vishnu-Dharma,* whilst analogy requires that it should be shorter by the same amount than bliss is smaller, i.e. by one-fourth. In this age, when offering to the fire, they begin to kill animals and to tear off plants, practices which before were unknown.

Thus the evil increases till, at the beginning of *dvapara,* evil and good exist in equal proportions, and likewise bliss and misfortune. The climates begin to differ, there is much killing going on, and the religions become different. Life becomes shorter, and lasts only 400 years, according to the *Vishnu-Dharma.* At the beginning of *Tishya,* i.e. *kaliyuga,* evil is thrice as much as the remaining good.

The Hindus have several well-known traditions of events which are said to have occurred in the *treta* and *dvapara yugas,* e.g. the story of Rama, who killed Ravana; that of Parasurama the Brahman, who killed every Kshatriya he laid hold upon, revenging on them the death of his father. They think that he lives in heaven, that he has already twenty-one times appeared on earth, and that he will again appear. Further, the story of the war of the children of Pandu with those of Kuru.

In the *kaliyuga* evil increases, till at last it results in the destruction of all good. At that time the inhabitants of the earth perish, and a new race rises out of those who are scattered through the mountains and hide themselves in caves, uniting for the purpose of worshipping and flying from the horrid, demoniac human race. Therefore this age is called *kritayuga,* which means "Being ready for going away after having finished the work."

In the story of Saunaka which Venus received from Brahman, God speaks to him in the following words: "When the Kaliyuga comes, I send Budhodana, the son of Suddhodana the pious, to spread good to the creation. But then *Muhammira,* i.e. the red-wearing ones, who derive their origin from him, will change everything that he has brought, and the dignity of the Brahmans will be gone to such a degree that a Sudra, their servant, will be impudent towards them. . . . The castes will be in uproar against each other, the genealogies will become confused and the four castes will be abolished, and there will be many religions and sects. . . .

Description of the *kaliyuga*

[Description of the *kaliyuga,* as given, in *Vishnu-Dharma* and some other sources, is presented. Pp. 380–382].

But finally, at the end of the *yuga*, when the evil will have reached its highest pitch, there will come forward Garga, the son of J-S-V (?) the Brahman, i.e. Kali, after whom this *yuga* is called, gifted with an irresistible force, and more skilled in the use of any weapon than any other. Then he draws his sword to make good all that has become bad; he cleans the surface of the earth of the impurity of people and clears the earth of them. He collects the pure and pious ones for the purpose of procreation. Then the *kritayuga* lies far behind them, and the time and the world return to purity, and to absolute good and to bliss.

This is the nature of the *yugas* as they circle round through the *caturyuga.*

The book *Caraka,* as quoted by Ali Ibn Zain of Tabaristan, says: "In primeval times the earth was always fertile and healthy, and the elements or *Mahabhuta* were equally mixed. Men lived with each other in harmony and love, without any lust and ambition, hatred and envy, without anything that makes soul and

The origin of medicine according to the book *Caraka*

body ill. But then came envy, and lust followed. Driven by lust, they strove to hoard up, which was difficult to some, easy to others. All kinds of thoughts, labours, and cares followed, and resulted in war, deceit, and lying. The hearts of men were hardened, the natures were altered and became exposed to diseases, which seized hold of men and made them neglect the worship of God and the furtherance of science. Ignorance became deeply rooted, and the calamity became great. Then the pious met before their anchorite Krisa (?) the son of Atreya, and deliberated; whereupon the sage ascended the mountain and threw himself on the earth. Thereafter God taught him the science of medicine."

[Similar Greek traditions are quoted, pp. 383–385].

CHAPTER XLIV

On The Manavantaras

As 72,000 *kalpas* are reckoned as the life of Brahman, the *manavantara*, i.e. period of Manu, is reckoned as the life of Indra, whose rule ends with the end of the period. His post is occupied by another Indra, who then rules the world in the new *manavantara*. . . .

The single *manavantaras*, their Indras, and the children of Indra

[A Table, showing the number (14) and names of the *manavantaras*, according to the *Vishnu-Purana*, *Vishnu-Dharma* and some other sources, and the names of Indra and the children of Manu, the king of the earth who ruled at the beginning of each period, is given. Explaining the variations in the names of some of the *manavantaras*, Al-Biruni comments on the excessive concern of the Hindus with names. He adds that they are more interested in names than the 'the order in which they are recorded for the posterity', pp. 387–388].

CHAPTER XLV

On The Constellation Of The Great Bear

The Great Bear is in the Indian lânguage called *Saptarshayas,* i.e. *the Seven Rishis.* They are said to have been anchorites who nourished themselves only with what it is allowable to eat, and with them there was a pious woman, *Al-suha* (*Ursa Major,* star 80 by z). They plucked off the stalks of the lotus from the ponds to eat of them. Meanwhile came *The Law (Dharma?)* and concealed her from them. Every one of them felt ashamed of the other, and they swore oaths which were approved of by *Dharma.* In order to honour them, *Dharma* raised them to that place where they are now seen *(sic).*

A tradition relating to Arundhati, the wife of Vasishtha

[A description of the Great Bear, as given in the *Samhita* of Varahamihira, is quoted. The differences in the statements of some Indian sources regarding the position of the Great Bear are examined and criticised. Al-Biruni makes an incidental but important remark that 'our time' (the time of the compilation of his account, i.e. 1030) corresponded with 952 of the Sakakala. This provides corroborative evidence on the concordance of the Saka era, pp. 389–392. He concludes the chapter by observing that:]

Mistakes and confusion such as we have here laid open arise, in the first place, from the want of the necessary skill in astronomical researches, and secondly, from the way of the Hindus of mixing up scientific questions with religious traditions.

Theological opinions mixed up with astronomy

For the theologians believe that the *Seven Rishis* stand higher than the fixed stars, and they maintain that in each *manavantara* there will appear a new Manu, whose children will destroy the earth; but the rule will be renewed by Indra, as also the different classes of the angels and the *Seven Rishis.* The angels are necessary, for mankind must offer sacrifices to them and must bring to the fire the shares for them; and the *Seven Rishis* are necessary, because they must renew the Veda, for it perishes at the end of each *manavantara.*

Our information on this subject we take from the *Vishnu-Purana.* From the same source we have taken the names of the *Seven Rishis* in each *manavantara,* as exhibited by the following Table:—

The *Seven Rishis* in the different *manavantaras*

[A Table showing *Seven Rishis* or the stars of the Great Bear in the 14 *manavantaras* is given. P. 394].

CHAPTER XLVI

On Narayana, His Appearance At Different Times And His Names

Narayana is according to the Hindus a supernatural power, which does not on principle try to bring about the good by the good, nor the bad by the bad, but to prevent the evil and destruction by whatever means happen to be available. For this force the good exists prior to the bad, but if the good does not properly develop nor is available, it uses the bad, this being unavoidable. In so doing, it may be compared to a rider who has got into the midst of a cornfield. When he then comes back to his senses, and wants to avoid evil-doing and to get out of the mischief he has committed, he has no other means but that of turning his horse back and riding out on the same road on which he has entered the field, though in going out he will do as much mischief as he has done in entering, and even more. But there is no other possibility of making amends save this.

On the nature of Narayana

The Hindus do not distinguish between this force and the *First Cause* of their philosophy. Its dwelling in the world is of such a nature that people compare it to a material existence, an appearance in body and colour, since they cannot conceive any other kind of appearance.

Besides other times, Narayana has appeared at the end of the first *manavantara* to take away the rule of the worlds from Valakhilya (?), who had given it the name, and wanted to take it into his own hands. Narayana came and handed it over to Satakratu, the performer of a hundred sacrifices, and made him Indra.

[A story is narrated about how Narayana appeared again at the end of the sixth *manavantara* and killed King Bali, son of Virocana, pp. 396–398].

In another passage of the same book [*Vishnu-Purana*] we read: "Vishnu, i.e. another name for Narayana, comes at the end of each *dvapara* to divide the Veda into four parts, because men are feeble and unable to observe the whole of it. In his face he resembles Vyasa."

[The names of the Vyasas of the seventh *manavantara* are enumerated, pp. 398–399].

CHAPTER XLVII

On Vasudeva And The Wars Of The Bharata

The life of the world depends upon sowing and procreating. Both processes increase in the course of time, and this increase is unlimited, whilst the world is limited.

Analogies of the course of nature to the history of mankind

When a class of plants or animals does not increase any more in its structure, and its peculiar kind is established as a *species* of its own, when each individual of it does not simply come into existence once and perish, but besides procreates a being like itself or several together, and not only once but several times, then this will as a single species of plants or animals occupy the earth and spread itself and its kind over as much territory as it can find.

The agriculturist selects his corn, letting grow as much as he requires, and tearing out the remainder. The forester leaves those branches which he perceives to be excellent, whilst he cuts away all others. The bees kill those of their kind who only eat, but do not work in their beehive.

Nature proceeds in a similar way; however, it does not distinguish, for its action is under all circumstances one and the same. It allows the leaves and fruit of the trees to perish, thus preventing them from realising that result which they are intended to produce in the economy of nature. It removes them so as to make room for others.

If thus the earth is ruined, or is near to be ruined, by having too many inhabitants, its ruler—for it has a ruler, and his all-embracing care is apparent in every single particle of it—sends it a messenger for the purpose of reducing the too great number and of cutting away all that is evil.

Story of the birth of Vasudeva

A messenger of this kind is, according to the belief of the Hindus, Vasudeva, who was sent the last time in human shape, being called Vasudeva. It was a time when the giants were numerous on earth and the earth was full of their oppression; it tottered, being hardly able to bear the whole number of them, and it trembled from the vehemence of their treading. Then there was born a child in the city of Mathura to Vasudeva by the sister of Kamsa, at that time ruler of the town. They were a Jatt family, cattle-owners, low Sudra people. Kamsa had learned, by a voice which he heard at the wedding of his sister, that he would perish at the hands of her child; therefore, he appointed people who were to bring him every child of hers . . . and he killed all her children . . . Finally, she gave birth to Balbhadra, and Yasoda, the wife of the herdsman Nanda, took the child to herself . . . Thereupon she became pregnant an eighth time, and gave birth to *Vasudeva* in a rainy night of the eighth day of the black half of the month of Bhadrapada . . . As the guards had fallen into deep sleep . . . the father stole the child and brought it to *Nandkula*, i.e. the stable of the cows of Nanda, near Mathura . . . Vasudeva grew up under the care of his foster-mother Yasoda without her knowing that he had been exchanged for her daughter . . . but Kamsa got some inkling of the matter. . . .

[The account of the war between the Kauravas and Pandus is as follows :]

The children of Kaurava (i.e Dhritarashtra) had the charge of their cousins (the children of Pandu). Dhritarashtra received them and played dice with them, the last stake being their whole property. They lost more and more, until he laid upon them the obligation of expatriation for more than ten years, and of concealment in the remotest part of the country, where nobody knew them. If they did not keep this engagement they would be bound to return into banishment for a like number of years. This engagement was carried out, but finally came the time of their coming forward for battle.

Now each party began to assemble their whole number and to sue for allies, till at last nearly innumerable hosts had gathered in the plain of Taneshar. There were eighteen *akshauhini.* Each party tried to gain Vasudeva as ally, whereupon he offered either himself or his brother Balabhadra together with an army. But the children of Pandu preferred him. They were five men—Yudhishthira, their leader, Arjuna, the bravest of them, Sahadeva, Bhimasena, and Nakula. They had seven *akshauhini,* whilst their enemies were much stronger. But for the cunning devices of Vasudeva and his teaching them whereby they might gain victory, they would have been in a less favourable situation than their enemies. But now they conquered; all those hosts were destroyed, and none remained except the five brothers. Thereafter Vasudeva returned to his residence and died, together with his family, who were called Yadava. Also the five brothers died before the year had reached its end, at the end of those wars.

[Al-Biruni gives some further details of the end of Vasudeva and of the five Pandu brothers. One among the brothers and relations of Vasudeva went to a Rishi, Durvasa, with a frying-pan hid under his coat and asked him about the result of his pregnancy. The Rishi, annoyed at thus being jeered at, said the thing in his belly would cause his, and his clansmen's, death. Vasudeva who knew that the curse would come true got the pan filed and thrown in a river. One small piece of it was eaten by a fish, and a fisherman who caught the fish and cut it got an arrow-head made of that bit. It was from this arrow that Vasudeva, while sitting cross-legged under a tree, was shot by a fisherman who mistook him for a gazelle. Out of the other bits of filed pan a *bardi* bush had grown. When the Yadavas reached near it and sat drinking, a quarrel occurred among them and they killed each other with the *bardi* bundles. Arjuna, who had been ordered by Vasudeva to burn his body and carry away the women was attacked by robbers on the way. Though he beat them off he felt that his strength was failing him. He and his brothers, therefore 'emigrated' to the north and entered the mountains. The cold killed them one after the other, (Pp. 404–406).

CHAPTER XLVIII

An Explanation Of The Measure Of An Akshauhini

Each	akshauhini	has	10	antkini.
"	antkini	"	3	camu
"	camu	"	3	pritana
"	pritana	"	3	vahini
"	vahini	"	3	gana
"	gana	"	3	gulma
"	gulma	"	3	senamukha
"	senamukha	"	3	patti
"	patti	"	1	ratha

In chess, the latter is called *rukh,* whilst Greeks call it *chariot of war.* It was invented by *Mankalus* (Myrtilos?) in Athens, and the Athenians maintain that they were the first who rode on chariots of war. However, before that time they had already been invented by Aphrodisias *(sic)* the Hindu, when he ruled over Egypt, about 900 years after the deluge. They were drawn by two horses. . . .

A *ratha* comprehends besides, one elephant, three riders, and five footmen.

All these orders and divisions are necessary for the preparation for battle, for pitching camp and breaking up camp.

An *akshauhini* has 21,870 chariots, 21,870 elephants, 65,610 riders, 109,350 footmen.

To each chariot there belong four horses and their conductor, the master of the chariot, armed with arrows, his two companions armed with spears, a guard who protects the master from behind, and a cartwright.

On each elephant there sits its conductor, and behind him the vice-conductor, a man who has to goad the elephant behind the chair, the master, armed with arrows, in the chair, and together with him his two spear-throwing companions and his jester, *hauhava* (?), who on other occasions runs before him.

Accordingly the number of people who ride on chariots and elephants is 284,323 *(sic)*. The number of those who ride on horses is 87,480. The number of elephants in an *akshauhini* is 21,870; the number of chariots, too, is 21,870; the number of horses is 153,090; the number of men, 459,283.

The sum-total of the living beings of one *akshauhini*, elephants, horses, and men, is 634,243; the same number for eighteen *akshauhini* is 11,416,374, viz. 393,660 elephants, 2,755,620 horses, 8,267,094 men.

This is an explanation of the *akshauhini* and of its single parts.

CHAPTER XLIX

A Summary Description Of The Eras

The eras serve to fix certain moments of time which are mentioned in some historical or astronomical connection. The Hindus do not consider it wearisome to reckon with huge numbers, but rather enjoy it. Still, in practical use, they are compelled to replace them by smaller (more handy) ones.

Enumeration of some of the eras of the Hindus

Of their eras we mention—

1. The beginning of the existence of Brahman.

2. The beginning of the day of the present nychthemeron of Brahman, i.e. the beginning of the *kalpa.*

3. The beginning of the seventh *manavantara,* in which we are now.

4. The beginning of the twenty-eighth *caturyuga,* in which we are now.

5. The beginning of the fourth *yuga* of the present *caturyuga,* called *kalikala* i.e. the time of Kali. The whole *yuga* is called after him, though, accurately speaking, *his* time falls only in the last part of the *yuga.* Notwithstanding, the Hindus mean by *kalikala* the beginning of the *kaliyuga.*

6. *Pandava-kala,* i.e. the time of the life and the wars of Bharata.

All these eras vie with each other in antiquity, the one going back to a still more remote beginning than the other, and the sums of years which they afford go beyond hundreds, thousands, and higher orders of numbers. Therefore not only astronomers, but also other people, think it wearisome and unpractical to use them.

The author adopts the year 400 of *Yazdajird* as a test-year

In order to give an idea of these eras, we shall use a first gauge or point of comparison that Hindu year the great bulk of which coincides with the *year* 400 of *Yazdajird.* This number consists only of hundreds, not of units and tens, and by this peculiarity it is distinguished from all other years that might possibly be chosen. Besides, it is a memorable time; for the breaking of the strongest pillar of the religion, the decease of the pattern of a prince, Mahmud, the lion of the world, the wonder of his time—may God have mercy upon him!—took place only a short time, less than a year, before it. The Hindu year precedes the Nauroz or new year's day of this year only by twelve days, and the death of the prince occurred precisely ten complete Persian months before it.

Now, presupposing this our gauge as known, we shall compute the years for this point of junction, which is the beginning of the corresponding Hindu year, for the end of all years which come into question coincides with it, and the Nauroz of the year 400 of *Yazdajird* falls only a little later (viz. twelve days).

[On the basis of extracts from various Indian scriptures and scientific treatises, Al-Biruni calculates the following: (a) how much of the life of Brahman has elapsed, (b) the period of Rama and (c) how much time has elapsed of the current *kaliyuga.*

He goes on to give brief explanatory account of the origin of the following more important and prevalent eras of (1) Sri Harsha, (2) Vikramaditya, (3) Saka, (4) Valabha, and (5) Gupta. [Pp. 2–5].

Era of Sri Harsha

The Hindus believe regarding Sri Harsha that he used to examine the soil in order to see what of hidden treasures was in its interior, as far down as the seventh earth; that, in fact, he found such treasures; and that, in consequence, he could dispense with oppressing his subjects (by taxes, etc). His era is used in Mathura and the country of Kanoj. Between Sri Harsha and Vikramaditya there is an interval of 400 years, as I have been told by some of the inhabitants of that region. However in the Kashmirian calendar I have read that Sri Harsha was 664 years later than Vikramaditya. In face of this discrepancy I am in perfect uncertainty, which to the present moment has not yet been cleared up by any trustworthy information.

Those who use the era of Vikramaditya live in the southern and western parts of India. It is used in the following way: 342 are multiplied by 3, which gives the product 1,026. To this number you add the years which have elapsed of the current *shashtyabda* or sexagesimal *samvatsara,* and the sum is the corresponding year of the era of Vikramaditya. . . .

Era of Sri Vikramaditya

The epoch of the era of Saka or Sakakala falls 135 years later than that of Vikramaditya. The here-mentioned Saka tyrannised over their country between the river Sindh and the ocean, after he had made Aryavarta in the midst of this realm his dwelling-place. He interdicted the Hindus from considering and representing themselves as anything but Sakas. Some maintain that he was a Sudra from the city of Almansura; others maintain that he was not a Hindu at all, and that he had come to India from the west. The Hindus had much to suffer from him, till at last they received help from the east, when Vikramaditya marched against him, put him to fight and killed him in the region of Karur, between Multan and the castle of Loni. Now this date became famous, as people rejoiced in the news of the death of the tyrant, and was used as the epoch of an era, especially by the astronomers. They honour the conqueror by adding Sri to his name, so as to say Sri Vikramaditya. Since there is a long interval between the era which is called the era of Vikramaditya and the killing of Saka, we think that Vikramaditya from whom the era has got its name is not identical with that one who killed Saka, but only a namesake of his.

The Sakakala

The era of Valabha is called so from Valabha, the ruler of the town Valabhi, nearly 30 *yojanas* south of Anhilvara. The epoch of this era falls 241 years later than the epoch of the Saka era. People use it in this way. They first put down the year of the Sakakala, and then subtract from it the cube of 6 and the square of 5 (216 + 25 = 241). The remainder is the year of the Valabha era. The history of Valabha is given in its proper place (cf. chap. xvii).

Era of Valabha

As regards the Guptakala, people say that the Guptas were wicked, powerful people, and that when they ceased to exist this date

Guptakala

was used as the epoch of an era. It seems that Valabha was the last of them, because the epoch of the era of the Guptas falls, like that of the Valabha era, 241 years later than the Sakakala.

Era of the astronomers

The *era of the astronomers* begins 587 years later then the Sakakala. On this era is based the canon *Khanda-khadyaka* by Brahmagupta, which among Muhammadans is known as *Al-arkand*. . . .

On the popular mode of dating by centennia or *samvatsaras*

Common people in India date by the years of a *centennium*, which they call *samvatsara*. If a *centennium* is finished, they drop it, and simply begin to date by a new one. This era is called *lokakala* i.e., the era of the nation at large. But of this era people give such totally different accounts, that I have no means of making out the truth. In a similar manner they also differ among themselves regarding the beginning of the year. On the latter subject I shall communicate what I have heard myself, hoping meanwhile that one day we shall be able to discover a rule in this apparent confusion.

[The different beginnings of the year, as current in the different parts of the country, are given Pp. 8–9].

Popular mode of dating in use among the Hindus and criticisms thereon

I have already before excused myself on account of the imperfection of the information given in this chapter. For we cannot offer a strictly scientific account of the eras to which it is devoted, simply because in them we have to reckon with periods of time far exceeding a *centennium*, and because all tradition of events farther back than a hundred years is confused. . . .

Origin of the dynasty of the Shahs of Kabul

The Hindus had kings residing in Kabul; Turks who were said to be of Tibetan origin. The first of them, Barhatakin, came into the country and entered a cave in Kabul, which none could enter except by creeping on hands and knees. The cave had water, and besides he deposited their victuals for a certain number of days. It is still known in our time, and is called *Var*. People who consider the name of Barhatakin as a good omen enter the cave, and bring out some of its water with great trouble.

Certain troops of peasants were working before the door of the cave. Tricks of this kind can only be carried out and become notorious, if their author has made a secret arrangement with somebody else—in fact, with confederates. Now these had induced persons to work there continually day and night in turns, so that the place was never empty of people.

Some days after he had entered the cave, he began to creep out of it in the presence of the people, who looked on him as a new-born baby. He wore Turkish dress, a short tunic open in front, a high hat, boots and arms. Now people honoured him as a being of miraculous origin, who had been destined to be king and in fact he brought those countries under his sway and ruled them under the title of a *shahiya of Kabul.* The rule remained among his descendants for generations, the number of which is said to be about sixty.

Unfortunately the Hindus do not pay much attention to the historical order of things, they are very careless in relating the chronological succession of their kings, and when they are pressed for information and are at a loss, not knowing what to say, they invariably take to tale-telling. But for this, we should communicate to the reader the traditions which we have received from some people among them. I have been told that the pedigree of this royal family, written on silk, exists in the fortress *Nagarkot,* and I much desired to make myself acquainted with it, but the thing was impossible for various reasons.

[There follows a story about how one of the rulers of this dynasty, Kanik, 'who is said to have built the *vihara* of Purushavar' was imprisoned and displaced by his Vazir. 'After him' ruled the Brahman kings.]

The last king of this race was *Lagaturman,* and his Vazir was Kallar, a Brahman. The latter had been fortunate, insofar as he had found by accident hidden treasures, which gave him much influence and power. In consequence, the last king of this Tibetan house, after it had held the royal power for so long a period, let it by degrees slip from his hands. Besides, Lagaturman had bad manners and a worse behaviour, on account of which people complained of him greatly to the Vazir. Now the Vazir put him in chains and imprisoned him for correction, but then he himself found ruling sweet, his riches enabled him to carry out his plans, and so he occupied the royal throne. After him

End of the Tibetan dynasty, and origin of the Brahman dynasty ruled the Brahman kings Samand[36] (Samanta), Kamalu, Bhim (Bhima), Jaipal (Jayapala), Anandapala, Tarojanapala (Trilocana-pala). The latter was killed A.H. 412 (A.D. 1021), and his son Bhimapala five years later (A.D. 1026).

This Hindu Shahiya dynasty is now extinct, and of the whole house there is no longer the slightest remnant in existence. We must say that, in all their grandeur, they never slackened in the ardent desire of doing that which is good and right, that they were men of noble sentiment and noble bearing. I admire the following passage in a letter of Anandapala, which he wrote to the prince Mahmud, when the relations between them were already strained to the utmost: "I have learned that the Turks have rebelled against you and are spreading in Khurasan. If you wish, I shall come to you with 5,000 horsemen, 10,000 foot-soldiers, and 100 elephants, or, if you wish, I shall send you my son with double the number. In acting thus, I do not speculate on the impression which this will make on you. I have been conquered by *you*, and therefore I do not wish that another man should conquer you."

The same prince cherished the bitterest hatred against the Muhammadans from the time when his son was made a prisoner, whilst his son Tarojanapala (Trilocanapala) was the very opposite of his father.

CHAPTER L

How Many Star-Cycles There Are Both In A "Kalpa" And In A "Caturyuga"

It is one of the conditions of a *kalpa* that in it the planets, with their apsides and nodes, must unite in 0° of Aries, i.e. in the point of the vernal equinox. Therefore each planet makes within a *kalpa* certain number of complete revolutions or cycles.

These star-cycles as known through *the canon* of Alfazari and Ya'kub Ibn Tarik, were derived from a Hindu who came to Bagdad as a member of the political mission which Sindh sent to the Khalif Almansur A.H. 154 (= A.D. 771). If we compare these secondary statements with the primary statements of the Hindus, we discover discrepancies, the cause of which is not known to me. Is their origin due to the translation of Alfazari and Ya'kub? Or to the dictation of that Hindu? Or to the fact that afterwards these computations have been corrected by Brahmagupta, or someone else? For, certainly, any scholar who becomes aware of mistakes in astronomical computations and takes an interest in the subject, will endeavour to correct them, as, e.g. Muhammad Ibn Ishak of Sarakhs has done. . . .

The tradition of Alfazari and Ya'kub Ibn Tarik

Muhammad Ibn Ishak of Sarakhs

Brahmagupta relates a different theory regarding the cycles of the apsides and nodes of the moon, on the authority of Aryabhata. We quote this from Brahmagupta, for we could not read it in the original work of Aryabhata, but only in a quotation in the work of Brahmagupta.

Aryabhatta quoted by Brahmagupta

[A Table showing the names of the planets, the number of their revolutions in a *kalpa,* and the number of the revolutions of their apsides and nodes, is given, p. 16].

. . . Alfazari and Ya'kub sometimes heard from their Hindu master expressions to this effect, that his calculation of the star-cycles was that of *the great Siddhanta, whilst Aryabhata reckoned with one-thousandth part of it.* They apparently did not understand him properly, and imagined that *Aryabhata* (Arab, *arjabhad*) meant *a thousandth part.* The Hindus pronounce the *d* of this word something between a *d* and an *r*. So the consonant became changed to an *r,* and people wrote *arjabhar.* Afterwards it was still more mutilated, the first *r* being changed to a *z,* and so people wrote *azjabhar.* If the word in this garb wanders back to the Hindus, they will not recognise it. . . .

Transformation of the word Aryabhatta among the Arabs

CHAPTER LI

An Explanation Of The Terms "Adhimasa" "Unaratra", And The "Aharganas", As Representing Different Sums Of Days

The months of the Hindus are lunar, their years solar; therefore their new year's day must in each solar year fall by so much earlier as the lunar year is shorter than the solar (roughly speaking, by eleven days). If this precession makes up one complete month, they act in the same way as the Jews, who make the year a leap year of thirteen months by reckoning the month Adar twice, and in a similar way to the heathen Arabs, who in a so-called *annus procrastinationis* postponed the new year's day, thereby extending the preceding year to the duration of thirteen months.

On the leap month

The Hindus call the year in which a month is repeated in the common language *malamasa. Mala* means the dirt that clings to the hand. As such dirt is thrown away, thus the leap month is thrown away out of the calculation, and the number of the months of a year remains twelve. However, in the literature the leap month is called *adhimasa*.

That month is repeated within which (it being considered as a solar month) two lunar months finish. If the end of the lunar month coincides with the beginning of the solar month, if, in fact, the former ends before any part of the latter has elapsed, this month is repeated, because the end of the lunar month, although it has not yet run into the new solar, still does no longer form part of the preceding month.

If a month is repeated, the first time it has its ordinary name, whilst the second time they add before the name the word *dura* to distinguish between them. If, e.g. the month *Ashadha* is repeated, the first is called *Ashadha*, the second *Durashadha.* The first month is that which is disregarded in the calculation. The Hindus consider it as unlucky, and do not celebrate any of the festivals in it which they celebrate in the other months. The most unlucky time in this month is that day on which the lunation reaches its end. . . .

As regards *adhimasa*, the word means *the first month*, for AD means *beginning* (i.e. *adi*). In the books of Ya'kub Ibn Tarik and of Alfazari this name is written *Padamasa. Pada* (in the orig. *P-Dh*) means *end,* and it is possible that the Hindus call the leap month by both names; but the reader must be aware that these two authors frequently misspell or disfigure the Indian words, and that there is no reliance on their tradition. I only mention this because Pulisa explains the latter of the *two* months, which are called by the same name, as the supernumerary one.

Explanation of the terms universal or partial months and days

The month, as the time from one conjunction to the following, is one revolution of the moon, which revolves through the ecliptic, but in a course distant from that of the sun. This is the difference between the motions of the two heavenly luminaries, whilst the direction in which they move is the same. If we subtract the revolutions of the sun, i.e. the solar cycles of a *kalpa,* from its lunar cycles, the remainder shows how many more lunar months a *kalpa* has than solar months. All months or days which we reckon as parts of whole *kalpas* we call here *universal*, and all months or days which we reckon as parts of a *kalpa.* e.g. of a *caturyuga,* we call *partial*, for the purpose of simplifying the terminology.

Universal *adhimasa* months

The year has twelve solar months, and likewise twelve lunar months. The lunar is complete with twelve months, whilst the solar year, in consequence of the difference of the two year kinds, has, with the addition of the *adhimasa,* thirteen months. Now evidently the difference between the universal solar and lunar months is represented by these supernumerary months, by which a single year is extended to thirteen months. These, therefore, are the *universal adhimasa* months. . . .

Explanation of the term *unaratra*

Regarding the cause which necessitates the *unaratra,* lit. the days *of the decrease*, we have to consider the following:

If we have one year or a certain number of years, and reckon for each of them twelve months, we get the corresponding number of solar months, and by multiplying the latter by 30, the corresponding number of the solar days. It is evident that lunar months or days of the same period is the same, *plus* an increase which forms one or several *adhimasa* months. If we reduce this increase to *adhimasa* months due to the period of time in question, according to the relation between the universal solar months and the universal *adhimasa* months, and add this to the months or days of the years in question, the sum represents the *partial* lunar days, i.e. those which correspond to the given number of years.

This however, is not what is wanted. What we want is the number of *civil* days of the given number of years which are *less* than the lunar days; for one *civil* day is greater than one *lunar* day. Therefore, in order to find that which is sought, we must subtract something from the number of lunar days, and this element which must be substract-ed is called *unaratra*. . . .

CHAPTER LII

On The Calculation Of "Ahargana" In General That Is, The Resolution Of Years And Months Into Days, And, Vice Versa, The Composition Of Years And Months Out Of Days

The general method of resolution is as follows:—

The complete years are multiplied by 12; to the product are added the months which have elapsed of the current year (and this sum is multiplied by 30); to this product are added the days which have elapsed of the current month. The sum represents the *savanahargana*, i.e. the sum of the partial solar days.

General rule on how to find the *savanahargana*

You write down the number in two places. In the one place you multiply it by 5311, i.e. the number which represents the *universal adhimasa* months. The product you divide by 172,800, i.e. the number which represents the *universal* solar months. The quotient you get, as far as it contains complete days, is added to the number in *the second place,* and the sum represents the *candrahargana*, i.e. the sum of the partial lunar days.

The latter number is again written down in two different places. In the one place you multiply it by 55,739, i.e. the number which represents the *universal unaratra* days, and divide the product by 3,562,220, ie. the number which represents the universal lunar days. The quotient you get, as far as it represents complete days, is subtracted from the number written in the second place, and the remainder is the *savanahargana,* i.e. the sum of *civil* days which we wanted to find.

However, the reader must know that this computation applies to dates in which there are only complete *adhimasa* and *unaratra* days, without any fraction. If, therefore a given number of years commences with the beginning of a *kalpa*, or a *caturyuga*, or a *kaliyuga,* this computation is correct. But if the given years begin with some other time, it may by chance happen that this computation is correct, but possibly, too, it may result in proving the existence of *adhimasa* time, and in that case the computation would not be correct. Also, the reverse of these two eventualities may take place. However, if it is known with what particular moment in the *kalpa, caturyuga,* or *kaliyuga,* a given number of years commences, we use a special method of computation, which we shall hereafter illustrate by some examples.

More detailed rule for the same purpose

[The following points are dicussed in the remaining portion of the chapter: (a) the latter method applied to (i) the *Sakakala* 953, (ii) a *caturyuga,* according to the theory of Pulisa, (b) the method of *ahargana* employed by Aryabhatta and by Ya'qub Ibn Tariq, (c) method for the computation of the *unaratra* days according to Brahmagupta, (d) method for the calculation of *adhimasa* for the years of a *kalpa, caturyuga* or *kaliyuga,* and (e) rules for constructing a chronological date from a certain given number of days, the converse of *ahargana.* Pp. 28–45.]

CHAPTER LIII

On The Ahargana, Or The Resolution Of Years Into Months, According To Special Rules Which Are Adopted In The Calendars For Certain Dates Or Moments Of Time

Method of *ahargana* as applied to special dates

Not all the eras which in the calendars are resolved into days have epochs falling at such moments of time when just an *adhimasa* or *unaratra* happens to be complete. Therefore, the authors of the calendars require for the calculation of *adhimasa* and *unaratra* certain numbers which either must be added or subtracted if the calculation is to proceed in good order. We shall communicate to the reader whatever of these rules we happened to learn by the study of their calendars or astronomical handbooks.

First, we mention the rule of the *Khandakhadyaka,* because this calendar is the best known of all, and preferred by the astronomers to all others.

[Al-Biruni explains the rule of the *Khandakhadyaka,* which work was 'preferred by the astronomers to all others' as also that of some other astronomical works and examines their application to the gauge year adopted by him. Pp. 46–56.]

CHAPTER LIV

On The Computation Of The Mean Places Of The Planets

General method for the determination of the mean place of a planet at any given time

If we know the number of cycles of the planets in a *kalpa* or *caturyuga*, and further know how many cycles have elapsed at a certain moment of time, we also know that the sum-total of the days of the *kalpa* or *caturyuga* stands in the same relation to the sum-total of the cycles as the past days of the *kalpa* or *caturyuga* to the corresponding amount of planetary cycles. The most generally used method is this:—

The past days of the *kalpa* or *caturyuga* are multiplied by the cycles of the planet, or of its apsis, or of its node which it describes in a *kalpa* or *caturyuga*. The product is divided by the sum-total of the days of the *kalpa* or *caturyuga* accordingly as you reckon by the one or the other. The quotient represents complete cycles. These, however, because not wanted, are disregarded.

The remainder which you get by the division is multiplied by 12, and the product is divided by the sum-total of the days of either *kalpa* or *caturyuga* by which we have already once divided. The quotient represents signs of the ecliptic. The remainder of this division is multiplied by 30, and the product divided by the same divisor. The quotient represents degrees. The remainder of this division is multiplied by 60, and is divided by the same divisor. The quotient represents minutes.

This kind of computation may be continued if we want to have seconds and minor values. The quotient represents the place of that planet according to its mean motion, or the place of that apsis or that node which we wanted to find.

[Mentions the method of Pulisa for the same purpose. Also mentions another method used by Brahmagupta and quotes extracts from *Khandakhadyaka, Karanatilaka,* etc. pp 58–60. Al-Biruni concludes by observing that,]

... But these methods are very subtle, and are so numerous, that none of them has obtained any particular authority. Therefore, we refrain from reproducing them, as this would detain us too long and be of no use.

The other methods of the computation of the mean places of the planets and similar calculations have nothing to do with the subject of the present book.

CHAPTER LV

On The Order Of The Planets, Their Distances And Sizes

When speaking of the *lokas,* we have already given quotation from the *Vishnu-Purana* and from the commentary of Patanjali, according to which the place of the sun is in the order of the planets below that of the moon. This is the traditional view of the Hindus. . . .

Traditional view on the sun being below the moon

We shall now give some quotations from the books of this school relating to the sun, the moon and the stars, and we shall combine herewith the views of the astronomers, although of the latter we have only a very slender knowledge.

[Quotes the *Vayu-Purana* regarding the shape of the sun, its heat, light, etc. Pp. 62–64.]

The Hindus believe regarding the bodies of all the stars that they have a globular shape, a watery essence, and that they do not shine, whilst the sun aloft is of fiery essence, self-shining, and *per accidens* illuminates other stars when they stand opposite to him. They reckon, according to eyesight, among the stars also such luminous bodies as in reality are not stars, but the lights

On the nature of the stars

into which those men have been metamorphosed who have received eternal reward from God, and reside in the height of heaven on thrones of crystal. . . .

All the stars are called *tara,* which word is derived from *tarana,* i.e. the passage. The idea is that those saints have *passed* through the wicked world and have reached bliss, and that the stars *pass* through heaven in a circular motion. The word *nakshatra* is limited to the stars of the lunar stations. As, however, all of these are called *fixed stars,* the word *nakshatra* also applies to all the fixed stars; for it means *not increasing and not decreasing.* I for my part am inclined to think that this increasing and decreasing refers to their number and to the distances of the one from the other, but the author of the last-mentioned book (*Vishnu-Dharma*) combines it with their light.

[Quotes from various Indian scriptures regarding the diameters of the planets and the circumference of the fixed stars (pp. 65–66), and observes,]

This is all we have been able to learn of the confused notions of the Hindus regarding these subjects. We shall now pass on to the views of the Hindu astronomers with whom we agree regarding the order of the planets and other topics, viz. that the sun is the middle of the planets, Saturn and the moon their two ends, and that the fixed stars are above the planets. Some of these things have already been mentioned in the preceding chapters. . . .

Views of the Hindu astronomers on the same subjects

Every educated man among the Hindu theologians, and much more so among their astronomers, believes indeed that the moon is below the sun, and even below all the planets.

The only Hindu traditions we have regarding the distances of the stars are those mentioned by Ya'kub Ibn Tarik in his book, *The Composition of the Spheres,* and he had drawn his information from the well-known Hindu scholar who, A.H. 161, accompanied an embassy to Bagdad.

Ya'kub Ibn Tarik on the distances of the stars

[A Table giving the names of the planets and showing their distances from the centre of the earth, their diameters, etc. is given. P. 68.]

It is well-known among all astronomers that there is no possibility of distinguishing between the higher and the lower one of two planets except by means of the *occultation* or the increase of the *parallax.*

On occultation and the parallax

However, the occultation occurs only very seldom. and only the parallax of a single planet, viz. the moon, can be observed. Now the Hindus believe that the motions are equal, but the distances different. The reason why the higher planet moves more slowly than the lower is the greater extension of its sphere (or orbit); and the reason why the lower planet moves more rapidly is that its sphere or orbit is less extended. Thus, e.g. one minute in the sphere of Saturn is equal to 262 minutes in the sphere of the moon. Therefore, the times in which Saturn and the moon traverse the same space are different, whilst their motions are equal.

I have never found a Hindu treatise on this subject, but only numbers relating thereto scattered in various books—numbers which are corrupt.

[In the remaining portion of the chapter, Al-Biruni discusses the following points: (a) radii of the planets or their distances from the earth, (b) diameters of the planets, (c) methods for the computation of the bodies of the sun and the moon at any given time, (d) Brahmagupta's method for the computation of the diameter of the shadow, and (e) the computation of the diameters of the sun and the moon according to some other Indian sources. Pp. 70–80.]

CHAPTER LVI

On The Stations Of The Moon

The Hindus use the lunar stations exactly in the same way as the zodiacal signs. As the ecliptic is, by the zodiacal signs, divided into twelve equal parts, so, by the lunar stations, it is divided into twenty-seven equal parts. Each station occupies 13⅓ degrees, or 800 minutes of the ecliptic. The planets enter into them and leave them again, and wander to and fro through their northern and southern latitudes. The astrologers attribute to each station a special nature, the quality of foreboding events, and other particular characteristic traits, in the same way as they attribute them to the zodiacal signs.

On the twenty-seven lunar stations

The number 27 rests on the fact that the moon passes through the whole ecliptic in 27⅓ days, in which number the fraction of ⅓ may be disregarded. In a similar way, the Arabs determine their lunar stations as beginning with the moon's first becoming visible in the west till her ceasing to be visible in the east. . . .

Lunar stations of the Arabs

However, the Arabs are illiterate people, who can neither write nor reckon. They only rely upon numbers and eyesight. They have no other medium of research than eyesight, and are not able to determine the lunar stations without the fixed stars in them. If the Hindus want to describe the single stations, they agree with the Araḥs regarding certain stars, whilst regarding others they differ from them. On the whole, the Arabs keep near to the moon's path, and use, in describing the stations, only those fixed stars with which the moon either stands in conjunction at certain times, or through the immediate neighbourhood of which she passes.

The Hindus do not strictly follow the same line, but also take into account the various positions of one star with reference to the other, e.g. one star's standing in opposition or in the zenith of another. Besides, they reckon also the Falling Eagle among the stations, so as to get 28.

Whether the Hindus have twenty-seven or twenty-eight lunar stations

It is this which has led our astronomers and the authors of *'anwa* books astray; for they say that the Hindus have twenty-eight lunar stations, but that they leave out one which is always covered by the rays of the sun. Perhaps they may have heard that the Hindus call that station in which the moon is, the *burning one;* that station which it has just left, *the left one after the embrace;* and that station in which she will enter next, *the smoking one.* Some of our Muslim authors have maintained that the Hindus leave out the station *Al-zubana,* and account for it by declaring that the moon's path is *burning* in the end of Libra and the beginning of Scorpio.

All this is derived from one and the same source, viz. their opinion that the Hindus have twenty-eight stations, and that under certain circumstances they drop one. Whilst just the very opposite is the case; they have twenty-seven stations, and under certain circumstances add one. . . .

The Hindus are very little informed regarding the fixed stars. I never came across any one of them who knew the single stars of the lunar stations from eyesight, and was able to point them out to me with his fingers. I have taken the greatest pains to investigate this subject, and to settle most of it by all sorts of comparisons, and have recorded the results of my research in a treatise *on the determination of the lunar stations.* Of their theories on this subject I shall mention as much as I think suitable in the present context. But before that I shall give the positions of the stations in longitude and latitude and their numbers according to the canon *Khandakhadyaka,* facilitating the study of the

Table of the lunar stations taken from the *Khandakhadyaka*

subject by comprehending all details in the following Table:—

[Table is given. Pp. 84–85.]

My remark relating to the confused notions of the Hindus regarding the stars is confirmed, though this is perhaps not apparent to the Hindus themselves, e.g. by the note of Varahamihira regarding *Alsharatan* = Asvini, one of the first-mentioned six stations; for he says that in it observation precedes calculation. Now the two stars of Asvini stand, in our time, in two-thirds of Aries (i.e. between 10° – 20° Aries), and the time of Varahamihira precedes our time by about 526 years. Therefore by whatever theory you may compute the motion of the fixed stars (or precession of the equinoxes), the Asvini did, in his time, certainly not stand in less than one-third of Aries (i.e. they had not come in the precession of the equinoxes farther than to 1° – 10° Aries).

The author criticises Varahamihira's statement

[Al-Biruni also criticises what he regards as the 'scantiness of the knowledge of the Hindus regarding the motion of the fixed stars', and as an example of it he quotes an extract from Varahamihira's *Samhita*. Pp. 88–89.]

CHAPTER LVII

On The Heliacal Risings Of The Stars, And On The Ceremonies And Rites Which The Hindus Practise At Such A Moment

The Hindu method for the computation of the heliacal risings of the stars and the young moon is, as we think, the same as is explained in the *canones* called *Sindhind.* They call the degrees of a star's distance from the sun which are thought necessary for its heliacal rising *kalamsaka.*

How far a star must be distant from the sun in order to become visible

Evidently the stars have, in this respect, been divided into three groups, the first of which seems to comprise the stars reckoned by the Greeks as stars of the first and second magnitude, the second the stars of the third and fourth magnitude, and the third the stars of the fifth and sixth magnitude.

Brahmagupta ought to have given this classification in his emendation of the *Khandakhadyaka,* but he has not done so. He expresses himself in general phrases, and simply mentions 14° distance from the sun as necessary for the heliacal risings of all lunar stations.

[The method for the computation of the heliacal rising of Agastya, i.e. Suhail or Canopus is given; also extracts from Brahmagupta's emendation of the *Khandakhadyaka.* P. 91.]

The book *Samhita* mentions certain sacrifices and ceremonies which are practised at the heliacal risings of various stars. We shall now record them, translating also that which is rather chaff than wheat since we have made it obligatory on ourselves to give the quotations from the books of the Hindus complete and exactly as they are.

On the ceremonies practised at the heliacal rising of certain stars

[Long extracts from Varahamihira's on the heliacal risings of Agastya, Rohini, Svati and Sravana, and the appropriate sacrifices for the occasion. Pp. 92–100.]

CHAPTER LVIII

How Ebb And Flow Follow Each Other In The Ocean

[The chapter begins by quoting the story of King Aurva from the *Matsya-Purana* 'with regard to the cause why the water of the ocean remains as it is.' The king had become very angry with the angels but was later conciliated and advised to throw 'the fire of his wrath' in the ocean. The fire absorbs the water and keeps it from overflowing.

Then follows the story of Prajapati's curse upon moon and its affliction with leprosy. Later, the moon repented and sought Prajapati's favour in getting the trace of the sin wiped off. Prajapati said that it could be done by erecting the shape of the *linga* of Mahadeva as an object of the moon's worship. That was done and the *linga* raised was the stone of Somanath.

Al-Biruni then, in a very rare reference to a political event, mentions the destruction of the Somanath temple by Sultan Mahmud. More important is the reference to the economic basis of the importance of Somanath—it being an important port used by the merchants trading with the people on the eastern African coast and with that of China, Pp. 101–102.]

. . . *soma* means the moon and *natha* means *master,* so that the whole word [Somanath] means *master of the moon.* The image was

The idol of Somanath

destroyed by the Prince Mahmud—may God be merciful to him!—A.H. 416. He ordered the upper part to be broken and the remainder to be transported to his residence, Ghaznin, with all its coverings and trappings of gold, jewels, and embroidered garments. Part of it has been thrown into the hippodrome of the town, together with the *Cakrasvamin*, an idol of bronze, that had been brought from Taneshar. Another part of the idol from Somanath lies before the door of the mosque of Ghaznin, on which people rub their feet to clean them from dirt and wet.

The *linga* is an image of the penis of Mahadeva, as follows:

Origin of the *linga*

[Al-Biruni then interjects a brief account of the origin of the *linga* and the specifications regarding its construction, as given in Varahamihira's *Brihatsamhita.*]

In the south-west of the Sindh country this idol is frequently met with in the houses destined for the worship of the Hindus, but

The worship of the idol of Somanath

Somanath was the most famous of these places. Every day they brought there a jug of Ganges water and a basket of flowers from Kashmir. They believed that the *linga* of Somanath would cure persons of every inveterate illness and heal every desperate and incurable disease.

The reason why in particular Somanath has become so famous is that it was a harbour for seafaring people, and a station for those who went to and fro between Sufala in the country of the Zanj and China.

Now as regards ebb and flow in the Indian Ocean, of which the former is called *bharna* (?), the latter *vuhara* (?), we state that, accord-

Popular belief about the cause of the tides

ing to the notions of the common Hindus, there is a fire called *Vadavanala* in the ocean, which is always blazing. The flow is caused by the fire's drawing breath and its being blown up by the wind, and the ebb is caused by the fire's exhaling the breath and the cessation of its being blown up by the wind.

It is flow and ebb to which Somanath owes its name (i.e. master of the moon); for the stone (or *linga*) of Somanath was originally erected on the coast, a little less than three miles west of the mouth of the river Sarsuti, east of the golden fortress Baroi, which had

Origin of the sacredness of Somanath

appeared as a dwelling-place for Vasudeva, not far from the place where he and his family were killed, and where they were burned. Each time when the moon rises and sets, the water of the ocean rises in the flood so as to cover the place in question. When, then, the moon reaches the meridian of noon and midnight, the water recedes in the ebb, and the place becomes again visible. Thus the moon was perpetually occupied in serving the idol and bathing it. Therefore the place was considered as sacred to the moon. The fortress which contained the idol and its treasures was not ancient, but was built only about a hundred years ago. . . .

CHAPTER LIX

On The Solar And The Lunar Eclipses

It is perfectly known to the Hindu astronomers that the moon is eclipsed by the shadow of the earth, and the sun is eclipsed by the moon. Hereon they have based their computations in the astronomical handbooks and other works.

[Extracts from Varahamihira's *Samhita* are quoted regarding the explanations for the phenomena of solar and lunar eclipses. Varahamihira is quoted as stating that "an eclipse of the moon is her entering the shadow of the earth, and an eclipse of the sun consists in this that the moon covers and hides the sun from us. Therefore the lunar eclipse will never revolve from the west, nor the solar eclipse from the east." Varahamihira also refers to the popular, unscientific notions about the eclipses, and states that, "However, common people are always loud in proclaiming the Head to be the cause of an eclipse, and they say, 'If the Head did not appear and did not bring about the eclipse, the Brahmans would not at that moment undergo an obligatory washing.'", (Pp. 107–09).

Al-Biruni expresses surprise as to why Varahamihira, who by his former explanation had 'already revealed himself to us as a man who accurately knows the shape of the world' was repeating such notions. Perhaps, he did so because he wanted 'to side with the Brahmans, to whom he belonged, and from whom he could not separate himself. Still, he could not be blamed too much, as on the whole, his foot stands firmly on the basis of truth'. . . . p. 110.]

Al-Biruni then refers to the views of Brahmagupta on the eclipses, and quotes the first chapter of *Brahmasiddhanta* as follows:—

Quotation from the *Brahmasiddhanta*

"Some people think that the eclipse is not caused by the Head. This, however, is a foolish idea, for it is *he* in fact who eclipses, and the generality of the inhabitants of the world say that it is the Head who eclipses. The *Veda*, which is the word of God from the mouth of Brahman, says that the Head eclipses, likewise the book *Smriti*, composed by Manu, and the *Samhita*, composed by Garga the son of Brahman. On the contrary, Varahamihira, Srishena, Aryabhatta, and Vishnucandra maintain that the eclipse is not caused by the Head, but by the moon and the shadow of the earth, in direct opposition to all (to the generality of men), and from enmity against the just-mentioned dogma. For if the Head does not cause the eclipse, all the usages of the Brahmans which they practise at the moment of an eclipse, viz. their rubbing themselves with warm oil, and other works of prescribed worship, would be illusory and not be rewarded by heavenly bliss. If a man declares these things to be illusory, he stands outside of the generally acknowledged dogma, and that is not allowed."

[Al-Biruni again expresses surprise as to why Brahmagupta, who was 'certainly one of the most distinguished among their astronomers' was reiterating such unscientific views, and remarks:]

Brahmagupta says, "The generality thinks thus." If he thereby means the totality of the inhabitants of the inhabitable world, we can only say that he would be very little able to investigate *their* opinions either by exact research or by means of historical tradition. For India itself is, in comparison to the whole inhabitable world, only a small matter, and the number of those who differ from the Hindus, both in religion and law, is larger than the number of those who agree with them.

Possible excuses for Brahmagupta

Or, if Brahmagupta means *the generality of the Hindus,* we agree that the uneducated among them are much more numerous than the educated; but we also point out that in all our religious codes of divine revelation the uneducated crowd is blamed as being ignorant, always doubting, and ungrateful.

I, for my part, am inclined to the belief that that which made Brahmagupta speak the above-mentioned words (which involve a sin against conscience) was something of a calamitous fate, like that of Socrates, which had befallen him, notwithstanding the abundance of his knowledge and the sharpness of his intellect and notwithstanding his extreme youth at the time. For he wrote the *Brahmasiddhanta* when he was only thirty years of age. If this indeed is his excuse, we accept it, and herewith drop the matter. . . .

[Al-Biruni also suggests a little earlier that Brahmagupta was presenting such an unscientific explanation probably because, as a Brahman, he was supporting the popular notions preached by them. Or, maybe, by repeating those silly ideas he was mocking the men who advocated them!].

CHAPTER LX

On The Parvan

The intervals between which an eclipse may happen and the number of their lunations are sufficiently demonstrated in the sixth chapter of Almagest. The Hindus call a period of time at the beginning and end of which there occur lunar eclipses, *parvan.*

Explanation of the term *parvan*

[Some information on the subject is quoted from Varahamihira's *Samhita,* and a Table showing the cycle of eclipses and the 'particular *dominant* and prognostics' of each one of them is given. On the latter point, Al-Biruni comments that what Varahamihira says of the astrological portents of the *parvans* does not 'well suit his deep learning.'

Rules for the computation of the *parvan* are quoted from the *Khandakhadyaka.* Pp. 115–117.]

CHAPTER LXI

On The Dominants Of The Different Measures Of Time In Both Religious And Astronomical Relations, And On Connected Subjects

Which of the different measures of time have dominants and which not

Duration, or time in general, only applies to the Creator as being *his* age, and not determinable by a beginning and an end. In fact, it is his eternity. They frequently call it *the soul*, i.e. *Purusha*. But as regards common time, which is determinable by motion, the single parts of it apply to beings beside the Creator, and to natural phenomena beside *the soul*. Thus *Kalpa* is always used in relation to Brahman, for it is his day and night, and his life is determined by it.

Each *manavantara* has a special dominant called *Manu*, who is described by special qualities, already mentioned in a former chapter. On the other hand, I have never heard anything of dominants of the *caturyugas* or *yugas*.

[Al-Biruni mentions the rules for the computation of the dominant of the year and the month, as given in the *Khandakhadyaka*, 'the most universally used among them.' Also gives Tables showing the dominants of the planets according to *Vishnu-Dharma*. Pp. 119–122.]

CHAPTER LXII

On The Sixty Years—Samvatsara, Also Called "Shashtyabda"

The word *samavatsara,* which means *the years,* is a technical term for cycles of years constructed on the basis of the revolutions of Jupiter and the sun, the heliacal rising of the former being reckoned as the beginning. It revolves in sixty years, and is therefore called *shashtyabda,* i.e. sixty years. . . .

Explanation of the terms *samvatsara* and *shashtyabda*

The great *yugas* begin with the heliacal rising of Jupiter in the beginning of the station Dhanishtha and the beginning of the month Magha. The small *yugas* have within the great ones a certain order, being divided into groups which comprehend certain numbers of years, and each of which has a special dominant. This division is represented by the following Table. . . .

Smaller cycles as contained in the cycle of sixty years

[Table given on p. 125.]

Further, every single one of the sixty years has a name of its own, and the *yugas*, too, have names which are the names of their dominants. All these names are exhibited in the following Table.

The names of the single years of a *samvatsara*

This Table is to be used in the same way as the preceding one, as you find the name of each year of the whole cycle (of sixty years) under the corresponding number. It would be a lengthy affair if we were to explain the meanings of the single names and their prognostics. All this is found in the book *Samhita.*

[Table given on pp. 127–28.]

When I heard, among these pretended names of *samvastras,* names of nations, trees, and mountains, I conceived a suspicion of my reporters, more particularly as their chief business was indeed to practise hocus-pocus and deception (as jugglers ?); . . . I used great care in examining every single one of them, in repeating the same questions at different times, in a different order and context. But lo! what different answers did I get! God is all-wise!

CHAPTER LXIII

On That Which Especially Concerns The Brahmans, And What They Are Obliged To Do During Their Whole Life

The life of the Brahman, after seven years of it have passed, is divided into four parts. The first part begins with the eighth year, when the Brahmans come to him to instruct him, to teach him his duties, and to enjoin him to adhere to them and to embrace them as long as he lives. Then they bind a girdle round his waist and invest him with a pair of *yajnopavitas,* i.e. one strong cord consisting of nine single cords which are twisted together, and with a third *yajnopavita,* a single one made from cloth. This girdle runs from the left shoulder to the right hip. Further, he is presented with a stick which he has to wear, and with a seal-ring of a certain grass, called *darbha,* which he wears on the ring-finger of the right hand. This seal-ring is also called *pavitra.* The object of his wearing the ring on the ring-finger of his right hand is this, that it should be a good omen and a blessing for all those who receive gifts from that hand. The obligation for wearing the ring is not quite so stringent as that of wearing the *yajnopavita,* for from the latter he is not to separate himself under any circumstances whatever. If he takes it off while

First period in the Brahman's life

works of piety, giving alms and receiving them. For that which the Brahmans give reverts to the *pitaras* (is in reality a benefit to the *Fathers*). He must continually read, perform the sacrifices, take care of the fire which he lights, offer before it, worship it, and preserve it from being extinguished, that he may be burned by it after his death. It is called *homa.*

The duties of Brahmans in general

Every day he must wash himself thrice: at the *samdhi* of rising, i.e. morning dawn, at the *samdhi* of setting, i.e. evening twilight, and between them in the middle of the day. The first washing is on account of sleep, because the openings of the body have become lax during it. Washing is a cleansing from accidental impurity and a preparation for prayer.

Their prayer consists of praise, glorification, and prostration according to their peculiar manner, viz. prostrating themselves on the two thumbs, whilst the two palms of the hands are joined, and they turn their faces towards the sun. For the sun is their *kibla,* wherever he may be, except when in the south. For they do not perform any work of piety with the face turned southward; only when occupied with something evil and unlucky they turn themselves towards the south.

The time when the sun declines from the meridian (the afternoon) is well suited for acquiring in it a heavenly reward. Therefore at this time the Brahman must clean.

The evening is the time of supper and of prayer. The Brahman may take his supper and pray without having previously washed himself. Therefore, evidently, the rule as to the third washing is not as stringent as that relating to the first and second washings.

A nightly washing is obligatory for the Brahman only at the times of eclipses, that he should be prepared to perform the rules and sacrifices prescribed for that occasion.

The Brahman, as long as he lives, eats only twice a day, at noon and at nightfall; and when he wants to take his meal, he begins by putting aside as much as is sufficient for one or two men as alms, especially for strange Brahmans who happen to come at evening-time asking for something. To neglect *their* maintenance would be a great sin. Further, he puts something aside for the cattle, the birds, and the fire. Over the remainder he says prayers and eats it. The remainder of his dish he places outside his house, and does not any more come near it, as it is no longer allowable for him, being destined for the chance passer-by who wants it, be he a man, bird, dog, or something else.

The Brahman must have a water-vessel for himself. If another one uses it, it is broken. The same remark applies to his eating-instruments. I have seen Brahmans who allowed their relatives to eat with them from the same plate, but most of them disapprove of this.

He is obliged to dwell between the river Sindh in the north and the river Carmanvati in the south. He is not allowed to cross either of these frontiers so as to enter the country of the Turks or of the Karnata. Further, he must live between the ocean in the east and west. People say that he is not allowed to stay in a country in which the grass which he wears on the ring-finger does not grow, nor the black-haired gazelles graze. This is a description for the whole country within the just-mentioned boundaries. If he passes beyond them he commits a sin.

In a country where not the whole spot in the house which is prepared for people to eat upon it is plastered with clay, where they, on the contrary, prepare a separate tablecloth for each person eating by pouring water over a spot and plastering it with the dung of cows, the shape of the Brahman's tablecloth must be square. Those who have the custom of preparing such tablecloths give the following as the cause of this custom:—The spot of eating is soiled by the eating. If the eating is finished, the spot is washed and plastered to become clean again. If, now, the soiled spot is not distinguished by a separate mark, you would suppose also the other spots to be soiled, since they are similar to and cannot be distinguished from each other.

Five vegetables are forbidden to them by the religious code:—Onions, garlic, a kind of gourd, the root of a plant like the carrots called *krncn* (?), and another vegetable which grows round their tanks called *nali.*

CHAPTER LXV

On The Sacrifices

Most of the Veda treats of the sacrifices to the fire, and describes each one of them. They are different in extent, so that certain of them can only be performed by the greatest of their kings. So, e.g. the *asvamedha*. A mare[37] is let freely to wander about in the country grazing, without anybody's hindering her. Soldiers follow her, drive her, and cry out before her: "She is the king of the world. He who does not agree, let him come forward." The Brahmans walk behind her and perform sacrifices to the fire where she castes dung. When she thus has wandered about through all parts of the world, she becomes food for the Brahmans and for him whose property she is.

Asvamedha

Further, the sacrifices differ in duration, so that only he could perform certain of them who lives a very long life; and such long lives do no longer occur in this our age. Therefore most of them have been abolished, and only few of them remain and are practised nowadays.

According to the Hindus, the fire eats everything. Therefore it becomes defiled, if anything unclean is mixed up with it, as e.g.

On fire-offerings in general

water. Accordingly they are very punctilious regarding fire and water if they are in the hands of non-Hindus, because they are defiled by being touched by them.

That which the fire eats for its share, reverts to the Devas, because the fire comes out of their mouths. What the Brahmans present to the fire to eat is oil and different cereals—wheat, barley, and rice—which they throw into the fire. Further, they recite the prescribed texts of the Veda in case they offer on their own behalf. However, if they offer in the name of somebody else, they do not recite anything.

[The story of the fire becoming leprous is narrated from the *Vishnu-Dharma.* Pp. 140–141.]

That which makes people do these things is usage and custom. However, religious commands are much more powerful, and influence much more the nature of man than usages and customs. The bases of the latter are investigated, explored, and accordingly either kept or abandoned, whilst the bases of the religious commands are left as they are, not inquired into, adhered to by the majority simply on *trust*. They do not argue over them, as the inhabitants of some sterile region do not argue over it, since they are born in it and do not know anything else, for they love the country as their fatherland, and find it difficult to leave it. If, now, besides physical differences, the countries differ from each other also in law and religion, there is so much attachment to it in the hearts of those who live in them that it can never be rooted out."

The Hindus have some places which are venerated for reasons connected with their law and religion, e.g. Benares (Baranasi). For their anchorites wander to it and stay there for ever, as the dwellers of the Ka'ba stay for ever in Mekka. They want to live there to the end of their lives, that their reward after death should be the better for it. They say that a murderer is held responsible for his crime and punished with a punishment due to his guilt, except in case he enters the city of Benares, where he obtains pardon. . . .

On Benares as an asylum

Another place of this kind is Taneshar, also called *Kurukshetra,* i.e. the land of Kuru, who was a peasant, a pious, holy man, who worked miracles by divine power. Therefore, the country was called after him, and venerated for his sake. Besides, Taneshar is the theatre of the exploits of Vasudeva in the wars of Bharata and of the destruction of the evil-doers. It is for this reason that people visit the place.

Mahura, too, is a holy place, crowded with Brahmans. It is venerated because Vasudeva was there born and brought up, in a place in the neighbourhood called *Nandagola.*

Nowadays the Hindus also visit Kashmir. Lastly, they used to visit Multan before its idol-temple was destroyed.

CHAPTER LXVII

On Alms, And How A Man Must Spend What He Earns

It is obligatory with them every day to give alms as much as possible. They do not let money become a year or even a month old, for this would be a draft on an unknown future, of which a man does not know whether he reaches it or not.

With regard to that which he earns by the crops or from the cattle, he is bound first to pay the ruler of the country the tax which attaches to the soil or the pasture-ground. Further, he pays him one-sixth of the income in recognition of the protection which he affords to the subjects, their property, and their families. The same obligation rests also on the common people, but they will always lie and cheat in the declarations about their property. Further, trading businesses,too, pay a tribute for the same reason. Only the Brahmans are exempt from all these taxes.

As to the way in which the remainder of the income, after the taxes have been deducted, is to be employed, there are different opinions. Some destine one-ninth of it for alms. For they divide it into three parts. One of them is kept in reserve to guarantee the heart against anxiety. The second is spent on trade to bring profit, and one-third of the third portion (i.e. one-ninth of the whole) is spent on

Why the meat of cows was forbidden

Some Hindus say that in the time before Bharata it was allowed to eat the meat of cows, and thai there then existed sacrifices part of which was the killing of cows. After that time, however, it had been forbidden on account of the weakness of men, who were too weak to fulfil their duties, as also the Veda, which originally was only one, was afterwards divided into four parts, simply for the purpose of facilitating the study of it to men. This theory, however, is very little substantiated, as the prohibition of the meat of cows is not an alleviating and less strict measure, but, on the contrary, one which is more severe and more restrictive than the former law.

Other Hindus told me that the Brahmans used to suffer from the eating of cows' meat. For their country is hot, the inner parts of the bodies are cold, the natural warmth becomes feeble in them, and the power of digestion is so weak that they must strengthen it by eating the leaves of *betel* after dinner, and by chewing the betel-nut. The hot betel inflames the heat of the body, the chalk on the betel-leaves dries up everything wet, and the betel-nut acts as an astringent on the teeth, the gums, and the stomach. As this is the case, they forbade eating cows' meat, because it is essentially thick and cold.

I, for my part, am uncertain, and hesitate in the question of the origin of this custom between two different views.

(*Lacuna in the manuscript*)

As for the economical reason, we must keep in mind that the cow is the animal which serves man in travelling by carrying his loads, in agriculture in the works of ploughing and sowing, in the household by the milk and the product made thereof. Further, man makes use of its dung, and in winter-time even of its breath. Therefore it was forbidden to eat cows' meat; as also Alhajjaj forbade it, when people complained to him that 'Babylonia became more and more desert. . . .'

CHAPTER LXIX

On Matrimony, The Menstrual Courses, Embryos, And Childbed

No nation can exist without a regular married life, for it prevents the uproar of passions abhorred by the cultivated mind, and it removes all those causes which excite the animal to a fury always leading to harm. Considering the life of the animals by pairs, how the one member of the pair helps the other, and how the lust of other animals of the same species is kept aloof from them, you cannot help declaring matrimony to be a necessary institution; whilst disorderly cohabitation or harlotry on the part of man is a shameful proceeding, that does not even attain to the standing of the development of animals, which in every other respect stand far below him.

Necessity of matrimony

Every nation has particular customs of marriage, and especially those who claim to have a religion and law of divine origin. The Hindus marry at a very young age; therefore the parents arrange the marriage for their sons. On that occasion the Brahmans perform the rites of the sacrifices, and they as well as others receive alms. The implements of the wedding rejoicings are brought forward. No gift is settled between them. The man gives

Law of marriage

only a present to the wife, as he thinks fit, and a marriage gift in advance, which he has no right to claim back, but the wife may give it back to him of her own will. Husband and wife can only be separated by death, as they have no divorce.

A man may marry one to four wives. He is not allowed to take more than four; but if one of his wives die, he may take another one to complete the legitimate number. However, he must not go beyond it.

The widow

If a wife loses her husband by death, she cannot marry another man. She has only to choose between two things—either to remain a widow as long as she lives or to burn herself; and the latter eventuality is considered the preferable, because as a widow she is ill-treated as long as she lives. As regards the wives of the kings, they are in the habit of burning them, whether they wish it or not, by which they desire to prevent any of them by chance committing something unworthy of the illustrious husband. They make an exception only for women of advanced years and for those who have children, for the son is the responsible protector of his mother.

Forbidden degrees of marriage

According to their marriage law it is better to marry a stranger than a relative. The more distant the relationship of a woman with regard to her husband the better. It is absolutely forbidden to marry related women both of the direct *descending* line, viz. a grand-daughter or great-grand-daughter, and of the direct *ascending* line, viz. a mother, grandmother, or great-grandmother. It is also forbidden to marry collateral relations, viz. a sister, a niece, a maternal or paternal aunt and their daughters, except in case the couple of relations who want to marry each other be removed from each other by five consecutive generations. In that case the prohibition is waived, but, notwithstanding, such a marriage is an object of dislike to them.

Number of wives

Some Hindus think that the number of the wives depends upon the caste; that, accordingly, a Brahman may take four, a Kshatriya three, a Vaisya two wives, and a Sudra one. Every man of a caste may marry a woman of his own caste or one of the castes or caste below his; but nobody is allowed to marry a woman of a caste superior to his own.

The child belongs to the caste of the mother, not to that of the father. Thus, e.g. if the wife of a Brahman is a Brahman, her child also is a Brahman; if she is a Sudra, her child is a Sudra. In our time, however, the Brahmans, although it is allowed to them, never marry any woman except one of their own caste.

Portus sequitur ventrem

The longest duration of the menstrual courses which has been observed is sixteen days, but in reality they last only during the first four days, and then the husband is not allowed to cohabit with his wife, nor even to come near her in the house, because during this time she is impure. After the four days have elapsed and she has washed, she is pure again, and the husband may cohabit with her, even if the blood has not yet entirely disappeared; for this blood is not considered as that of the menstrual courses, but as the same substance-matter of which the embryos consist.

Duration of the menstrual courses

It is the duty (of the Brahman), if he wants to cohabit with a wife to get a child, to perform a sacrifice to the fire called *garbhadhana;* but he does not perform it, because it requires the presence of the woman, and therefore he feels ashamed to do so. In consequence he postpones the sacrifice and unites it with the next following one, which is due in the fourth month of the pregnancy, called *simamtonnayanam.* After the wife has given birth to the child, a third sacrifice is performed between the birth and the moment when the mother begins to nourish the child. It is called *jatakarman.*

On pregnancy and childbed

The child receives a name after the days of the childbed have elapsed. The sacrifice for the occasion of the name-giving is called *namakarman.*

As long as the woman is in childbed, she does not touch any vessel, and nothing is eaten in her house, nor does the Brahman light there a fire. These days are eight for the Brahman, twelve for the Kshatriya, fifteen for the Vaisya, and thirty for the Sudra. For the low-caste people which are not reckoned among any caste, no term is fixed.

The longest duration of the suckling of the child is three years, but there is no obligation in this matter. The sacrifice on the occasion of the first cutting of the child's hair is offered in the third, the perforation of ear takes place in the seventh and eighth years.

People think with regard to harlotry that it is allowed with them.

On the causes of prostitution

Thus, when Kabul was conquered by the Muslim and the Ispahbad of Kabul adopted Islam, he stipulated that he should not be bound to eat cows' meat nor to commit sodomy (which proves that he abhorred the one as much as the other). In reality, the matter is not as people think, but it is rather this, that the Hindus are not very severe in punishing whoredom. The fault, however, in this lies with the kings, not with the nation. But for this, no Brahman or priest would suffer in their idol-temples the women who sing, dance, and play. The kings make them an attraction for their cities, a bait of pleasure for their subjects, for no other but financial reasons. By the revenues which they derive from the business both as fines and taxes, they want to recover the expenses which their treasury has to spend on the army.

In a similar way the Buyide prince Adud-aldaula acted, who besides also had a second aim in view, viz. that of protecting his subjects against the passions of his unmarried soldiers.

CHAPTER LXX

On Lawsuits

The judge demands from the suitor a document written against the accused person in a well-known writing which is thought suitable for writs of the kind, and in the document the well-established proof of the justice of his suit. In case there is no written document the contest is settled by means of witnesses without a written document.

On procedure

The witnesses must not be less than four, but there may be more. Only in case the justice of the deposition of a witness is perfectly established and certain before the judge, he may admit it, and decide the question alone on the basis of the deposition of this sole witness. However, he does not admit prying about in secret, deriving arguments from mere signs or indications in public, concluding by analogy from one thing which seems established about another, and using all sorts of tricks to elicit the truth, as 'Iyas Ibn Muawiya used to do.

Number of witnesses

If the suitor is not able to prove his claim, the defendant must swear, but he may also tender the oath to the suitor by saying, "Swear thou that thy claim is true and I will give thee what thou claimest."

There are many kinds of the oath, in accordance with the value of the object of the claim. If the object is of no great importance, and the suitor agrees that the accused person shall swear, the latter simply swears before five learned Brahmans in the following words: "If I lie, he shall have as recompense as much of my goods as is equal to the eightfold of the amount of his claim."

Different kinds of oaths and ordeals

[Some other kinds of oaths and ordeals are described. These included the methods of (i) asking the accused person to take a poisonous drink, (ii) throwing him in a river, and (iii) putting a red-hot piece of iron in his hand. If he was not a culprit he would remain unharmed in all these cases. Pp. 159–160.]

CHAPTER LXXI

On Punishments And Expiations

In this regard the manners and customs of the Hindus resemble those of the Christians, for they are, like those of the latter, based on the principles of virtue and abstinence from wickedness, such as never to kill under any circumstance whatsoever, to give to him who has stripped you of your coat also your shirt, to offer to him who has beaten your cheek the other cheek also, to bless your enemy and to pray for him. Upon my life, this is a noble philosophy; but the people of this world are not all philosophers. Most of them are ignorant and erring, who cannot be kept on the straight road save by the sword and the whip.

The Brahmans originally the rulers of the nation

India has developed in a similar way. For the Hindus relate that originally the affairs of government and war were in the hands of the Brahmans, but the country became disorganised, since they ruled according to the philosophic principles of their religious codes, which proved impossible when opposed to the mischievous and perverse elements of the populace. They were even near losing also the administration of their religious affairs. Therefore, they humiliated themselves before the lord of their religion. Whereupon Brahman entrusted them exclusively with the functions which they now have, whilst he entrusted the Kshatriyas with the duties of ruling and fighting. Ever since the Brahmans live by asking and begging, and the penal code is exercised under the control of the kings, not under that of the scholars.

The law about murder is this: If the murderer is a Brahman, and the murdered person a member of another caste, he is only bound to do expiation consisting of fasting, prayers, and alms-giving.

Law of murder

If the murdered person is a Brahman, the Brahman murderer has to answer for it in a future life; for he is not allowed to do expiation, because expiation wipes off the sin from the sinner, whilst nothing can wipe off any of the mortal crimes from a Brahman, of which the greatest are: the murder of a Brahman, called *vajrabrahmahatya;* further, the killing of a cow, the drinking of wine, whoredom, especially with the wife of one's own father and teacher. However, the kings do not for any of these crimes kill a Brahman or Kshatriya, but they confiscate his property and banish him from their country.

If a man of a caste under those of the Brahman and Kshatriya kills a man of the same caste, he has to do expiation, but besides the kings inflict upon him a punishment in order to establish an example.

The law of theft directs that the punishment of the thief should be in accordance with the value of the stolen object. Accordingly, sometimes a punishment of extreme or of middling severity is necessary, sometimes a course of correction and imposing a payment, sometimes only exposing to public shame and ridicule. If the object is very great, the kings blind a Brahman and mutilate him cutting off his left hand and right foot, or the right hand and left foot, whilst they mutilate a Kshatriya without blinding him, and kill thieves of the other castes.

Law of theft

An adulteress is driven out of the house of the husband and banished.

Punishment of an adulteress

I have repeatedly been told that when Hindu slaves (in Muslim countries) escape and return to their country and religion, the Hindus order that they should fast by way of expiation, then they bury them in the dung, stale, and milk of cows for a certain number of days, till they get into a state of fermentation. Then they drag them out of the dirt and give them similar dirt to eat, and more of the like.

Hindu prisoners of war, how treated after returning to their country

I have asked the Brahmans if this is true, but they deny it, and maintain that there is no expiation possible for such an individual, and that he is never allowed to return into those conditions of life in which he was before he was carried off as a prisoner. And how should that be possible? If a Brahman eats in the house of a Sudra for sundry days, he is expelled from his caste and can never regain it.

CHAPTER LXXII

On Inheritance, And What Claim The Deceased Person Has On It

The chief rule of their law of inheritance is this, that women do not inherit, except the daughter. She gets the fourth part of the share of a son, according to a passage in the book *Manu.* If she is not married, the money is spent on her till the time of her marriage, and her dowry is bought by means of her share. Afterwards she has no more income from the house of her father.

Law of inheritance

If a widow does not burn herself, but prefers to remain alive, the heir of her deceased husband has to provide her with nourishment and clothing as long as she lives.

The debts of the deceased must be paid by his heir, either out of his share or of the stock of his own property, no regard being had whether the deceased has left any property or not. Likewise he must bear the just-mentioned expenses for the widow in any case whatsoever.

As regards the rule about the male heirs, evidently the descendants, i.e. the son and grandson, have a nearer claim to the inheritance than the ascendants, i.e. the father and grandfather. Further, as regards the single relatives among the descendants as well as the ascendants, the nearer a man is related, the more claim he has on inheriting. Thus a son has a nearer claim than a grandson, a father than a grandfather.

The collateral relations, as, e.g. the brothers, have less claim, and inherit only in case there is nobody who has a better claim. Hence it is evident that the son of a daughter has more claim than the son of a sister, and that the son of a brother has more claim than either of them.

If there are several claimants of the same degree of relationship, as, e.g. sons or brothers, they all get equal shares. A hermaphrodite is reckoned as a male being.[38]

If the deceased leaves no heir, the inheritance falls to the treasury of the king, except in the case that the deceased person was a Brahman. In that case the king has no right to meddle with the inheritance, but it is exclusively spent on alms-giving.

Duties of the heir towards the deceased

The duty of the heir towards the deceased in the first year consists in his giving sixteen banquets, where every guest in addition to his food receives alms also, viz. on the fifteenth and sixteenth days after death; further, once a month during the whole year. The banquet in the sixth month must be more rich and more liberal than the others. Further, on the last but one day of the year, which banquet is devoted to the deceased and his ancestors; and finally, on the last day of the year. With the end of the year the duties towards the deceased have been fulfilled.

If the heir is a son, he must during the whole year wear mourning dress; he must mourn and have no intercourse with women, if he is a legitimate child and of a good stock. Besides, you must know that nourishment is forbidden to the heirs for one single day in the first part of the mourning-year.

Besides the almsgiving at the just-mentioned sixteen banquets, the heirs must make, above the door of the house, something like a shelf projecting from the wall in the open air, on which they have every day to place a dish of something cooked and vessel of water, till the end of ten days after the death. For possibly the spirit of the deceased has not yet found its rest, but moves still to and fro around the house, hungry and thirsty.

Parallel from Plato

A similar view is indicated by Plato in *Phaedo,* where he speaks of the soul circling round the graves, because possibly it still retains some vestiges of the love for the body. . . .

On the tenth of the last-mentioned days, the heir spends, in the name of the deceased, much food and cold water. After the eleventh day, the heir sends every day sufficient food for a single person and a *dirham* to the house of the Brahman, and continues doing this during all the days of the mourning-year without any interruption until its end.

CHAPTER LXXIII

About What Is Due To The Bodies Of The Dead And Of The Living (i.e. About Burying And Suicide)

Primitive burial customs

In the most ancient times the bodies of the dead were exposed to the air by being thrown on the fields without any covering; also sick people were exposed on the fields and in the mountains, and were left there. If they died there, they had the fate just mentioned; but if they recovered, they returned to their dwellings.

Thereupon there appeared a legislator who ordered people to expose their dead to the wind. In consequence they constructed roofed buildings with walls of rails, through which the wind blew, passing over the dead, as something similar is the case in the grave-towers of the Zoroastrians.

After they had practised this custom for a long time, Narayana prescribed to them to hand the dead over to the fire, and ever since they are in the habit of burning them, so that nothing remains of them, and every defilement, dirt, and smell is annihilated at once, so as scarcely to leave any trace behind. . . .

[Greek parallels are referred to. The ancient Greeks 'had both customs, that of burning and that of burying'.]

. . . In a similar way the Hindus express themselves. There is a point in man by which he is what he is. This point becomes free when the mixed elements of the body are dissolved and scattered by combustion.

Regarding this return (of the immortal soul to God), the Hindus think that partly it is effected by the rays of the sun, the soul attaching itself to them and ascending with them, partly by the flame of the fire, which raises it (to God). Some Hindus used to pray that God would make his road to himself as a straight line, because this is the nearest road, and that there is no other road upwards save the fire or the ray.

Fire and the sunbeam as the nearest roads to God

Similar to this is the practice of the Ghuzz Turks with reference to a drowned person; for they place the body on a bier in the river, and make a cord hang down from his foot, throwing the end of the cord into the water. By means of this cord the spirit of the deceased is to raise himself for resurrection. . . .

People relate that Buddha had ordered the bodies of the dead to be thrown into flowing water. Therefore his followers, the Shamanians, throw their dead into the rivers.

According to the Hindus, the body of the dead has the claim upon his heirs that they are to wash, embalm, wrap it in a shroud, and then to burn it with as much sandal and other wood as they can get. Part of his burned bones are brought to the Ganges and thrown into it, that the Ganges should flow over them, as it has flowed over the burned bones of the children of Sagara, thereby forcing them from hell and bringing them into paradise. The remainder of the ashes is thrown into some brook of running water. On the spot where the body has been burned they raise a monument similar to a milestone, plastered with gypsum.

Hindu manner of burial

The bodies of children under three years are not burned.

Those who fulfil these duties towards the dead afterwards wash themselves as well as their dresses during two days, because they have become unclean by touching the dead.

Those who cannot afford to burn their dead will either throw them somewhere on the open field or into running water.

Now as regards the right of the body of the living, the Hindus would not think of burning it save in the case of a widow who chooses to follow her husband, or in the case of those who are tired of their life, who are distressed over some incurable disease of their body, some irremovable bodily defect, or old age and infirmity. This, however, no man of distinction does, but only Vaisyas and Sudras, especially at those times which are prized as the most suitable for a man to acquire in them, for a future repetition of life, a better form and condition than that in which he happens to have been born and to live. Burning oneself is forbidden to Brahmans and Kshatriyas by a special law. Therefore these, if they want to kill themselves, do so at the time of an eclipse in some other manner, or they hire somebody to drown them in the Ganges, keeping them under water till they are dead.

Modes of suicide

At the junction of the two rivers, Yamuna and Ganges, there is a great tree called *prayaga*[39], a tree of the species called *vata*. It is peculiar to this kind of tree that its branches send forth two species of twigs, some directed upward, as is the case with all other trees, and others directed downward like roots, but without leaves. If such a twig enters into the soil, it is like a supporting column to the branch whence it has grown. Nature has arranged this on purpose, since the branches of this tree are of an enormous extent (and require to be supported) Here the Brahmans and Kshatriyas are in the habit of committing suicide by climbing up the tree and throwing themselves into the Ganges. . . .

The tree of *Prayaga*

CHAPTER LXXIV

On Fasting, And The Various Kinds Of It

Fasting is with the Hindus voluntary and supererogatory. Fasting is abstaining from food for a certain length of time, which may be different in duration and in the manner in which it is carried out.

Various methods of fasting

The ordinary middle process, by which all the conditions of fasting are realised, is this: A man determines the day on which he will fast, and keeps in mind the name of that being whose benevolence he wishes to gain thereby and for whose sake he will fast, be it a god, or an angel, or some other being. Then he proceeds, prepares (and takes) his food on the day before the fast-day at noon, cleans his teeth by rubbing, and fixes his thoughts on the fasting of the following day. From that moment he abstains from food. On the morning of the fast-day he again rubs his teeth, washes himself, and performs the duties of the day. He takes water in his hand, and sprinkles it into all four directions, he pronounces with his tongue the name of the deity for whom he fasts, and remains in this condition till the day after the fast-day. After the sun has risen, he is at liberty to break the fast at that moment if he likes, or, if he prefers, he may postpone it till noon.

This kind is called *upavasa,* i.e. the fasting; for the not-eating from one noon to the following is called *ekanakta,* not fasting.

Another kind, called *kricchra,* is this: A man takes his food on some day at noon, and on the following day in the evening. On the third day he eats nothing except what by chance is given him without his asking for it. On the fourth day he fasts.

Another kind, called *paraka,* is this: A man takes his food at noon on three consecutive days. Then he transfers his eating-hour to the evening during three further consecutive days. Then he fasts uninterruptedly during three consecutive days without breaking fast.

Another kind, called *candrayana,* is this: A man fasts on the day of full moon; on the following day he takes only a mouthful, on the third day he takes double this amount, on the fourth day the three-fold of it, etc., etc., going on thus till the day of new moon. On that day he fasts; on the following days he again diminishes his food by one mouthful a day, till he again fasts on the day of full moon.

Another kind, called *masavasa* (*masopavasa*), is this: A man uninterruptedly fasts all the days of a month without ever breaking fast. . . .

If a man fasts all the days of Caitra, he obtains wealth and joy over the nobility of his children. If he fasts in Vaisakha, he will lord over his tribe. . . . If he fasts in Jyaishtha, he will be a favourite of the women. If he fasts in Ashadha, he will obtain wealth. If he fasts in Sravana, he obtains wisdom. If he fasts in Bhadrapada, he obtains wealth and valour, riches and cattle. If he fasts in Asvayuja, he will always be victorious over his enemies. If he fasts in Kartikka, he will . . . obtain his wishes. If he fasts in Margasirsha, he will be born in the most beautiful and fertile country. If he fasts in Pausa, he obtains a high reputation. If he fasts in Magha, he obtains innumerable wealth. If he fasts in Phalguna, he will be beloved.

He who fasts, however, during all the months of the year, only twelve times breaking the fast, will reside in paradise 10,000 years, and will thence return to life as the member of a noble, high and respected family. . . .

CHAPTER LXXV

On The Determination Of The Fast-Days

The reader must know in general that the eighth and eleventh days of the white half of very month are fast-days, except in the case of the leap month, for it is disregarded, being considered unlucky.

The eighth and eleventh days of each half of a month are fast-days

The eleventh is specially holy to Vasudeva, because on having taken possession of Mahura, the inhabitants of which formerly used to worship Indra one day in each month, he induced them to transfer this worship to the eleventh, that it should be performed in his name. ... Therefore they fast on this day in the state of the most punctilious cleanness, and they stay awake all the night, considering this as an obligatory performance, though in reality it is not obligatory. ...

[Some of the single fast-days throughout the year are mentioned. Among these are:]

The sixth day of Caitra is a fast-day holy to the sun.

The day of full moon in the month Sravana is a fast-day holy to Somanath. ...

The eighth of the same month is a fast-day holy to Bhagavati. Fasting is broken when the moon rises.

The fifth day of Bhadrapada is a fast-day holy to the sun, called *shat*. . . .

When in the month Karttika the moon stands in Revati, the last of her stations, it is a fast-day in commemoration of the waking up of Vasudeva. It is called *deotthini*, i.e. the rising of the Deva. Others add, besides, the condition that it must be the eleventh of the white half. . . .

On the sixth day of Pausha is a fasting in honour of the sun.

On the third day of Magha there is fasting for the women, not for the men. It is called *Gaur-t-r (gauri-tritiya?)*, and lasts the whole day and night. On the following morning they make presents to the nearest relatives of their husbands.

CHAPTER LXXVI

On The Festivals And Festive Days

Yatra means travelling under auspicious circumstances. Therefore a feast is called *yatra.* Most of the Hindu festivals[40] are celebrated by women and children only.

The 2nd Caitra

The 2nd of the month Caitra is a festival to the people of Kashmir, called *Agdus* (?), and celebrated on account of a victory gained by their king, Muttai, over the Turks. According to their account he ruled over the whole world. But this is exactly what they say of most of their kings. However, they are incautious enough to assign him to a time not much anterior to our time, which leads to their lie being found out. It is, of course, not impossible that a Hindu should rule (over a huge empire), as Greeks, Romans, Babylonians, and Persians have done, but all the times not much anterior to our own are well known. (If, therefore, such had been the case, we should know it.) Perhaps the here mentioned king ruled over the whole of India, and they know of no other country but India and of no other nations but themselves.

On the 11th there is a festival called *Hindolicaitra,* when they meet in the *devagriha,* or temple of Vasudeva, and swing his image to and

fro, as had been done with him when he
11th Caitra was an infant in the cradle. They
perform the same in their houses during
the whole day and make merry.

On the full moon's day of Caitra there is a feast called *Bahand* (*vasanta*?), a festival for the women,
Full moon's day when they put on their ornaments and
demand presents from their husbands.

The 22nd is a festival called *caitra-cashati*, a day of merriment
22nd Caitra holy to Bhagavati, when people used
to wash and to give alms.

The 3rd Vaisakha is a festival for the women called *Gaur-t-r* (*gauri-tritiya*?), holy to Gauri, the daughter of the mountain Himavant, the wife of Mahadeva. They wash and
3rd Vaisakha dress gaily, they worship the image of
Gauri and light lamps before it, they offer perfumes, abstain from eating, and play with swings. On the following day they give alms and eat.

On the 10th Vaisakha all the Brahmans whom the kings have invited proceed forth to the open fields, and there they light great fires for the sacrifices during five days till full moon. They make the fires in sixteen different spots and in four different groups. In each group a Brahman performs the sacrifice, so that there are *four* performing priests as there are four Vedas. On the 16th they return home.

In this month occurs the vernal equinox, called *Vasanta*. They determine the day by calculation and
Vernal equinox make it a festival, when people invite
the Brahmans.

On the 1st Jyaishtha, or new moon's day, they celebrate a festival and throw the first-fruits of all seeds
1st Jyaishtha into the water in order to gain thereby a
favourable prognostic.

The full moon's day of this month is a festival to the women,
Full moon's day called *Rupa-panca* (?)

All the days of the month Ashadha are devoted to alms-giving. It
Ashadha is also called *Ahari*. During this time the
household is provided with new vessels.

On the full moon day of Sravana, they give banquets to the
15th Sravana Brahmans.

On the 8th Asvayuja, when the moon stands in the nineteenth

station, Mula, begins the sucking of the sugarcane. It is a festival holy to Mahanavami, the sister[41] of Mahadeva, when they offer the first fruits of sugar and all other thing to her image which is called Bhagavati. They give much alms before it and kill kids. He who does not possess anything to offer, stands upright by the side of the idol, without ever sitting down, and will sometimes pounce upon whomsoever he meets and kill him. . . .

8th Asvayuja

In the month Bhadrapada, when the moon stands in the tenth station, Magha, they celebrate a festival which they call *Pitripaksha*[42], i.e. the half of the month of the Fathers because the moon's entering this station falls near the time of new moon. They distribute alms during fifteen days in the name of the Fathers.

Bhadrapada, new moon

On the 3rd Bhadrapada is the festival *Harbali* (?), for the women. It is their custom that a number of days before they sow all kinds of seeds in baskets, and they bring the baskets forward on this day after they have commenced growing. They throw roses and perfumes on them and play with each other during the whole night. On the following morning they bring them to the ponds, wash them, wash themselves, and give alms.

3rd Bhadrapada

On the 6th of this month, which is called *Gaihat* (?), when people give food to those who are in prison.

6th Bhadrapada

On the 8th, when the moonlight has reached half of its development, they have a festival called *Dhruvagrihá* (?); they wash themselves and eat well growing grain-fruit that their children should be healthy. The women celebrate this festival when they are pregnant and desire to have children. . . .

8th Bhadrapada

When the moon stands in her fourth station, Rohini, they call this time *Gunalahid* (?), celebrating a festival during three days and making merry by playing with each other, from joy over the birth of Vasudeva. . . .

16th Bhadrapada

. . . The 1st Karttika, or new moon's day, when the sun marches in Libra, is called *Dibali*[43]. Then people bathe, dress festively, make presents to each other of betel-leaves and areca-nuts; they ride to the temples to give alms and play merrily with each

1st Karttika

other till noon. In the night they light a great number of lamps in every place so that the air is perfectly clear. The cause of this festival is that Lakshmi, the wife of Vasudeva, once a year on this day liberates Bali, the son of Virocana, who is a prisoner in the seventh earth, and allows him to go out into the world. Therefore the festival is called *Balirajya,* i.e. the principality of Bali. . . .

In the same month, when full moon is perfect, they give banquets and adorn their women during all the days of the black half. . . .

15th Margasirsha

On full moon's day of the same month there is another festival of the women.

On most of the days of the month Pausha they prepare great quantities of *puhaval* (?) i.e. a sweet dish which they eat.

8th Pausha

On the eighth day of the white half of Pausha, which is called *Ashtaka,* they make gatherings of the Brahmans, present them with dishes prepared from the plant *Atriplex hortensia,* i.e. *sarmak* in Arabic (= orache), and show attentions to them.

On the eighth day of the black half, which is called *Sakartam,* they eat turnips.

3rd Magha

The 3rd Magha, called *Mahatriji* (*Magha-tritiya* ?), is a feast for the women, and sacred to Gauri. They meet in the houses of the most prominent among them before the image of Gauri, place before it various sorts of costly dresses, pleasant perfumes, and nice dishes. In each meeting-place they put 108 jugs full of water, and after the water has become cool, they wash with it four times at the four quarters of that night. On the following day they give alms, they give banquets and receive guests. The women's washing with cold water is common to all the days of this month. . . .

15th Phalguna

The full moon's day of Phalguna is a feast to the women, called *Odas* (?), or also *dhola*[44], (i.e. *dola*), when they make fire on places lower than those on which they make it on the festival *Camaha,* and they throw the fire out of the village.

16th Phalguna

On the following night, i.e. that of the 16th, called *Shivaratri*[45], they worship Mahadeva during the whole night; they remain awake, and do not lie down to sleep, and offer to him perfumes and flowers.

On the 23rd, which is called *Puyattan* (?), they eat rice with butter and sugar.

23rd Phalguna

The Hindus of Multan have a festival which is called *Sambapura-yatra;* they celebrate it in honour of the sun, and worship him. . . .

A festival in Multan

CHAPTER LXXVII

On Days Which Are Held In Special Veneration, On Lucky And Unlucky Times, And On Such Times As Are Particularly Favourable For Acquiring In Them Bliss In Heaven

The single days enjoy different degrees of veneration according to certain qualities which they attribute to them. They distinguish, e.g. the Sunday, because it is the day of the sun and the beginning of the week, as the Friday is distinguished in Islam.

The days of new moon and full moon

To the distinguished days further belong *amavasya* and *purnima,* i.e. the days of conjuction (new moon) and opposition (full moon), because they are the limits of the wane and the increase of the moonlight. In accordance with the belief of the Hindus regarding this increase and wane, the Brahmans sacrifice continually to the fire in order to earn heavenly reward. They let the portions of the angels accumulate, which are the offerings thrown into the fire at moonlight during the whole time from new moon to full moon. Then they begin distributing these portions over the angels in the time from full moon to new moon, till at the time of new moon nothing any more remains of them. We have already mentioned that new moon and full moon are noon and midnight of the nychthemeron of the Fathers. Therefore the uninterrupted almsgiving on these two days is always done in honour of the Fathers.

The four days on which the four *yugas* are said to have commenced

Four other days are held in special veneration, because, according to the Hindus, with them the single *yugas* of the present *caturyuga* have commenced, viz.:—

The 3rd Vaisakha, called *kshairita* (?), on which the *kritayuga* is believed to have commenced.

The 9th Karttika, the beginning of the *tretayuga.*

The 15th Magha, the beginning of the *dvaparayuga.*

The 13th of Asvayuja, the beginning of the *kaliyuga.*

According to my opinion, these days are festivals, sacred to the *yugas*, instituted for the purposes of almsgiving or for the performance of some rites and ceremonies, as, e.g. the commemoration-days in the year of the Christians. However, we must deny that the four *yugas* could really have commenced on the days here mentioned.

[Al-Biruni criticises the basis of the calculations for determining the actual day of the commencement of the four *yugas.* He thinks that such an exact determination could only be made by 'resorting to very artificial ways of interpretation.']

The days called *punyakala*

The times which are specially favourable to earn a heavenly reward in them are called *punyakala*. . . .

No doubt, most of the feast days enumerated in the preceding belong to this kind of days, for they are devoted to almsgiving and banqueting. If people did not expect to gain thereby a reward in heaven, they would not approve of the rejoicings and merriments which are characteristic of these days.

Notwithstanding the nature of the *punyakala* is such as here explained, some of them are considered as lucky, others as unlucky days.

Those days are lucky when the planets migrate from one sign into the other, especially the sun. These times are called *Samkranti.* The most propitious of them are the days of the equinoxes and solstices, and of these the most propitious is the day of the vernal equinox. It is called *bikhu* or *shibu (vishuva)*, as the two sounds *sh* and *kh* may be exchanged for each others, and may also, by a *metathesis,* change their place.

Samkranti

As, however, a planet's entering a new sign does not require more than a moment of time, and during it, people must offer to the fire the offering *santa* (?) with oil and corn, the Hindus have given a greater extent to these times, making them *begin* with the moment when the eastern edge of the body of the sun touches the first part of the sign; reckoning as their *middle* the moment when the sun's centre reaches the first part of the sign, which is in astronomy considered as the time of the migration (of the planet from one sign to the other), and reckoning as the *end* that moment when the western edge of the sun's body touches the first part of the sign. This process lasts, in the case of the sun, nearly two hours.

[Two different methods for calculating the moment of *Samkranti* are mentioned. Pp. 188–191.]

. . . Most propitious times are, further, the times of solar and lunar eclipses. At that time, according to their belief, all the waters of the earth become as pure as that of the Ganges. They exaggerate the veneration of these times to such a degree that many of them commit suicide, wishing to die at such a time as promises them heavenly bliss. However, this is only done by Vaisyas and Sudras, whilst it is forbidden to Brahmans and Kshatriyas, who in consequence do not commit suicide. [*Vide,* however, p. 253.]

Times of eclipses

Further, the times of *Parvan* are propitious, i.e. those times in which an eclipse may take place. And even if there is no eclipse at such a time, it is considered quite as propitious as the time of an eclipse itself.

Parvan and yoga

The times of the *yogas* are as propitious as those of the eclipses. We have devoted a special chapter to them (chap. lxxix). . .

. . . Times which are considered as unlucky, to which no merit whatsoever is attributed, are e.g. the times of earthquakes. Then the Hindus beat with the pots of their households against the earth and break them, in order to get a good omen and to banish the mishap. As times of a similar ill nature, the book *Samhita* further enumerates the moments of landslips, the falling of stars, red glow in the sky, the combustion of the earth by lightning, the appearance of comets, the occurrence of events contrary both to nature and custom, the entering of the wild beasts into the villages, rainfall when it is not the season for it, the trees putting forth leaves when it is not the season for it, when the nature of one season of the year seems transferred to another, and more of the like. . . .

Times of earthquakes

CHAPTER LXXVIII

On The Karanas

We have already spoken of the lunar days called *tithi,* and have explained that each lunar day is shorter then a civil day, because the lunar month has thirty lunar days, but only a little more than twenty-nine and half civil days.

Explanation of *karana*

As the Hindus call these *tithis* nychthemera, they also call the former half of a *tithi* day, the latter half night. Each of these halves has a separate name, and they all of them (i.e. all the halves of the lunar days of the lunar month) are called *karanas.*

[The rule for finding out a *karana* is given. P. 195.]

The word *buht* is of Indian origin. In the Indian language it is *bhukti* (= the daily motion of a planet). If the corrected motion is meant, it is called *bhukti sphuta.* If the mean motion is meant, it is called *buhkti madhyama,* and if the *buht* which renders equal is meant, it is called *bhuktyantara,* i.e. the difference between the two *bhuktis.*

Explanation of *bhukti*

The lunar days of the month have special names, which we exhibit in the following diagram. If you know the lunar day in which you are,

Names of the lunar days of the half of a month

you find, by the side of the number of the day, its name, and opposite it the *karana* in which you are. If that which has elapsed of the current day is less than half a day, the *karana* is a diurnal one; if that which has elapsed of it is more than half a day, it is a nocturnal one. This is the diagram:—

[The diagram is given, p. 197.]

The Hindus attribute to some of the *karanas* dominants, as is their custom. Further they give rules showing what during each *karana* must be done or not, rules which are similar to collection of astrological prognostics (as to lucky or unlucky days, etc.). If we give here a second diagram of the *karanas,* we thereby simply mean to confirm what we had said already, and to repeat a subject which is unknown amongst us, because learning is the fruit of repetition.

Table of *karanas* with their dominants and prognostics

[Diagrams showing the prognostics of the four fixed and seven movable *karanas* are given.

Al-Biruni goes on to point out that Alkindi and some other Arab authors have adopted the Indian system of the *karanas* but they had not quite fully understood it. Though they had improved upon it in some ways but 'the thing' had become 'totally different from what it originally was.' Both the methods, that of the Hindus and that of Alkindi must be treated separately. Pp. 198–203.]

CHAPTER LXXIX

On The Yogas

These are times which the Hindus think to be most unlucky and during which they abstain from all action. They are numerous. We shall here mention them.

There are two *yogas* regarding which all Hindus agree, viz.:—

Explanation of *vyatipata* and *vaidhrita*

(1) The moment when sun and moon together stand on two circles, which are, as it were, *seizing* each other, i.e. each pair of circles, the declinations of which, on one and the same side (of either solstice), are equal. This *yoga* is called *vyatipata.*

(2) The moment when sun and moon stand together on two *equal* circles, i.e. each pair of circles, the declinations of which, on different sides (of either solstice), are equal. This is called *vaidhrita.*

[Different methods for computing the *vyatipata* and *vaidhrita,* as given by Pulisa and the author of *Karanatilaka* are given. Al-Biruni also refers to two books which he prepared on the subject, including one titled *Arabic Khandakhadyaka* which he had 'composed for' a Kashmiri named Sayavabala.[46] A Table showing the names and the qualities of the *yogas* is also given. Pp. 204–210.]

CHAPTER LXXX

On The Introductory Principles Of Hindu Astrology, With A Short Description Of Their Methods Of Astrological Calculations

Our fellow-believers in these (Muslim) countries are not acquainted with the Hindu methods of astrology, and have never had an opportunity of studying an Indian book on the subject. In consequence, they imagine that Hindu astrology is the same as theirs and relate all sorts of things as being of Indian origin, of which we have not found a single trace with the Hindus themselves. As in the preceding part of this our book we have given something of everything, we shall also give as much of their astrological doctrine as will enable the reader to discuss questions of a similar nature with them. If we were to give an exhaustive representation of the subject, this task would detain us very long, even if we limited ourselves to delineate only the leading principles and avoided all details.

Indian astrology unknown among Muhammadans

First, the reader must know that in most of their prognostics they simply rely on means like auguring from the flight of birds and physiognomy, that they do not—as they ought to do—draw conclusions, regarding the affairs of the sublunary world, from the seconds (*sic*) of the stars, which are the events of the celestial sphere.

Regarding the number seven as that of the planets, there is no difference between us and them. They call them *graha.* Some of them are throughout lucky, viz. Jupiter, Venus and the Moon, which are called *saumyagraha.* Other three are throughout unlucky, viz. Saturn, Mars, and the Sun, which are called *kruragraha.* Among the latter, they also count the dragon's head, though in reality it is not a star. The nature of one planet is variable and depends upon the nature of that planet with which it is combined, whether it be lucky or unlucky. This is Mercury. However, alone by itself, it is lucky.

On the planets

[Table listing the names of the seven planets, the various information obtainable from them regarding the sex and character of human beings, the elements and the seasons indicated by them, etc. as also some explanatory notes, on the Table, are given. A Table showing the peculiar qualities of each zodiacal sign is given, pp. 213–219.]

The *height* or *altitude* of a planet is called, in the Indian language, *uccastha,* its particular degree *paramoccastha.* the *depth* or *dejectio* of a planet is called *nicastha.* its particular degree *paramanicastha. Mulatrikona* is a powerful influence, attributed to a planet, when it is in the *gaudium* in one of its two houses. . . .

Explanation of some technical terms of astrology

They do not refer the *aspectus trigoni* to the elements and the elementary natures, as it is our custom to do, but refer them to the points of the compass in general, as has been specified in the Table.

They call the *turning* zodiacal sign (*tropikon*) *cararasi,* i.e. moving, the *fixed* one (*stereon*) *sthirarasi,* i.e. the *resting* one, and the *double-bodied* one (*disoma*) *dvisvabhava,* i.e. both together.

As we have given a table of the zodiacal signs, we next give a table of the *houses* (*domus*), showing the qualities of each of them. The one half of them above the earth they call *chatra,* i.e. parasol, and the half under the earth they call *nau,* ie. ship. Further, they call the half ascending to the midst of heaven and the other half descending to the *cardo* of the earth, *dhanu,* i.e. the bow. The *cardines* they call *kendra* (*kentron*), the next following houses *panaphara* (*epanaphora*), and the *inclining* houses apoklima (*apoklima*):-

The houses

[Table given. Pp. 221–222.]

The hitherto mentioned details are in reality the cardinal points of Hindu astrology, viz. the planets, zodiacal signs, and *houses*. He who knows how to find out what each of them means or portends deserves the title of a clever adept and of a master in this art.

[Al-Biruni then goes on to describe the 'division of the zodiacal signs in minor portions', the Indian astrologer's ideas about 'the friendship and enmity' of planets, 'the four forces of each planet', 'the years of life which the single planets bestow' and 'the three species of these years', etc. Pp. 222–231.]

Special methods of inquiry of the Hindu astrologers

From the description given in the preceding pages, the reader learns how the Hindus compute the duration of human life. He learns from the positions of the planets, which they occupy on the origin (i.e. at the moment of birth) and at every given moment of life in what way the years of the different planets are distributed over it. To these things Hindu astrologers join certain methods of the astrology of nativities, which other nations do not take into account. . . .

On comets

I mention these things in order to show the reader the difference between the astrological methods of our people and those of the Hindus. Their theories and methods regarding aerial and cosmic phenomena are very lengthy and very subtle at the same time. As we have limited ourselves to mentioning in their astrology of nativities, only the theory of the determination of the length of life, we shall in this department of science limit ourselves to the species of the comets, according to the statements of those among them who are supposed to know the subject thoroughly. The analogy of the comets shall afterwards be extended to other more remote subjects.

The head of the Dragon is called *rahu*, the tail *ketu*. The Hindus seldom speak of the tail, they only use the head. In general, all comets which appear on heaven are also called *ketu*.

[Quotation from Varahamihira's *Samhita* regarding different kinds of comets, their prognostics, etc. are given. A Table showing the names of the comets, the number of stars each one of them has, the directions from which they appear, their prognostics, etc. is also given.

A conscientious scholar, Al-Biruni notes that the manuscript at his disposal was defective and so certain entries in some of the columns had to be left blank. Pp. 234–238.]

Further quotations from the *Samhita* of Varahamihira

The author (Varahamihira) had divided the comets into three classes: the *high* ones near the stars; the *flowing* ones near the earth; the *middle* ones in the air, and he mentions each one of the *high* and *middle* classes of them in our Table separately. . . .

The Jews hold the same opinion regarding the comets as we hold regarding the stone of the Ka'ba (viz. that they all are stones which have fallen down from heaven). Accordiing to the same book of Varahamihira, comets are such beings as have been on account of their merits raised to heaven, whose period of dwelling in heaven has elapsed and who are then redescending to the earth.

[A Table giving similar information, as above, in regard to these three types of comets is given. Pp. 241–244.]

This is the doctrine of the Hindus regarding the comets and their presages.

On meteorology

Only few Hindus occupy themselves in the same way as physical scholars among the anicient Greeks did, with exact scientific researches on the comets and on the nature of the other phenomena of heaven (*tameteōra*), for also in these things they are not able to rid themselves of the doctrines of their theologians. . . .

As regards the phenomena of the sky, they say, for instance, that the thunder is the roaring of *Airarata,* i.e. the riding-elephant of Indra the ruler when it drinks from the pond Manasa, rutting and roaring with a hoarse voice.

The rainbow (lit. bow of Kuzah) is the bow of Indra, as our common people consider it as the bow of Rustam.

Conclusion

We think now that what we have related in this book will be sufficient for any one who wants to converse with the Hindus, and to discuss with them questions of religion, science, or literature, on the very basis of their own civilisation. Therefore, we shall finish this treatise, which has already, both by its length and breadth, wearied the reader. We ask God to pardon us for every statement of ours which is not true. We ask Him to help us that we may adhere to that which yields Him satisfaction. We ask Him to lead us to a proper insight into the nature of that which is false and idle, that we may sift it so as to distinguish the chaff from the wheat. All good comes from Him, and it is He who is clement towards His slaves. Praise be to God, the Lord of the worlds, and His blessings be upon the Prophet Muhammad and his whole family!

Select References*

1. Edward C. Sachau, *The Chronology of Ancient Nations,* London, 1879, Introduction, pp. V-XIV.
2. Edward C. Sachau. *Albiruni's India,* London, 1888 (Delhi reprint, 1964), Introduction. pp. VII-L.

   (Both these Introductions by Sachau, the scholar who introduced Al-Biruni to the wider English-speaking world, contain a very exhaustive account of the life of Al-Biruni and significance of his work.)
3. *Al-Biruni Commemoration Volume,* Iran Society, Calcutta, 1951.
4. *Indo-Iranica,* Vol. V, no. 4, 1952, 'Al-Biruni Millenary Celebrations'.

4A. Hakim Mohammad Said, Ed., *Al-Biruni Commemoration Volume,* Karachi, 1979.

   (These volumes contain some very good articles on the life and works of Al-Biruni. These articles have not been separately listed here.)

5. K.A. Nizami, *ed. Politics and Society During the Early Medieval Period* (Collected Works of Professor M. Habib), 'Abu Raihan Alberuni on the National Character of the Hindus', pp. 25–32; *ibid,* 'Hindu Society in the Early Middle Ages', pp. 137–57; *ibid.,* 'Indian Culture and Social Life at the Time of the Turkish Invasions', pp. 152–228.

   (These articles of Professor Habib were written in 1930–31 and 1940, and have been reproduced in this volume. They contain some very incisive comments on Al-Biruni's observations, and present summarised version of some portions of the text.)
6. Elliot and Dowson, *History of India As Told By Its Own Historians,* Vol. II, Aligarh Reprint, 1952, with Introduction by M. Habib, pp. 1–8 and Notes.
7. *Encyclopaedia of Islam,* article by D.J. Boilot entitled 'Al-Biruni', new ed. London, 1960, 1, 1236–38.
8. C.C. Gillespie, *ed., Dictionary of Scientific Biography*, article by E.S. Kennedy entitled 'Al-Biruni', New York, 1970, 11, 147–58.
9. Ainslie T. Embree, *Alberuni's India,* (abridged edition), New York, 1971, Introduction, pp. V-XIX. (See also p. XI. note 2).

* The articles listed here are from among those relating to the life of Al-Biruni and some aspect of his work on India. For a fuller list of articles on Al-Biruni see J.D. Pearson, *Index Islamicus,* 1906–55, Cambridge, 1958, pp. 146–48 and its subsequent issues. Also serial nos. 7, 23 and 24 above.

10. R.C. Majumdar, 'A Passage in Alberuni's India—A Nanda Era?', *J.B.O.R.S.*, IX, 1923, pp. 417–18.
11. Abdullah Yusuf Ali, *Albiruni's India, I.C.*, 1, no. 1, 1927, pp. 31–35; *ibid.*, no. 2, pp. 223–30; *ibid.*, no. 3, pp. 473–87.
12. Z. Ahmad, *Al-Biruni, I.C.*, V, 1931, pp. 343–51, *ibid.*, VI, 1932, pp. 363–69.
13. F. Kerenkow, 'Abu'r Rahman Al-Biruni', *I.C.*, VI, 1932, pp. 528–34.
14. S.H. Barni, 'Al-Biruni's Scientific Achievements', *ibid.*, 1952–53, pp. 37–48.
15. A.H. Dani, 'Al-Biruni on Sanskrit Literature', *J.P.H.S.*, 1, 1953, pp. 301–17.
16. S.A. Ali, 'Al-Biruni, the Scholar and the Writer', *Progs. Vol. Pakistan Historical Conference*, 1953, pp. 243–52.
17. M.L. Roy Choudhury, 'Abu Raihan Al-Biruni and his Indian Studies', *I.I.* Vol. VII, 1954, pp. 9–22.
18. B.C. Law, 'Al-Biruni's Knowledge of Indian Geography', *I.I.*, Vol. VII, 1954, pp. 1–26.
19. M. Yasin, 'Al-Biruni in India', *I.C.*, XLIX, 1975, pp. 207–13.
20. M.S. Khan, 'Al-Biruni on Indian Metaphysics', *ibid.*, LV, 1981, pp. 161–68.
21. Gonindar Kaur, 'Al-Biruni: An Early Student of Comparative Religions', *ibid.*, LVI, 1982, pp. 149–63.
22. M.S. Khan, 'Al-Biruni and the Political History of India', *Oriens.*, E.J. Brill, Leiden, Vol. 25–26, pp. 86–115.
23. Maqbul Ahmad, *et. al.*, 'Al-Biruni, An Introduction to his life and Writings', paper presented at the New Delhi Symposium on Al-Biruni, 1971.
24. M. Ghiyasuddin, unpublished Ph. D. thesis (1968), 'A Critical Analysis of the Writings of Al-Biruni Pertaining to India', Maulana Azad Library, A.M.U., Aligarh.

Notes

1. 'Abu-Sahl 'Abd-Almun'im Ibn 'Ali Ibn Nuh At-Tiflisi (p.4).[1] It is rather surprising that Al-Biruni does not give any biographical particulars about this apparently important personage at whose suggestion and for whose pleasure he prepared his great work on India. On the basis of the respectable prefix of *Ustad* (master), added generally to the names of high civil officers, not generals, Sachau suggests that he was a high civil functionary in Sultan Mahmud's Court, and was probably of Persian origin.

2. *Mu'tazila* sect (p. 4). One of the early religio-philosophical movements in Islam. The founder of this school of rationalism was Wasil Ibn Ata (d. 748).

The *Mu'tazilites* asserted the principle of free-will as against predestination, and maintained that the divine attributes of God should not be regarded as co-existent with God, because that would destroy the concept of the unity of God. They also believed in the dogma of the 'creation' of the Quran. The movement gained influence and importance during the *Khilafat* of Al-M'amun (813–33).

Its doctrines were influenced by the Greek philosophy, and evoked strong controversies and produced much polemical literature. Al-Biruni wanted his own book on India to be free from any such polemical bias.

3. Abu-Al-'Abbas Aleranshahri (p.5). Author of a general work on the history of religions, including some account of Hinduism and Buddhism. One of the rare instances in which Al-Biruni approvingly refers to the work of an earlier Muslim writer on Indian culture.

---

[1] This and the subsequent references to page numbers within brackets indicate the pages of the present abridged edition.

Al-Biruni's study of the Indian society and religion is otherwise almost entirely based on indigenous sources or personal information and observation.

To some early Arab geographers Eranshahr denoted the whole area of the Sasanid empire but here it indicates a smaller region or a town.

4. Zarkan (p.5). Al-Biruni does not give any particulars about him except that he was the author of a treatise on Buddhism which Eranshahri (no. 3 above) had incorporated in his own book. Al-Biruni does not think very highly about the authenticity of Zarkan's account but Sachau suggests that whatever brief information Al-Biruni gives about Buddhism is based on Zarkan's book.

5. *Samkhya* (p. 6) (Reasoning). It is the name of a school of thought founded by the legendary saint Kapila. It is characterised by a rigid dualism (between matter and spirit) and a fundamental atheism. For Al-Biruni's description of the ideas of the *Samkhya* school of philosophers, see pp. 23–24.

Al-Biruni mentions *Samkhya* as a book composed by Kapila (p. 60). He had translated this book into Arabic and has quoted from it extensively on matters of religion and philosophy. Discussing its identification, Sachau draws attention to the "so-called *Samkhya-pravacanam* ('The Sankhya Aphorism of Kapila')" and two other works, the *Samkhya Karika* of Isvara Krishna (probably of the 4th century A.D.) and the *Bhashya* of Gaudapada (see note 17 A below). He writes that though there are similarities in these works they are not identical.

It may be added that the earliest document of *Samkhya* school is the *Shashtitantra* composed by Varshagnya in the 1st or 2nd century A.D. The *Samkhya* school offers salvation to both the twice-born and the once-born, whereas the *Purva Mimamsa* and *Vedanta* restrict it to the twice-born only.

6. Patanjali (Patanjala ?) (p. 6). Sachau notes that the Arabic text generally has *kitab-i batanjal* (in Arabic there is no letter for *p,* for which the letter *b* is used), which may be translated as 'the book of (the author) Patanjali' or 'the book (which is called) Patanjali or Patanjala.' Only at one place, Al-Biruni writes *Sahib-i kitab-i Batanjal,* or the author of the book of Patanjali, where Batanjal means the title of the book, not the name of the author. At two other places, the word Batanjal, however, indicates the name of the author (p. 37). Sachau, therefore suggests that the name of the author was probably

taken to indicate the title of his book too. Regarding the pronunciation, Sachau points out that in the Arabic text it is written with a long *a,* but there was no uniformity in the transliteration on this point. He therefore wrote it as Patanjali, as written in Sanskrit generally.

Like the *Samkhya,* mentioned above, this is one of the books translated into Arabic by Al-Biruni, and extensively quoted by him on matters of religion and philosophy (p. 60).

Patanjali was the author of *Yugasutra* which is assigned to the 4th century A.D. Sachau, however, points out that 'Alberuni's Patanjali is totally different from "The Yoga Aphorisms of Patanjali".

7. 'The book *Gita,* a part of the book *Bharata*' (p. 13). Like the above-mentioned two books, Al-Biruni quotes extensively from it on matters of religion and philosophy. It may be noted that he calls it a part of the *Bharata,* and does not mention the title *Mahabharata.*

Sachau draws attention to the differences in the text used by Al-Biruni and the present *Bhagwad Gita.* He thinks that Al-Biruni's copy of the text was 'more ancient' and fuller, and expresses surprise that no trace of that copy has survived. (See last para of note 12 below on the question of the original Sanskrit texts used by Al-Biruni.)

Sachau also suggests that Al-Biruni was probably using a commentary, not the text of the *Gita.*

8. *Jabriyya* sect (p. 14). Derived from the word *Jabr* (compulsion), the followers of this school of thought emphasised the all-powerfulness of God, and opposed the Mu'tazilite doctrine of free-will.

9. Abu-alfath Albusti (p. 17). A famous poet in the court of Sultan Mahmud and Mas'ud. He belonged to Bust (Afghanistan), and had served earlier under the Samanids. He died in 1039.

10. Buddhodana and the Shamanians (p. 19). Sachau's suggestion that the word Buddhodana is a misreading of Suddhodana, the father of Gautam Buddha, is not very acceptable because it does not fit in the context in which it occurs. His other suggestion, that the work of Eranshahri (see note 3 above) which is obviously Al-Biruni's source on this point, perhaps contained the word Suddhodana, not Buddhodana (they look similar in Arabic writing), and that Suddhodana 'would be Sauddhodani, i.e. the son of Suddhodana, or Buddha', is more acceptable. In fact, at another place (p. 177) Al-Biruni himself writes this—'Buddhodana, the son of Suddhodana.' Sachau seems to have missed this clear reference.

The word *Shamanians* is used in Arabic to denote the Buddhists. It is derived from a Prakritic form of Sanskrit, *Sramana.* Al-Biruni also called them the *Muhammira* (p. 177), or the red-robed ones, which obviously refers to the red-brown cloaks of the Buddhists.

11. The *Vishnu-Purana* (p. 29). It is the name of one of the *Puranas* (see note 16A below). It is divided into six parts, five of which deal with cosmic matters. The sixth book which is the central portion of the work gives an account of the sports and exploits of a youthful Krishna whom it regards as an incarnation of Vishnu.

12. *Vishnu Dharma* (p. 35). Al-Biruni mentions this work in the chapter on the religious literature of the Hindus (Chapter XII), and explains that it means 'Religion of God who in this case is understood to be Narayana'.

Sachau finds himself unable to identify this work, and he writes that 'it is a sort of *Purana,* full of those legends and notions characteristic of the literature of the Puranas', but points out that Al-Biruni does not include it in his list of the Puranas (p. 60). He writes that the traditions of Saunaka, often quoted by Al-Biruni (p. 233) were probably taken from the *Vishnu Dharma.* He adds that the work may be the same as *Vishnu-Dharmottara-Purana* which 'is said to have comprehended Brahmagupta's *Brahmasiddhanta.*' Al-Biruni had a copy of this work, and Sachau suggests that 'he (Al-Biruni) had it perhaps as a portion of this larger work.'

For a discussion of the general problem of the authenticity of the Sanskrit texts used by Al-Biruni, and the identification of some of the works cited by him, see Dr J. Gonda, 'Remarks on Al-Biruni's Quotations from Sanskrit Texts', *ACV,* Pp. 111–18. Dr Gonda writes that the accuracy of these extracts has generally been vindicated with the discoveries of more copies of such texts and a better understanding of the Puranic traditions. On the identification of this particular work, Sachau's surmise has been confirmed by other writers.

13. The four castes and the *Antyaja* (pp. 45–46). This portion relating to the caste hierarchy and the one relating to the rites and customs observed by members of the different castes (Chapters IX, LXIII & LXIV) constitute in many ways the most important part of Al-Biruni's account. No such detailed and perceptive account of the caste system as it prevailed in early medieval India is available in any other non-Indian source.

B.P. Mazumdar (*Socio-Economic History of Northern India, (1030–*

1194 A.D.), 1960, p. 79) comments that Al-Biruni must have been stating the position as it was given in the ancient scriptures and not what actually obtained in the Hindu society at the time. He adds that at the beginning of the 11th century there was much caste proliferation, and there were a number of mixed castes too.

Actually, Al-Biruni's account also gives some glimpses of the actual situation. He writes, for example, in regard to the 'latter two classes' (Vaisya and Sudra) that much as they differed from each other 'they live together in the same towns and villages, mixed together in the same houses and lodgings.' This may also be taken as indicative of inter-caste marriages to some extent.

As regards the *Antyajas,* Professor Mazumdar writes that at the time when the early *smritis* were composed the untouchables were called *antyajas,* and adds that the enumeration of their subdivisions varied, some sources mentioning 7, others 12. Al-Biruni mentions them 'after the Sudras' and adds that they were 'not reckoned amongst any caste, but only as members of a certain craft or profession'. He enlists them as 'the fuller, shoe-maker, juggler, the basket and shield maker, the sailor, fisherman, the hunter of wild animals and of birds and the weaver.' Professor Mazumdar identifies them with the Rajaka, Charmakara, Nata or Sailushika, Buruda, Navika, Kaivarta, Bhillas and Kuvindaka, and adds that they were regarded as Candala or Antyaja in early *smriti* literature but Manu regarded them as Sudra.

14. Karmatians (p. 53). A well-organised extremist sect which appears at first to have been associated with the Isma'ili movement but whose origins remain obscure. It laid stress on esoteric interpretation of some religious doctrines and was characterised by some communistic tendencies. Its followers, called the 'Bolsheviks of Islam' by some modern writers, stressed religious tolerance, organised workers and artisans into guilds, and advocated community of property and wives.

Hamdan Qarmat, an Iraqi peasant, was the founder of the sect, and its followers came to be known as Qarmatians. They established a state on the western shore of Persian Gulf (899) which became a constant source of trouble to the Abbasid Caliphate. In 930 they attacked and seized the sacred city of Makka and carried away the holy Black Stone which was returned 20 years later by the order of the Fatimid Khalifa al Mansur (946–52).

Later they established their rule over the greater part of upper

Sind. They were defeated and suppressed by Sultan Mahmud (to which Al-Biruni is referring here) but regained their position after his death, and had to be suppressed again in 1175 by Sultan Muizuddin Muhammad Ghori (1173–1206).

15. Varahamihira (p. 53). The famous Indian astronomer of the 6th century A.D., and author of the well-known works *Pancha-siddhantika* and *Brihat Samhita* both of which are frequently referred to by Al-Biruni. The latter book is on astrology, but also contains information about many other subjects, including architecture, iconography, gardening, erotics, etc. H. Kern edited it in the *Bibliotheca Indica* series (1864, 1865) and also translated it into English in *Journal of Royal Asiatic Society,* London, New Series, Vols. IV–VII.

16. Vasuḳra, the Kashmirian, putting the Veda into writing (p. 58). This reference to the Veda being put to writing sometime around 10-11th century is very significant. It is a great pity that no copy of the work has survived.

16A. The Puranas (p. 60). The word *Purana* means ancient. As a category of literature these are ancient religious poems, as also a corpus of legends and religious instructions. Content-wise, these were originally a book of origins, which is evident from their five characteristic features, viz. creation, re-creation, genealogies of gods and sages, the four cardinal aeons (*yugas*) and genealogy of kings. In their present form the texts, according to A.L. Basham (*The Wonder that Wȧs India,* paperback edition, 1967, p. 301) do not go beyond the Gupta period (319-550 A.D.), but their legendary material is very old.

Al-Biruni gives a list of the names of 18 Puranas as he had heard and noted down, and another somewhat different list, also of 18 names, read to him from the *Vishnu-Purana.* He adds that of these he had seen portions only of the Matsya, Aditya and Vayu Puranas.

17. *Smriti* (p. 60). The *Smriti* (Remembered, or Tradition) denotes a category of religious literature comprising law-books. The most famous among these is the *Manu-Smriti* (Law Book of Manu) composed in its final form during the 2nd to 3rd century A.D. Al-Biruni however mentions *Smriti* here as a particular book containing 'commandments and prohibitions'.

It may be noted that the list of *Smriti* books given by Al-Biruni is very important in one respect. It contains the names of some minor *Smritis,* such as Atri, Harita and Daksha. This helps us to determine the lower time-limit of the period of their compilation. He lists Likhita and Sankha (nos. 14 and 15, p. 60). as two separate books, but they are one—*Sankha 'Likhita.*

17A. Gauda the anchorite (p. 60). Al-Biruni does not mention specifically the name of Gaudapada, the preceptor of the great Sankaracharya, but Sachau suggests that Gauda the anchorite mentioned here may be identified with Gaüdapada. The absence of any reference by Al-Biruni to Sankaracharya is surprising.

18. *Nyayabhasa* composed by Kapila (p. 60). Sachau writes that he is not sure about the transliteration of this word in the Arabic text, where it looks like *Naybhash.* He also writes that the contents of the book bear no relation to the *Nyaya* philosophy of Gautama but are identical with the *Mimamsa* philosophy of Jamini whose name is mentioned just a little later.

The *Nyaya* is one of the six traditional schools of Hindu philosophy, of which the chief document is the *Nyayasutra* of Akshapada Gautam (4th century A.D.). It was commented upon by another scholar in the 16th century and this commentary is known as the *Nyayabhashya.* The author of this commentary is unknown but Al-Biruni states here that it was written by Kapila.

19. *Mimamsa* (p. 61) (Inquiry). A school of thought founded by the sage Jaimini. Its original objective was to explain the *Veda*, which it regarded as primeval and superhuman. There are two schools of *Mimamsa* philosophy derived from the Vedas. One, known as *Purva Mimamsa,* deals with Vedic rituals, while the other, *Uttara Mimamsa* (also known as Vedanta) concentrates on the spiritual side of the Vedic literature.

Al-Biruni is referring here to the former. The *Purva Mimamsa Sutra* of Jaimini is a work of the 4-5th century A.D.

20. The book *Laukayata* (*sic*) (p. 61). Sachau notes that the Lokayata school of thought was founded by Brihaspati, author of *Barhaspatyasutram.* Its followers were materialist thinkers who did not believe in any self or entity beyond the material body and its needs. They believed that perception alone was the source of proof or knowledge. Al-Biruni who uses the term as the name of a book seems to be referring to some book by a writer of this school.

20A. The book *Agastymata* (p. 61). There are two books whose titles bear the prefix Agastya. The first is the *Agastya-Sutiveshna-Samvada,* a work of the Ramaite sect of the Bhakti school which is assigned to the period between the 6th and 10th century A.D. The other text is the *Agastyasutra* which together with the *Devi Bhagwata* constitutes the chief document of a sect of the Sakta school which seeks release through a total devotion to a supreme goddess, Devi. It may be assigned to the latter half of the early middle ages. It is not clear as to whether Al-Biruni is referring here to either of these two works or some other one.

21. Panini (p. 63). The name of the famous Indian grammarian of the 4th century B.C., and the author of the great Sanskrit grammar, *Astadhyayi* (Eight Chapters).

22. Abul'aswad Addu'ali (p. 64). The originator of Arabic grammar according to literary tradition. He died in 681.

23. *Sindhind* (p. 70). Al-Biruni writes that the Indians called every standard work on astronomy a *Siddhanta*. One such work, the *Brahmasiddhanta* of Brahmagupta (note 25, below) was translated into Arabic by Al-Fazari by the order of Khalifa Mansur (754-75) and it was called *Sindhind*. It was the earliest work which acquainted the Arabs with Indian astronomy.

24. Paulisa and Pulisa (p. 70). Al-Biruni uses the two names for two different persons. The former was a Greek, and the author of a work on astronomy, the *Paulisa Siddhanta*. He has been identified with the classical astronomer Paul of Alexandria. The latter was a commentator of that work.

25. Brahmagupta (p. 70). A famous Indian astronomer and mathematician who flourished in the 7th century A.D. His well-known work on astronomy, the *Brahmasiddhanta* was partly translated into Arabic by Al-Biruni (p. 70) who has also given a description of the contents of this book (pp. 70–71). He also refers to another work of Brahmagupta, called *Khandakhadyaka*, which was known among the Arabs as *Al-Arkand* (p. 192). There was a commentary on this work called *Khandakhadyaka-tippa* which Al-Biruni has taken to be a work of Balbhadra. It may also be noted here that Al-Biruni refers to a book which he wrote for a Kashmiri Syavabala (?), whose title he gives as *Arabic Khandakhadyaka* (p. 268).

Al-Biruni praises Brahmagupta for the 'abundance of his knowledge and the sharpness of his intellect' and calls him 'the most distinguished of their (Hindu's) astronomers', but also criticises him for having compromised with certain scientific truths, of which he was convinced, in order to placate uneducated priests. Al-Biruni adds that Brahmagupta had to do so probably because of some strong compulsion and in order to avoid the fate of Socrates (p. 218).

He also condemns him for using 'offensive terms' against another distinguished astronomer, Aryabhatta (p. 174).

26. Aryabhatta (p. 72). Famous Indian astronomer and mathematician of the 5th century A.D. He was the first to treat mathematics as a distinct subject; his most important contribution in this field being the notation system based on decimal place-value system. His well-known work *Aryabhatiya* was composed in 499 A.D. It has been edited with commentary by H. Kern (Leiden, 1874) and more recently by Pandit Baldeva Mishra with commentary in Sanskrit and Hindi (published by Bihar Research Society, Patna, 1966). Al-Biruni writes that he had not seen any of his works but knew of him through the quotations given by Brahmagupta.

Aryabhatta held that the earth was a sphere and it rotated on its axis. He criticised the traditional explanation of the eclipses, and explained that 'an eclipse of the moon is her entering the shadow of the earth, and an eclipse of the sun consists in this that the moon covers and hides the sun from us' (p. 216). For these views he was strongly criticised by Brahmagupta (p. 174, 217).

It may be noted that Al-Biruni refers to two different persons bearing the name Aryabhatta. He describes them as 'Aryabhatta the elder', and as 'Aryabhatta of Kusumpura, who belongs to the school of the elder Aryabhatta' (pp. 116, 172). The latter was the author of a book called *Al-ntf* (?) and also another book which was commented upon by Balbhadra.

27. Caraka (p. 74). Author of *Caraka Samhita,* was the court physician of the Kusana ruler Kanishka (1st century A.D.). Caraka's work has been regarded as one of the basic texts on early Indian medical science.

Al-Biruni refers to and quotes from an Arabic translation of this work which was done for a prince of the Barmaki family (p. 74).

28. Barmecides (p. 74). The descendants of Khalid ibn Barmak the powerful and influential Wazir of Khalifa Mansur. Khalid was the son of the chief priest (*Barmak*) of a Buddhist monastery in Balkh. His descendants called *Barmaki* or Barmecides wielded great influence during the Khilafat of Mansur and Mahdi (775–85), but met with a violent end in the Khilafat of Harun Rashid (786–809). The Barmecides were great patrons of learning, and the period of their dominance witnessed a marked increase in Persian and Indian cultural influences in the Abbasid court.

29. *Kalila wa Dimna* (p. 74). An Arabic translation, from an

earlier Persian translation, of a Sanskrit work. Both the Sanskrit original and the Persian translation are now lost, and the Arabic version by Ibn al-Muqaffa (d. 757) is the basis of many other translations in different languages. The work contains didactic stories meant to instruct princes in morals and polity.

Some material of the lost Sanskrit original is available in an expanded form in the *Pancatantra.*

30. Abdullah ibn al-Muqaffa (p. 74). A Zoroastrian convert to Islam. He was put to death by fire in *c.* 757 on account of his suspect orthodoxy.

30A. Udunpur is Purvadesa (p. 81). Udunpur may be identified with the *Odantavihara,* one of the four principal universities in early medieval Bihar (600–1200). It was founded around 725 and stood on the rocky hill at the outskirt of modern Biharsharif town (Nalanda district), see Yogendra Mishra, 'The Odantapuri Vihara', Annual Number of Journal of Rama Krishna Mission, Patna, 1984, pp. 93–114. It is to be distinguished from the earlier, more well-known, Nalanda *vihara* situated nearby.

31. Kanoj and Bari (p. 94). This is a valuable piece of information regarding the decline and ruin of the famous capital-city of Kanauj and the transfer of the capital to another place named Bari, on the eastern side of the Ganges. The transfer took place on the eve of Mahmud's invasion of Kanauj (1018).

R.S. Tripathi (*History of Kanauj,* 1964 edition, pp. 285, 287) notices this information but does not make any comment on it. Professor Y. Mishra (*The Hindu Shahis of Afghanistan and the Punjab, A.D. 865–1026,* Patna, 1972. p. 197 and note) suggests that Bari (which he reads as *Vari*) was only a camp of the *skandhvari* ('owner of the camp') Pratihara king, and that after its sack by Mahmud nothing of it remained. It may, however, be pointed out that Al-Biruni writing some 12 years after the invasion uses the terms 'city' and 'town' for Bari.

32. *Farsakh* (p. 94). A measure of distance, equal to 4 miles.

33. Yakub and Alfazari (p. 137). Yaqub ibn Tariq and Muhammad Ibn Ibrahim Al-Fazari were pioneers in introducing Indian astronomical works to the Muslim world. The former belonged to the second half of the 8th century A.D., and was the author of a book on astronomy and mathematical geography which Al-Biruni quotes, and also criticises for the wrong understanding of some concepts of Indian astronomy and incorrect rendering of some Sanskrit words.

The latter was the translator of the *Brahmasiddhanta* (no. 25 above), and Sachau suggests that he also translated the other work of Brahmagupta, the *Khandakhadyaka,* which was known among the Arabs as *Al-Arkand.*

34. Rama and Ramayana (p. 140). C. Bulcke 'Al-Beruni and the Rama-Katha' *ACV,* pp. 77–83, points out that although Al-Biruni does not mention the Ramayana in the chapter dealing with the Indian religious literature (Chap. XII) it is evident from his various references to 'the story of Rama and Ramayana' (pp. 53, 55, 100–101, 139–141, 176) that he knew a good deal about the contents of the great epic.

35. Muhammad Ibn Zakariyya Alrazi (p. 144). Abu Bakr Muhammad ibn Zakariya Al-Razi (anglicised as Rhazes) (865–925) was the chief physician of the hospital at Baghdad, and the author of a number of books on medicine—the most famous of these being the *Hawi* (the comprehensive book).

36. The Brahman kings Samand . . . Bhimpala (p. 194). Sachau comments upon the dissimilarity in the nature and contents of the two portions of this Chapter (XLIX), and observes that the earlier portion, relating to the eras is taken from the *Vishnu-Dharma* (see note 12 above). For the latter portion, information of a historical character (dynasty of the Shahs of Kabul) Al-Biruni does not mention any written source. This is unlike Al-Biruni; had he consulted some book he would have named it. It appears therefore that this portion is based on oral information and 'is to be considered as the *vulgata* among the educated Hindus in the north-west of India in his time.' Al-Biruni often writes about the unreliability of such historic tradition, and on this topic particularly he admits that the historic chronology as given by him was not fully satisfactory. Sachau concludes by remarking that 'whatever blame or praise' was to be attached to this chapter was to be laid to the charge of Al-Biruni's informants.

For a recent comprehensive study of the Hindu Shahis, see Professor Yogendra Mishra, *The Hindu Sahis of Afghanistan and the Punjab, A.D. 865–1026,* Patna, 1972. Professor Mishra regards the list of rulers given here as correct, but points out that the Shahis were Kshatriyas, not Brahmans as stated by Al-Biruni.

37. A mare is let freely to wander . . . (p. 230). According to the standard sources on the point a horse was used for the purpose but Al-Biruni refers to a mare.

38. (p. 249). This is an interesting piece of information. The number of such persons must have been considerable in order to justify a provision regarding them in the law of inheritance.

39. There is a great tree called *prayaga* . . . (p. 253). What seems to be meant here is that there was a tree of the species called *vata* at the point of confluence of the Ganga and the Jamuna at Prayaga which was known as the *prayaga* tree, or the tree at Prayaga.

40. Hindu festivals (p. 258). Sachau suggests a comparison of this portion relating to the Indian festivals with H.H. Wilson's essay on 'The Religious Festivals of the Hindus' in his *Essays and Lectures,* Vol. II, and points out that this chapter was translated into Persian in Abu Sayeed Abdul Hayy Gardezi's work (Bodleian *ms.* copy).

It may be added that Gardezi was a contemporary of Sultan *Zainul Millat* Abdur Rashid bin Sultan Mahmud (1049–52) to whom he dedicated his book, the *Zainul Akhbar.* The book contains an account of the ancient kings of Iran, early Islamic history, chronological eras, and festivals of the Muslims, Jews. Christians, Zoroastrians and Hindus. The last-mentioned portion, as Sachau points out, is a translation of this chapter of Al-Biruni. Barthold, commenting on the importance of *Zainul Akhbar* for the history of Khurasan area also writes that the portion relating to India is 'entirely dependent on Arabic sources', and that the translation is incorrect in some cases.

The Bodleian *ms.* copy is a transcript of the Cambridge *ms.* copy.

41. Mahanavami, the sister of Mahadeva (p. 260). The goddess Mahanavami is equated with Bhagwati whose festival is celebrated on the 8th *Asvayuja,* but she is wrongly described as the sister, not consort, of Mahadeva. The festival obviously corresponds with the Durga Puja festival of the present times. The sacrifice of a goat is also mentioned.

42–45. (p. 260–61). Some doubts may arise in the mind of the readers about the period of certain ceremonies such as the *pitripaksha,* and dates of some festivals such as *Divali* and *Shivratri,* etc. For a better understanding and appreciation of this whole account, B.P. Mazumdar's *The Socio-Economic History of Northern India.* (*1030–1194 A.D.*), pp. 274–315, may be seen where a well-documented account of the Indian festivals based on a comparative study of the Hindu digests and Al-Biruni's book has been given. Professor Mazumdar rightly draws attention to the points that there are differences in regard to the date, and manner, of celebrating some festivals, that the association of some festivals with certain gods and goddesses has undergone changes, that Al-Biruni mentions certain practices which are 'unknown to Indian digest-makers', that some festivals then observed have now become extinct, and that some important present-day festivals, such as *Chath*, were not known to the northern Indians upto the 12th century.

The following point about the Hindu calendar may also be kept in mind in this connection;

(i) *Pitripaksha* (p. 260). There are two methods of calculating a month in a year (a) from the new moon to the *amawasya*, called the *amant*, and (ii) from the full moon to the full moon, called the *purnimant*. The period of *shukla paksh* or the bright half of the month, may be common to both the methods. Al-Biruni describes this festival as occurring 'when the moon stands in the tenth station, Magha,' and goes on to add that 'the moon's entering this station falls near the time of the new moon.' Under the *purnimant* method of calculating the months, *Bhadrapada* which Al-Biruni mentions here would be inclusive of *Asvin* (*Asvayuja*), in which the festival is celebrated.

(ii) *Dibali* (p. 260). Al-Biruni mentions it as being celebrated on 'the 1st Kartikka, or new moon's day, when the sun marches in Libra'. According to L.D.S. Pillai (*Indian Ephemeris*, vol. 1, Madras, 1922, p. 31) 'a lunation or synodical month is divided into thirty *tithis* or lunar days of equal mean length. The first fifteen *tithis*, corresponding to the bright-half of the month are called *shukla paksha*, and the second fifteen *tithis* are called *krishna paksha*. The last or the 30th *tithi* is the new moon or *Amawasya* (emphasis added), and it is called sometimes by the name of the month of which it marks the end, and sometimes by the name of the following month. Further, it may be added that the new moon or *amawasya* is a particular moment of time, not a particular day or date. The 'new moon', technically, does not indicate its visibility on the horizon.

(iii) *Dhola (i.e. dola)* and *Shivratri* (p. 261). The *Dola* festival is the *Holi* festival of the present times, as indicated by its date (15th *Phalguna*) and the manner of its observation.

(iv) The Shivratri (p. 261) is mentioned as occurring 'on the following night, i.e. that of the 16th (*Phalguna*)'. As we know, there is one *Mahashivratri*, which is an annual festival observed 16 days before the *Holi* or *Dola*, and, according to the *Panchangs* there is a *Shivratri* in every month, on the 13th day. Al-Biruni is not mentioning the *Mahashivratri* but *Shivratri*, which may be one of the monthly *Shivratris*. The discrepancy of the dates (13th and 16th), however, still remains, and it might be due to error of transcription.

One other small discrepancy may be noted. The festivals are described month-wise, in the usual order. Al-Biruni does not specify that the months are listed in the serial order, but all of them are, except one, which is listed out of turn—after *Sravana* comes *Asvayuja*, not *Bhadrapada*.

46. Syavabala (?) (p. 268). Sachau in his annotations suggests that Syavabala (the Arabic text has the name Siyawpal) seems to have been a Kashmiri Hindu who was converted to Islam. Irrespective of this being correct or not, the important point to note is that there were some Indians, at least in the border areas on the west, who could read books in Arabic, and who tried to obtain some information through them.

At another place Al-Biruni has referred to his 'being occupied in composing for the Hindus a translation of the books of Euclid and of the Almagest, and dictating to them a treatise on the construction of the astrolabe' (p. 65). These references are very significant, for they have a bearing on the rather neglected question of the Indian readers of Al-Biruni.

Index

D

E

Q

R

Z

Printed at New Kings Offset Press, Meerut.